B2G
Pricing

B2G Pricing

Best Practices in Business-to-Government Pricing Strategies

By Stephan M. Liozu PhD

Value Innoruption Advisors Publishing • Anthem AZ • 2020

B2G Pricing: Best Practices in Business-to-Government Pricing Strategies
By Stephan M. Liozu

Published by Value Innoruption Advisors Publishing
1946 W Eastman Court
Anthem, Arizona 85086
USA
www.valueinnoruption.com

EVE® and Economic Value Estimation® are registered trademarks of Monitor Company Group Limited Partnership. Vested® is a registered trademark of Kate Vitasek. The Software Pricing Framework® is a registered trademark of Miller Advisors, Inc.

ISBN: 978-1-945815-06-5 trade paperback
        978-1-945815-07-2 electronic book

First printing

Design and composition: www.dmargulis.com

MANUFACTURED IN THE UNITED STATES OF AMERICA

I dedicate my tenth book to my wife, Katie, and my son, Lorenzo. Both are my true loves and my inspiration to keep going in my quest for research and dissemination. They both provide encouragement and support when I need it the most! I love you both!

Contents

SECTION 2: VALUE-BASED PRICING

SECTION 3: PRICE-TO-WIN

SECTION 4: INNOVATION IN PRICING

Preface

EACH YEAR, AROUND THE world, governments spend trillions of dollars to acquire products, services, knowledge, and software. Hundreds of thousands of companies compete for these opportunities under very strict procurement regulations that vary greatly, not only from country to country but also within national procurement agencies. After many years working in the business-to-business (B2B) pricing space and recently in the business-to-government (B2G) pricing space, I wanted to produce a reference book on the topic of B2G pricing. This was done with humility and respect as well as the hope that additional content will be produced in the future to address this vast and complex topic. I thank the countless Thales Group employees who have worked with me over the years and helped me understand the government space. I've learned as much from them as they've learned from me.

I thank all the contributors to this project. I'm truly inspired by their work and appreciate their sharing of their great knowledge.

- Katie Ashton
- Dennis Berg
- Michele Flynn
- Andreas Hinterhuber
- Kim Kelly
- Alex King
- Marsha Lindquist
- Michael Mansard
- Scott Miller
- Larry Newman
- Michael O'Guin
- Emmanuel Poidevin
- Chris Street
- Kate Vitasek

Introduction

IN 2015 I BEGAN working for the Thales Group as a consultant. It was my very first exposure to the B2G and more particularly to the defense world. I found it highly intriguing, and I truly
enjoyed learning a different side of the business world. After one
year of intense work with various divisions of Thales, I wanted to
dive more deeply into this complex and technology-driven world.
So I joined Thales as a full-time Chief Value Officer focusing
on value-based pricing, customer value, segmentation, business
model innovation, and digital pricing. The next four years in this
assignment were intense and enriching. I learned a lot from working with highly analytical, talented teams. I trained thousands
of professionals and certified hundreds more. I was able to coach
hundreds of teams working diligently on value-based strategies
for the public sector. Like with many of my new assignments, I
began it by researching the field of B2G pricing to uncover anything on the topic. To my surprise, little had been published.
I uncovered another empty knowledge space. I found great inspiration from the work of Shipley Associates on the topic of capture management as well as the work of Michael O'Guin and Kim

Kelly, partners at Knowledge Link. In 2012 they authored a must-read book, *Winning the Big Ones—How Teams Capture Large Contracts*. They agreed to share a chapter on price-to-win for this book. That is a real honor. I continued to search for more B2G pricing content and found only bits and pieces on multiple websites, on blogs, and by attending conferences of the Association of Proposal Management Professionals (APMP). I was shocked at the lack of readily available knowledge in the field of B2G pricing. As a result, I embarked on a personal mission to become trained and certified in the capture process, price-to-win, and black hat facilitation. I wanted to experience the training and be exposed to all the content so that I could modify it, put it into action, and eventually build a repository of knowledge in B2G pricing. Fast forward four years, and you have this new book entirely aimed at closing this knowledge gap.

Many contributors

To write this book, I connected my 10 years of experience in B2B pricing with my limited experience in the B2G world. I have much more to learn, and I can't pretend to have absorbed everything there is to know about the public sector. To improve the richness and depth of this book, and as I've done in previous books, I've called on the expertise of people who've spent many decades dealing with pricing, estimating, and contracting with the public sector. I'm grateful that they agreed to collaborate on and contribute to this piece of work. I'm grateful that they trusted me to deliver what might be a first step in closing the knowledge gap. You can find bios and contact information for each of these experts at the end of their respective contributions. I encourage you to connect with them and see how they can help your B2G pricing projects.

Focus of the book

The government sector is vast, complicated, and global. There's no way to cover the topic of pricing in a single book. When I conceptualized this project, I wanted to focus on pricing for differentiated, high-value, and complex offers to the government. I purposely excluded the pricing of commodity products and services. There's no great value in writing a book on how to price ink, paper, or paper clips. I wanted to focus on best-value contracts when there's an opportunity to position superior performance and extract a bit more value. That's already a challenge for many government vendors. I also wanted to zoom in on critical topics of B2G pricing and provide practical guidelines to practitioners in the fields of pricing, contracting, estimating, and bid management. Many people get involved in B2G pricing, and many vendors lack dedicated pricing teams. That's a major difference between B2B and B2G pricing.

Structure of the book

This book has 22 chapters organized in four sections that feature different types of chapters:

Lightning strikes These are shorter chapters highlighting one area of pricing in a very pragmatic format. They present best practices, tips, and techniques.

Expert interviews There are three expert interviews in this book: Larry Newman, from Shipley Associates; Marsha Lindquist, from Granite Leadership Strategies; and Emmanuel Poidevin, from e-Attestations.com. All three provide great insights on the capture process, on B2G pricing, and on how to position a startup in the public sector.

Regular chapters These chapters go deep into a specific area of B2G pricing.

Section 1 focuses on B2G pricing in general. It includes a chapter on B2G trends affecting pricing; key differences between B2B and B2G pricing; key considerations for successful B2G pricing; the interview with Marsha Lindquist; a contribution from Dennis Berg, from Shipley Associates, on how to prepare cost/volume analysis; and an essay by Scott Miller on how to manage government RFPs in the digital era. That's a very rich start!

Section 2 covers the vast topic of performing value-based pricing in the government world. The section begins with important considerations in performing B2G value-based pricing. The other five chapters focus on individual steps of the value-based pricing process: segmentation, competitive analysis, value quantification. Finally, Chris Street covers the topic of conducting black hat sessions to support the price-to-win or position-to-win analysis.

Section 3 is the largest of the book. Over five chapters, this section focuses on price-to-win analysis. It begins with a short essay on the differences and similarities between price-to-win and value-based pricing. Then, Alex King and Andreas Hinterhuber share their experiences in performing price-to-win analysis to win large government contracts. The pearl in this section is the reprint of the price-to-win chapter written for the 2012 book *Winning the Big Ones—How Teams Capture Large Contracts*. Michael O'Guin and Kim Kelly agreed to let me reprint this chapter to bring more power to this book focused on B2G pricing. Their book is a must-have for any professionals engaged in government contracting.

Finally, section 4 addresses the topic of performing innovation in B2G pricing. I wanted to have a section dedicated to new topics in the pricing area. In this section, Kate Vitasek discusses best practices in outcome-based pricing, while Scott Miller focuses on best practices in B2G software pricing. I invited Michael Mansard from Zuora to tell us why he thinks subscription-based pricing will eventually enter the B2G world. We finish with an interview with Emmanuel Poidevin, the CEO of e-Attestations.com, in France, who describes his successful scaling in the SaaS business with 55 percent of the company's revenues to the public space.

Final remarks

So there you have it. This book and all 22 chapters are dedicated to the topic of B2G pricing. This is the first such book, and I hope more work will be done to inform this space in the future. Some people might tell you that it's impossible to cover this topic in one book because of the specificities of the B2G world and the differences between all government agencies in one country and across all countries. I acknowledge the difficulty in doing so. But it's essential to occupy the space and to provide more knowledge to the pricing community at large. I don't want to be defeated by naysayers. I encourage them to publish their own contribution to the field of pricing and to engage in more dissemination activities. There are some great blogs out there. I encourage you to spend time on Marsha Lindquist's blog. It was a great inspiration to me and allowed to me to learn from her 40 years in government contracting and pricing. Of course, there are other sources of information, but they're fragmented. This book can be used as a reference manual or can be read from cover to cover. I hope you enjoy it. It took six months of hard work, and it was very enriching for the simple reason that I had the opportunity to engage with great experts. They taught me a lot about their craft, and that was humbling. I thank them from the bottom of my heart.

Abbreviations and acronyms used in the book

ANN	Artificial neural networks	**KPI**	Key performance indicators
APMP	Association for Proposal Management Professionals	**LCC**	Life-cycle costing
B2B	Business to business	**M&S**	Maintenance and support
B2C	Business to consumer	**MEAT**	Most economically advantageous tender
B2D	Business to defense		
B2G	Business to government	**MFC**	Most-favored customer
B2G2C	Business to government to consumer	**NBCA**	Next best competitive alternatives
BAFO	Best and final offer	**O&S**	Operations and support
CC	Creative Commons	**PaaS**	Platform as a service
CI	Competitive intelligence	**PECO**	Pricing ecosystem
CMA	Certified Management Accountant	**PMIC**	Pricing Model Innovation Canvas
CPA	Chartered Professional Accountant	**PPS**	Professional Pricing Society
CPI	Competitive pricing intelligence	**PTW**	Price-to-win
		Q&A	Question and answer
CPP	Certified Pricing Professional	**RFI**	Request for information
CVM	Customer Value Modeler	**RFP**	Request for proposal
DTC	Design-to-cost	**RTS**	Reagan Test Site
EDS	Explosive Detection System	**SaaS**	Software as a service
ERP	Enterprise resource planning	**SEI**	Subscription Economy Index
EVE	Economic Value Estimation		
FAR	Federal Acquisition Regulations	**SME**	Small and medium enterprises
FEI	Front end of innovation	**SWAP**	Software Acquisition and Practices
FPA	Focal plane array		
GMP	Guaranteed maximum price	**T&M**	Time and materials
ILS	International Launch Services	**TBO**	Total benefits of ownership
ISPMA	International Software Product Management Association	**TCO**	Total cost of ownership
		VBP	Value-based pricing
		VfM	Value for money
IT	Information technology	**WBS**	Work-breakdown structure
JDAM	Joint Direct Attack Munitions		
		WTP	Willingness-to-pay

Section 1

PRICING

1

Trends Affecting
B2G Pricing

THE BUSINESS WORLD IS changing. For the past five years, I've written and spoken about the topic of disruption in the business world. Forces of change cannot be stopped. Some of these forces are related to business dynamics, global geopolitics, and technological advancements. The B2G world is not immune to such changes. Over the past 10 years, changes in the way governments conduct business have affected how vendors must manage their go-to-market strategies, including pricing. As things rapidly change, government agencies have had to adapt and embrace new pricing concepts. I list some of these trends below to start the conversation.

1 **E-commerce is entering the B2G world.** Some procurement agencies have embraced the boom in e-commerce using publicly available platforms such as Google Supply or

Amazon Business Services. Much of commodity procurement is funneled through e-commerce or e-procurement platforms that are developed internally or available through marketplaces. For smaller contracts that are non-commodity-based, some governments in developing countries are providing an e-procurement platform to allow vendors to upload their information and pricing and to respond directly to smaller requests for proposals (RFPs). This is the case in the Philippines, for example.

2 **Technology as a source of differentiation is forcing best-value discussions.** In recent years, the generation of RFPs and the evaluation of vendor responses have been somewhat industrialized through the use of tools. From the vendor side, some estimating and contracting software is designed to match the procurement agency's automated process of evaluation. From the government side, templates and tools are growing increasingly popular. They reinforce a level of standardization to assist evaluators in the comparison of proposals. Some government agencies also force very structured and short responses to require vendors to get to the point!

3 **There's a movement from best-in-class vendors to best-in-class customers.** Some B2G vendors are developing new technologies specifically for embedding with customers and encouraging interaction in the design and costing of advanced solutions. This is, in a way, a step toward creating technical or marketing switching costs. An example of this trend is GE's Brilliant Pricing technology, used to cost single-sourced contracts with the US Air Force.

> GE calls it Brilliant Pricing both because the system uses artificial neural networks (ANNs) and because it can slash the time needed to produce pricing estimates

by 85 percent. When the government enters into a sole-source contract, suppliers must document how they arrived at a price, an excruciatingly time-consuming exercise that produces reams of paperwork and can take months to complete. If the Air Force or a foreign part-ner wants to buy more F110 jet engines, for instance, GE must document the cost of every single component—down to the last screw. ("GE's 'Brilliant Pricing' Technol-ogy Makes Acquisition Go Faster," 2020)

4 Cost modeling software is readily available. In 2019 I attended the Association of Proposal Management Profes-sionals (APMP) conference and noticed a variety of software solutions for industrializing and standardizing cost estimat-ing for government procurement. Most vendors call them-selves providers of government contract pricing and proposal analysis software, but they are in fact offering software to enable estimating and costing. Using off-the-shelf software allows one to analyze complex cost proposals while greatly reducing the time and likelihood of mistakes that come with spreadsheet-based pricing systems. So it's a real advancement in costing and pricing that was unavailable just 10 years ago. This level of professionalization in costing and proposal anal-ysis is good news for the profession. I hope it doesn't stop here and that we begin to see similar software focused on best-value pricing and customer-value propositions for govern-ment work.

5 B2B procurement best practices have gained wider acceptance in the B2G world. Over the past 10 to 20 years, the B2B procurement function has dramati-cally invested in systems and professional processes. Driven by some of the largest original equipment manufacturers in the world, vendors must adhere to rules, regulations, and tremendous level-of-process requirements. Over the past 10 years, some public procurement agencies have adopted some of these best practices, usually following the recommendations of strategic procurement consultants. B2B procurement experts are joining government agencies to do the same. This is not a general trend around the world, however, and it's very agency-dependent. It's important for a vendor to know when they're facing a professional buyer.

6   **B2B pricing techniques have reached the B2G world.** Similarly, procurement agencies that are behaving like price buyers have adopted procurement mechanisms from the B2B world. These include auctions, reverse auctions, sealed-bid auctions, open-room competitive discussions, and competitive dialogues. The goal of these techniques is to prevent vendors from interacting with procurement agents and to create a level of uncertainty aimed at breaking vendors' confidence.

7   **There's a shift toward anticipatory government.** More progressive and sophisticated government agencies have put themselves on high alert for trends in the public sectors and are anticipating their acceptance by the public. The goal of this approach is to be ready when there's high public demand for a service or a particular form of payment, for example. Later in this book, we discuss the penetration of subscription-based pricing into the public space. Some agencies have already embraced this trend, as it has taken the business-to-consumer (B2C) world by storm.

8   **There's a greater focus on outcomes.** In several countries and for specific government agencies, the shift to outcome-based business models has already happened. The UK's armed forces, for example, have already outsourced a large

part of their supply chain to outside vendors. Sodexo provides services to cafeterias and canteens around the world. For these services, vendors are prepared to sign performance-based or outcome-based contracts. Please read chapter 19, by Kate Vitasek, on contract best practices.

9 **There's a greater focus on improving the lives of citizens.** In Scandinavian countries, the relationship between the government and the public is closer and much more focused on quality of life. It's not unusual to see citizens engaging in brainstorming with particular agencies and/or serving on public initiatives. The result is the development of services and technologies aimed at improving quality of life. One example of this is the rapid penetration of cashless payment apps, replacing the need for cash and making life easier. Denmark, Sweden, and Norway have the highest rates of adoption of such technologies.

10 **There's a greater focus on sustainability to preserve scarce resources.** More governments around the world are sensitive to sustainable technologies and are introducing environmentally friendly requirements in RFPs. I wouldn't call this a general trend, but it might become one over the next decade. That will influence the nature of products and services offered and their costing. Offering sustainable solutions might eventually become a differentiating criterion for states like California or the Scandinavian countries.

11 **There's a greater focus on improving the speed and ease of bidding for government vendors.** Governments understand that they need to move fast in some critical areas. They cannot continue to rely on procurement and innovation processes that can last years. Some have created parallel accelerated programs to engage innovators and entrepreneurs. The result is the attribution of bid awards in a matter of hours

or days to avoid long delays for time-critical contracts. This is more the exception than the rule. The US Air Force, for example, awarded 100 contracts in 40 hours! (Ripple, 2018).

12 Agencies are implementing more cost-cutting programs by leveraging big data and analytics. Optimizing costs and expenses is an ongoing goal in the public space. We often hear about cost reductions or budget cuts. These are a reality, but agencies are also focused on using spending and costing data to learn and optimize. Data-drive procurement is increasingly a reality in the B2G space. Agencies might make data management a new requirement in RFPs, as cyber is today. There's an opportunity for more mature B2G vendors to create a competitive advantage in this space by demonstrating data leadership at a price premium. Budget cuts can be politically charged, but cost optimization might be a solution to this.

13 An improved purchasing toolbox reduces costs, waste, and time. Data and analytics are part of the growing toolbox adopted by some governments to fight waste and accelerate procurement. The goal of this progressive toolbox is to improve design, drive transparency, and manage suppliers. Some of these tools, commonly used in B2B, are increasingly embraced in the public sector: creativity and design sessions, product benchmarking, value analysis, supplier workshops, online bidding events, total cost of ownership, and so forth. The drive toward greater cost and price transparency is a both a blessing and a curse for B2G vendors.

14 It's important to be willing to accept new revenue models from vendors through innovation and co-development. This is growing topic in the B2G space. We discuss the adoption of subscription-based pricing in section 4 of this book. Usage-based pricing, outcome-based pricing, and subscription-based pricing have become popular in the B2C world and more widely adopted in B2B. As more government agencies work with Amazon, Google, and Microsoft, it's inevitable that new business and revenue models will come into play. They already exist in the education space, for example.

15 It's important to provide equal business opportunities to small and medium enterprises (SMEs) with modernization initiatives and new types of procurement processes. Public agencies may launch competitions in the form of a hackathon to encourage SMEs' participation. During these competitions, agencies give the SMEs and startups an actual challenge to solve that includes a desired end state and available budgets. In France, hackathons of a few days are held with a single incentive/premium to promote the winner. Real minimum viable product contracts are awarded to the winners after a few months of "racing" following a proof of concept, following a mockup, and with a funnel of competitors being short-listed at each stage. A similar concept was organized in Singapore with the KPMG Innovation Ignite Summit, which focused on encouraging outcome-based procurement and crowdsourcing.

16 Intentional government participation in ecosystems of innovation is increasing. Here I refer to Government 4.0. PricewaterhouseCoopers coined the term *innovation-driven government*. In this situation, government agencies play a very active role in the ecosystems of innovation by driving the speed and nature of investments and by engaging nontraditional partners like startups, incubators, and other innovation labs. They bypass traditional B2G vendors to discover nuggets of innovation directly and to capture them early in the development cycle.

17 There's an increasing focus on outsourcing to specialist partners. There are specific areas where government agencies are unwilling to invest or are incapable of investing over the long term. The result is the development of strong partnership with critical vendors and co-investments in new technologies. Areas like artificial intelligence, cybersecurity, and cloud computing are potential areas of collaboration and outsourcing. Competition to gain such a positional advantage with agencies is fierce, and long-term contracts can be in the billions. The JEDI contract in the US is a good example of a large-scale contract worth $10 billion over 10 years.

18 There's an increasing focus on developing local and national prosperity by requiring local production and industrial offsets. Government agencies are increasingly concerned about the development of local capabilities and prosperity. They often include in their RFPs the need to transfer technology, to work with local industrial partners, or to compensate the attribution of a contract with the creation of local jobs or wealth. These requirements need to be taken seriously and must be quantified in terms of value and wealth. Vendors might need to create offset teams to track and deploy the components and programs of a winning bid. A strategic and intentional approach in this area can create strong differentiation when vendors are willing to invest in joint ventures and local industrial partnerships.

19 Incumbents must beware! The perception of safety as an incumbent when contracts are being renewed is no longer relevant. When the renewal process is focused on cost reduction or innovation, incumbents must work twice as hard as potential competitors to defend their business. Agencies understand the cost of disruption when switching vendors, but they're willing to assume the risk. Often, they refuse to consider the cost of disruption in their comparative analysis. Although incumbents still have an advantage in terms of customer knowledge and access to data, they cannot be complacent and must be competitive. Rigorous analysis is essential to anticipating competitors' positioning and pricing.

20 There is increasing rationalization of service providers under the platform-thinking umbrella. This trend is accelerating in Western countries. The whole premise is the simplification and rationalization of the number of service contractors used for large contracts and ongoing service agreements. With the emergence of digital platforms, some governments are open to a process of "platformization" of services under the leadership of a third-party partner.

These 20 trends are not an exhaustive list. But they're a good start. Interestingly, while I was searching for trends and discussing them with a variety of experts, they all agreed that there are not one or two trends that can be generalized to the entire world. Trends are regional or national. There might be collaboration between countries and allies on various advanced technologies or in the military world, but the B2G world seems to be fragmented. Government procurement can be complex. And it's being changed by B2B procurement methods and digital technologies. This forces B2G vendors to keep up and to make sure they have a very well-prepared capture strategy including pricing.

References

GE's "Brilliant Pricing" technology makes acquisition go faster. (2020). *Air Force Magazine,* February 19. Retrieved from www.airforcemag.com/ges-brilliant-pricing -technology-makes-acquisition-go-faster/

Ripple, B. (2018). Air Force moves at the speed of startups with 100 contract awards in 40 hours. *Wright-Patterson AFB*, November 28. Retrieved from www.wpafb.af.mil/News /Article-Display/Article/1700007/air-force-moves-at -the-speed-of-startups-with-100-contract-awards-in-40 -hours/

Key Notes

Key Actions

_____

_____

_____

_____

_____

_____

_____

_____

_____

_____

_____

_____

2

Key Differences between B2B and B2G Pricing

MOST PRICING BOOKS FOCUS on the B2C and B2B worlds. The B2G sector is integrated into the wider B2B world because of their similar environments. Although B2B and B2G pricing use some of the same methodologies, there are fundamental differences between them that can affect their relevance and applicability. The same can be said when comparing the B2C and B2B worlds. Below I list 25 key differences between B2B and B2G pricing to illustrate this point. There are potentially more of them, but I believe I cover the most important ones, in no particular order.

1 **Fewer customers.** In the B2G world, you're essentially dealing with just a few entities or agencies per country. That doesn't mean that the business opportunities are smaller in terms of size or number of transactions. It means that you have

a limited number of strategic accounts to pursue. Your total addressable market might be very large in dollar value, but it will be very narrow in terms of the number of customers. For example, there are about 75 active navies in the world. Some are very small and not very interested in capability development. Of those 75, 20 to 25 might actively invest in and focus on border security. Finally, 10 to 15 may have available budgets in a given fiscal year or budgeting period.

2 **More qualitative approaches.** In many areas, the B2G world requires deeper qualitative analysis. In a specific geographic area (whether regional or national), the number of actors or entities will be small. You cannot therefore hope to have a significant amount of information and data points with which to conduct quantitative analysis. A buying-center analysis of a municipal transportation authority, for example, will rely on qualitative, social, and psychological details for a few stakeholders. It requires deeper customer intimacy to uncover formal and informal information. Qualitative analysis does not necessarily mean simplicity. You might have to deal with very complex interactions or communications between stakeholders of a particular entity. In addition, what might be formal and in plain sight might have less weight than what is informal and unsaid. The need for social and emotional intelligence in analyzing these accounts is critical.

3 **Request-for-proposal (RFP) nature and process.** The request-for-information (RFI) and RFP processes can be complex, detailed, and lengthy. They might include dozens or hundreds of technical specifications and long lists of commercial conditions. The processes might be open and flexible, or closed and tight. There's a need to pay great attention to what documents are received from public customers to ensure compliance with the process and with financial considerations.

Understanding the RFP process is a critical piece of the customer-insight process. Each agency might have a different RFP process with significant changes in timelines, evaluation criteria, response requirements, and types of interaction with vendors. An RFP does not come unexpectedly. It is generally announced and developed over time. Capture teams therefore need to anticipate and influence the RFI and RFP process early in the customer development process. This situation might also happen in B2B large-scale commercial contracts, but perhaps not as frequently as with B2G projects and contracts.

4 **Complex buying-center/stakeholder maps.** In B2G and large B2B contracts, the buying center might be more complex, with a variety of actors or agencies playing different roles. That complexity needs to be studied and captured in a key account plan as well as in the capture plan (Gold and Blue Sheet, for examples). In a complex buying-center situation or when dealing with an industrial consortium, you might have to create multiple buying-center and stakeholder maps. Your account team must be consistently gathering new information about the account and updating relevant documents. For example, a joint air force contract between the German and the Dutch air forces will require several of these deliverables for your capture plan. I often also recommend designing a relationship matrix to match the vendor's stakeholders to the customer's stakeholders.

5 **Complex ecosystems.** The B2G ecosystem might span industries and geographies. It's essential to understand all the actors, whether public or private, and to map all existing relationships (joint ventures, consortia, and partnerships). There are formal and information connections in the ecosystem that might influence pricing and value management. A competitor might become a partner for another customer, for example.

Experienced account managers and business development managers will bring that wealth of knowledge to your capture plan. You might be required to conduct activities with your ecosystem partners (black hat and value proposition sessions, for example).

6 **Influence of national preference.** In the B2G and B2D worlds, the influence of government affairs, lobbying, and national protectionism is greater than in B2B. Norms and regulations might impact the ability of vendors to bid. Informal influences also need to be understood, especially when powerful countries have zones of influence around the world in the form of relationships, subsidies, and doctrines. For examples, governments of countries in the Commonwealth will cooperate much more among themselves and will participate actively in technological collaboration. Military alliances will also influence the attribution of specific contracts.

7 **Sole-source contracts.** Being a sole-source provider in a B2G and/or B2D market or region increases customers' scrutiny of cost and profit levels. It might also erode the level of trust between vendor and customer and lead to the publication of an unforeseen competitive tender. In the B2B sector, sole-source contracts are rare. You'd have to possess a remarkable positional advantage or a strong patent to be a sole supplier. In reality, procurement teams select from a list of approved strategic suppliers and diversify their position. In the B2G world, sole-source contracts are more frequent because of point 6 above. However, the difficulty is remaining the incumbent when contracts are extended or renewed. Vendors are often fully embedded in government operations, making switching costs very high. In my experience, public entities are increasingly aware of the strength position of incumbents and tend to discard the cost of disruption and switching costs in the

analysis and comparison of bids. Vendors can no longer justify their premiums on the basis that a government will incur switching costs.

8 **Required cost transparency.** National procurement agencies might require that vendors sign an agreement to adhere to cost and profit principles. Vendors must open their books and guarantee a maximum profit level. There, mandatory pricing structures are unchangeable. Of course, working in a profit-controlled environment is constraining, but that doesn't mean that it's impossible to generate healthy margins. This is rarely the case in the B2B world. In some sectors such as automotive and OEM avionics, vendors are required to justify their cost base. But this is more the exception than the general case.

9 **Predominance of financial pricing.** Financial costing and pricing are critical in the B2G world, especially for very large, customized, and complex contracts that might last decades and that might be very risky. Financial pricing might be influenced by source currency, cash flow, cost escalation, and risk predictability. Risk management and contingency planning are an important dimension of financial pricing models and the overall bid presentation pack. Being able to manage risks and contingency is often a source of incremental gross margin when profit is under the microscope, as mentioned in point 8 above. Many government contracts involving new and complex technologies must account for these risks. In the space business, for example, often new technologies are theoretical until they're actually produced. This is the nature of technological gaps based on science and capabilities.

10 **Complexity of pricing proposals.** Some B2G contracts might have straightforward pricing models and structures.

The longer the timeline of the agreement and the more complex the offer, the more complex the pricing proposals. Some customers might require base-dated pricing, and others, full life-cycle pricing with full escalation. Vendors must be able to create innovative pricing and payment models as well as manage complex pricing structures over time and for very advanced solutions. Pricing proposals might also include capital injections, industrial offsets in the country of destination, and advanced financing instruments. These are all part of a pricing strategy that's rare in the B2B world. A highly sophisticated B2G pricing strategy is often the source of true differentiation.

11 **Open specifications.** In B2G pricing, all technical and commercial conditions are open. Vendors have access to the same level of information, which sometimes makes positional advantage irrelevant. In addition, customers may enter into competitive dialogues with vendors to extract valuable information from them and to communicate widely all findings to ensure the lowest price. This is a tricky situation to be in. A vendor might decide to participate or not in these rounds of competitive dialogue. Doing so often means falling into the trap of "poker playing" accounts (those that act like value buyers but procure like price buyers). These accounts have one thing in mind: developing the most advanced technical requirements that take the best from all suppliers, and then letting the vendors compete on pure price.

12 **Set budgets.** Given competing priorities within government branches, budgets for large contracts might be set in advance, inflexibly and arbitrarily. Customers communicate a set budget while seeking the best technological solution. Part of the price-to-win analysis is discovering the customer's maximum budget, realistic budget, and addressable budget.

Capture teams also need to work in anticipation of customers' setting their budget so that they can influence the budget-setting process and influence it up or down. Competitive intelligence teams also must search for any published budget numbers in the media or through official government channels. These must be included in the capture plan along with other relevant information.

13 **Length and nature of contracts.** When supplying heavy equipment or complex systems to the public sector, vendors must be proficient in the art and science of total-cost-of-ownership and life-cycle costing modeling. These are essential, internal value- and financial-quantification capabilities. Some companies have developed a center of excellence in these capabilities and have deployed advanced simulation tools.

14 **Flexibility in pricing process.** Because of long lead times and changing specifications, the first internal pricing analysis might not be the last one. Customers might require several pricing proposals over the RFP response period. For long-term pursuits, changes in technologies, budget levels, and geopolitical dynamics might radically change the RFP process and the relevant pricing/costing levels. For example, changes in administration and leadership might change a project's specifications and require the creation of jobs to support manufacturing. The implication for pricing and bidding teams is that pricing evolves over time as project information also evolves.

15 **Pricing timeframe.** Traditionally, very large and complex public contracts have longer commercial cycles between the RFI and the deployment of technology. Cycles might be three to five years long, making pricing and costing rapidly obsolete as technology evolves. Contracts must include some parameters to address risk, cost escalation, and changes in the business dynamics. Think about the latest JEDI cloud contract

that was attributed to Microsoft for $10 billion in the US. The formal procurement process lasted two years. The preformalization process might have also lasted another two years in order to define contract parameters and specifications. One can only imagine the changes in cloud technology during four to five years. The contract is expected to last 10 years.

16 The power of incumbents. In very complex B2G contract renewals, incumbents often have a positional advantage over newcomers. Because of risk aversion and a lack of operational performance data, new entrants often have difficulty establishing a solid and tested business case. The level of disruption is often a barrier to entry.

17 Competitive pricing information. Some governments publish public contracts and therefore communicate bid pricing. The information is public but somewhat difficult to access. One must have the skills necessary to access public databases and locate the relevant information. It's hard but not impossible. However, for complex bids, it might be difficult to extract the pricing of components as well as hardware versus software pricing. Most of the time in B2B, the bid process is closed and pricing is confidential. It's impossible to exactly identify competitors' net prices before and after the contract is attributed.

18 Willingness-to-pay. The concept of willingness-to-pay (WTP) in the public sector is not as straightforward and researchable as it is in the B2B sectors. Some B2G accounts are not willing or able to express their willingness-to-pay for products and services. In the case of technological innovations and/or complex customized contracts, technical users often lack precise knowledge of performance requirements in the early stages of the conceptualization. Similarly, because of a lack of appropriate samples for conducting WTP testing, qualitative interviews might be able to gauge interest in a solution but not a specific WTP. In the public, WTP is still important, as is ability to pay: that is, the existence of an addressable budget.

19 Value discussion that is too personal. Discussing cost savings and incremental revenues of a solution with B2G accounts might be difficult or impossible. For example, in health care and defense, value-of-life discussions are often not appropriate when human lives and survivability are being discussed. Similarly, discussing head-count reductions and labor cost savings is generally not recommended when government employees are unionized and protected from termination. So customer-value quantification must be done carefully, keeping these sensitive areas in mind. Selecting the right value drivers must be done with account managers who understand the do's and don'ts of the specific account.

20 Difficulty dollarizing differentiation. Dollarizing differentiated value propositions for B2G accounts requires detailed knowledge of their operations and applications. Often these are secretive environments, not open to vendors. It's often difficult to model the end-use application for new products and services and/or to obtain comparative performance test results. Deep knowledge of "conops" comes from the presence of business advisors and retired government personnel. This situation makes the co-development of innovations with the B2G world essential. The sooner one can collaborate, the sooner one can understand the customer's needs and the potential value-in-use of the solution.

21 Difficulty validating cost savings. Equally difficult is the ability to validate true savings in the customer's operations. In the B2D world, each customer operates differently, and each mission might be different. Therefore, the validation process might require using a specific mission scenario or developing academic research projects with a reputable university. Usually, the government agency might deny access to the equipment once it's in pilot trials in the field. Some agencies keep these trials and performance verification pilots secret.

22 **Shaping of customer needs.** Vendors to B2G and B2D accounts must spend significant time and resources shaping and influencing customer needs very early in the capture process, and even before a formal RFP is considered. This is an area where account management and business development play essential roles, and where continuity in relationships is important. This encompasses influencing the customer's technical specifications, shaping commercial conditions, co-creating long-term roadmaps, and shaping budget planning. The economic value pool calculations post-dollarization exercise is important to guiding the customer's budget-forming process.

23 **Subject of political sensitivity.** Pricing for large B2G contracts is often a controversial subject discussed in the highest political spheres. Large infrastructure or military spending bills can receive greater scrutiny than others, especially when budgets are not respected and programs are severely delayed. It's often the cause of negative press for vendors, although the fault might reside with the government in the end. Two famous examples of this situation are the exposure by the US president of the overall cost of the F35 program in 2017 or the delays in delivering the A400M aircraft to European air forces.

24 **Impact of industrial/technology policies.** Some countries have strong industrial/technology policies that need to be understood and that might influence costing, pricing, and the overall capture process. Those aspects are not always public, which makes understanding and compliance tricky. Vendors need to discover and understand B2G customer technology

roadmaps and their intention in localizing intellectual property (IP) and developing local capabilities. For example, Airbus has had to localize production in China and supply IP information to local producers. This is an essential part of the capture process.

25 Interaction between customers. Besides national entities, many business opportunities might exist for larger institutions such as the EU, WTO, WHO, UN, or NATO. These projects can be fully or partially funded by these institutions, who might interact well with national agencies. These situations complicate the discovery of customer needs and of who might have the power in the buying center. They may also trigger conflicts between stakeholders and thus increase the complexity of the sales process.

As you can see, the public sector is somewhat different from the traditional B2B sector. These differences affect how pricing is set and managed. Some of the methodologies must be adapted to reflect these differences. As in B2B, pricing in B2G must be formally organized to respect the parameters of RFPs and to deliver pricing proposals that fit in the overall bid proposal. In the end, B2B and B2G pricing both need to respond to customer needs and make an impact in the customer's business. We delve much deeper into the topics of value-based pricing and price-to-win in the rest of the book.

Key Notes

_____

_____

_____

_____

_____

_____

Key Actions

_____

_____

_____

_____

_____

_____

Lightning Strike

3

15 Considerations for Progressive B2G Pricing

B2G PRICING REQUIRES SPECIAL attention and unique capabilities. B2G pricing also has unique rules and vocabulary. In the B2B world, pricing is usually hosted by marketing, sales, or finance organizations. In the B2G world, pricing most likely resides within finance, bid management, offer management, or proposal teams. It's not unusual to find people participating in pricing work scattered across the organization, without formalized and coordinated roles. Pricing is often one of many roles in a job description that includes other elements of the bid analysis or capture process.

I've worked in the B2G world for five years and have listed important best practices to make B2G pricing successful. I call them considerations in this chapter. Some are common sense to the world of pricing, marketing, and offer management.

1 **B2G pricing does require a strategy.** As in B2C and B2B, B2G pricing requires a strategy. And that strategy must be aligned with some of the strategic objectives of the organization: deal realization, win/loss ratio, gross margin, gross margin of order intake, earnings before interest and taxes. A good pricing strategy sets the role of pricing in the offer management and capture process and defines some of the tools needed to evaluate customer opportunities.

2 **Must-win contracts or very large government contracts must be prepared intensively.** In a project-oriented business, there are potentially thousands of requests for proposals (RFPs) coming from the B2G world. Not all RFPs are created equal. A vendor must be able to sort through the project pipeline and quickly identify must-win opportunities. For these, there must be a strategic allocation of resources to study the RFP, assemble a team, conduct the necessary pricing analysis (using the four C's: cost, competition, customer, change), and develop the capture plan. Often in the B2G world, proper segmentation is not done, which means that all offers are considered equal. This is not good news.

3 **Value-based pricing (VBP) is 90 percent value and 10 percent pricing.** Performing VBP in the public sector is different but not impossible. I often face objections when discussing VBP in B2G. I must remind people that VBP is a methodology requiring discipline and a great focus on the customer. In the B2G world and for differentiated offerings, VBP is even more focused on customer value. When this is done well, pricing is often easier to do. Depending on the level of pricing sophistication in an organization, the 90/10 ratio might change. But every government project must include the right customer analysis: customer profile,

customer journey, customer-value proposition, customer-value model, customer proposal, and more. There's no going around that.

4   **Doing pricing after the RFP comes out is too late.** Often, pricing is considered and discussed too late in the capture process. After the RFP is published, pricing can still be done, of course. But there's very little opportunity to influence the RFP process or the customer's budget, or to shape the customer's needs. So once the RFP is out, pricing must be compliant in order to play. It's too late to discuss value and to take the risk of making an offer that does not comply with the specifications and the evaluation criteria.

5   **Pricing begins very early in the capture and pursuit process.** The work should begin as soon as the customer has expressed the desire and need to acquire a certain technology or solution. Several years can elapse between that stage and the production of the official RFP. During this period, the account management and business development organizations must focus on shaping the customer's needs, the perceptions of value, the understanding technological worth, and the budget definition. This is an ongoing effort that is part of the value-selling process. Some organizations call this "early capture" or the "left-shift" process. This exercise on shaping and anticipating is essential with must-win opportunities and with customers who are partnership-seekers or value buyers. Such customers might be more open to co-developing and modifying their internal processes.

6   **Pricing touches many functions in the organization.** Because B2G pricing needs a strategy, it also needs formal coordination, as it touches many functions in the organization: costing, finance, marketing, product management, bidding, proposal development, and engineering. When a vendor

lacks a formal pricing team, such coordination is also lacking. Pricing is fragmented across these actors, and information might not flow smoothly.

7   **Project pricing needs the right teaming.** Vendors need to be able to assemble the right team to work on the pricing of specific B2G contracts. Of course, not all RFPs are the same, and teams might vary depending on the nature and complexity of the opportunity. For very demanding opportunities, a capture leader will be named; this person needs to assemble the right team with the relevant internal and external professionals. For specific contracts, external price-to-win experts might be mobilized.

8   **Pricing decisions must be informed by the three C's of pricing.** It's essential to balance the sources of input and information when making bid-pricing decisions. Traditionally, industrial and B2G vendors are competitor- or costs-oriented in their pricing strategy. The information on customer needs and customer value doesn't often enter in the gate review for specific bids. This is why I developed a pricing model innovation canvas (PMIC) based on the four C's of pricing: cost, customer, competitors, and change. The foundation of this canvas is to develop pricing intelligence to make better pricing decisions. Chapter 18 focuses on PMIC in detail.

9   **Pricing must evolve as your value proposition and offer do.** Because of the long B2G commercial cycles, the customer's needs and requirements will change over time. The value proposition will be adapted to these changing customer dynamics. Often, pricing remains static along the way. While the price levels might stay the same, the pricing strategy and model might not evolve enough. Successful B2G pricing requires agile and innovative pricing strategies that match the customer's changing needs.

10 The pricing process needs to be included in your bidding and capture process. Vendors may have very professional and managed process management rules covering capture management and bid management. Often, pricing is integrated into one or more of these process streams. It's critical to ensure that the pricing process be as robustly managed either as an independent process or under another process. All rules, responsibilities, process documents, educational documents, and references to relevant tools must be included in this process description.

11 Pricing and value must be part of a good proposal as a crisp story. A good customer proposal is built based on a customer-value proposition and a series of winning themes. Even after the proper homework is done for a specific bid or offer, the work is still not done. Proposal managers must create a strong storyline tying together all the elements of the offers: customer needs, value proposition, winning themes, customer value, and pricing. The design of this customer proposal is equally important.

12 Confidence in the data and analysis affects your internal pricing decision. Internally, top management reviewing your big pricing and approving the gate reviews needs to have confidence in the analysis of the bid components and ultimately pricing. The typical emphasis is on cost modeling and risk management for the offer. Less attention and discipline are given to competitive review and customer-value analysis or to price-to-win. To change this paradigm, it's important to balance the focus on the three C's of pricing to give equal attention and discipline to all C's. Your customer will also perceive your degree of preparation and depth of analysis when you deliver their proposal. So it's all about discipline in preparation.

13 Innovation in pricing is required, but it's different.
The public sector is typically not very receptive to new pricing models, but it's changing. Some government agencies have outsourced asset operations to third-party vendors and pay them based on outcome or performance. Other vendors have been very creative and aggressive with payment terms, financing schemes, industrial offset strategies, and shared R&D expenses. Pricing innovation isn't just about pricing models. In B2G, financing and payment structures are essential. Working with financial institutions and collaborating with experts is also a form of innovation for B2G customers.

14 Mastering and anticipating risk impact your pricing.
Managing B2G pricing means excellence in mastering risk management. Most of the cost modeling tools for advanced and complex bids will have a strong risk management module. Bid and capture managers need to manage a risk register for each offer. Risk is potentially everywhere when designing a solution for a potential 20 years: risks in partnership, risks in customer dynamics, risks in the technology roadmap, risks in currency and geopolitics. All vendors to the B2G world need to price customer proposals with the right level of risk. The difference when everything goes well with a specific project ends up in the gross margin. When everything goes wrong, it can quickly reduce margins to zero and cost in program overruns.

15 Language doesn't matter, but principles do. B2G pricing uses different vocabulary. For example, what are referred to as differentiators in B2B pricing are called discriminators in B2G. Successful B2G pricing requires nimbleness and agility. It's best not to fall in love with methodologies, languages, or philosophies. I encourage teams to embrace methodologies and to absorb their principles: customer needs, value proposition, differentiators, willingness and ability to pay, and pricing.

These 15 considerations are based on my experience with B2G pricing over the past five years. I'm far from an expert, but they've resonated with many pricing practitioners. I hope they will with you too. Most of the rest of this book focuses on these considerations. We'll dive deeply into B2G value-based pricing, price-to-win best practices, and innovation in pricing.

Key Notes

_____

_____

_____

_____

_____

_____

Key Actions

_____

_____

_____

_____

_____

_____

4

Interview with an Expert

Marsha Lindquist, CP APMP, APMP Fellow, NCMA Fellow, Granite Leadership Strategies, Inc.

Stephan   Thanks very much for talking with me today. To begin our conversation, please introduce yourself, and then tell us what you've done in pricing all these years.

Marsha   It's exciting to hear that we're going to be more vocal about pricing to the government, because it's not an area that's very well written about. I've been in government contracting and pricing since 1982, and I love it. I've been doing pricing since that time.

I make a distinction between pricing and pricing strategy, which, as we will talk about, gets into a little bit more than just putting the math together and putting spreadsheets together. I've also served on the side as a controller for a few companies in the Washington, DC, area, and I was also Director of Contracts and Pricing. So I've served in the pricing world in many different roles in order to be able to draw on that experience, to talk about pricing strategy, and to talk about pricing.

Stephan   You have a wealth of experience, and I really appreciate you sharing some of that with us. Why is it, do you think, that there's never been a book written about the B2G pricing process and methodologies whereas we have over 110 books on B2C and B2B pricing?

Marsha   Very little has been written in this area—mostly blogs and newsletters. It's a wide area to cover, and usually specific to each agency. It's hard to talk about pricing or pricing strategy because the landscape changes over time a little bit. But what you can touch is what's in your toolbox. Those tend to be the same kinds of things, but it changes from procurement to procurement. It's hard to make generalizations about pricing, just like it's hard to generalize about each company's accounting system. You can't, because each company is unique, just like each procurement process is unique.

Stephan   That makes sense. So, with all your years of experience, how would you characterize the evolution of B2G pricing over time? Is it more sophisticated? Is it still the same? Is it still very fragmented?

Marsha   Things change and things do stay the same. There are tools out there to help contractors with their pricing. Most often the government is asking for their pricing in Excel formats. That's to make sure that the government's price analyst can evaluate everybody in the same way. So they ask for that because, let's face it, Excel's fairly user-friendly, and one contractor can respond to the requirement using Excel, and so can the next one and the next one and the next one. But contractors now have software tools at their disposal to do pricing. But again, you're still going to be responding to the government probably in an Excel format. Agencies have gotten a little bit more sophisticated in what they ask for and how they ask for it. Often, we see the government giving us the format that they want back, so that makes it easier for them to evaluate all the contractors on the same basis. I've walked in the shoes of a price evaluator and done that analysis, and when you come back with everybody's tables and Excel looking the same, it makes the process of evaluating each and against one another a lot faster.

Stephan   That's interesting. Coming from the B2B world, there are thousands of software companies offering cloud-based pricing optimization, value-based pricing (VBP) dynamically, but then when you go into the B2G space, the contracting space, most of the software is cost-driven: they call it pricing software, but it's really a cost modeling software, which was puzzling to me.

Marsha   I think there are some database-driven systems out there that larger companies tend to use to do the estimating. I make this distinction between estimating and pricing because they're not the same thing. You can't do the pricing without the estimates, but you need the basic estimates behind the data to do the pricing. Pricing strategy is the wisdom that goes into actually putting the price together. It's not the estimates. People like to confuse estimates with pricing and they're not the same thing. But there are software tools out there that do estimating and some of them, in addition to that, do the pricing.

Stephan   Thanks for clarifying that. And I was asking Larry Newman, from Shipley, why it's extremely cost-driven, and it was a bit shocking for me coming from more of a value-based background. But most of the processes that vendors go through are dominated by cost. Would you agree?

Marsha   I would agree, but that's also because the government is geared towards you justifying your costs. Again, government contracting tends to be very cost-driven. They want you to justify your costs to determine whether the price you're offering in the end is reasonable, accurate, and complete. They want to determine whether the cost that you come up with is, in fact, based on history, based on actuals, based on things that you know you can justify. So in that regard, yes it is. Although there are parts of the government world where commercial pricing comes into play, in which case cost never comes into account.

Stephan   Besides pricing, have you seen sort of a major trend at the high level in government procurement?

Marsha   The government is getting smarter in the way they put out the pricing requirements. They put out the tables they want to see. They go to great lengths where they largely ask for specifically what they want: give me this table, this table, and that table and the documentation behind it. So I'm seeing more and more of that. I've seen that over the years, probably for more than 20 years from places like NASA to some degree, and from some of DOD. NASA has always been a front leader in my book for how they do procurements and how they put out the requirements. They're also a lot more advanced in their thinking about the justification that goes into those. So if I were to say there's a trend, I'm seeing more of government agencies specifying the format in which they want you to return the answer to their pricing.

Stephan   Obviously you mentioned profits control and the transparency on cost, and that's another surprise coming from the B2B. How difficult is it to do VBP in the B2G environment?

Marsha   I think when you get into anything other than a low price technically acceptable in the LPTA [low-priced, technically acceptable] bid, you have an opportunity to show your value. If it's *truly* best-value procurement, then you have an opportunity to advance your pricing to show the additional value you bring and the price associated with it. I often talk about the business side of proposal management. You must show in the cost volume to the government where you've added value that you're offering and how you plan to deliver that additional value and what it's worth to the government. Am I saving time, money, and people? That's what it comes down to. If the government doesn't care about any of those things, then there's no point in offering it. I will say that a true price-to-win analysis will show you on a continuum where the value is that a contractor can add. The more value you offer, the more your price will go up. But you can't do that without describing to the government the value proposition you offer. That's a differentiator that the government cares about.

Stephan This is pretty much the principle of VBP, which is also the case for best-value deals. But one of the most common objections I get from people at the vendor side is that even if you have that situation, you can never get above the limit authorized to make profits in the B2G environment. They conclude by saying, "You can't do VBP in government work." Obviously I reject this position. Do you know what I mean?

Marsha I reject that too. I think there are parts of the government where they aren't looking for low price. Just-low-price procurements are going to go away, as there's a new regulation for highly technical procurement. If that's truly going to happen more and more, we're going to see the pendulum swing back on those. We'll begin to see where the government will be buying that value because it means something to them. But again, you can't do that if you don't even know whether the government cares about that. You can't guess that. You've got to know that—it's got to be something that you know in your bones—that the government cares about and is willing to pay for it.

Stephan That's amazing because the key word that you highlighted was *truly*—is it truly the best-value deal, and sometimes it's not clear, right?

Marsha Well, it's not usually clear, but you don't know that unless you've done your homework with that government customer to know whether they even care about it or not.

Stephan Let me switch gears. You have amazing content in your blog, and I invite readers to read it, and it's in your bio at the end of this interview. Let's talk a little bit about professional pricing expertise, which you mentioned is highly important in the capture plan. And much of the time we don't see that expertise in the capture process. Please tell us your view on that.

Marsha You really hit one of my hot-button issues. Some of my colleagues and I are adamant that contractors need to focus on the strategic pricing elements and actions that must accompany the capture phase. If they don't, you're behind the eight ball because of all the strategy things that sometimes get decided in the 11th hour. Management says "cut 10 percent off that" or "let's change this," and they make big, sweeping emotional changes at the end, whereas all those last-minute decisions need to be moved to the front of the plan. They need to be part of a capture plan, and if you don't invite strategic pricing in at that stage, you're starting off behind the eight ball. I can't count the number of times someone says "We're going to call on you and Marsha for some help and when the RFP comes out, we'll give you a call." That's too late. Even worse than that is when someone calls and says "I have two weeks left: I need your help." That's even more disastrous, because the strategy includes all the various decisions that go into helping you decide the right price. Put those decisions up front. If you make those same decisions at the end it's going to be madness. And so you may be making the wrong decisions. You may even be offering a price even lower than you should have, had you not talked about it in the capture phase.

Stephan   Is that what you refer to in your multiple posts as having a great pricing strategy over time?

Marsha   Yes. The strategy does develop over time. You begin it way back in the capture phase. You refine it as you begin to advance through the capture phase and into the proposal phase. Just like Larry Newman talks about the various stages of a proposal, pricing has to be involved throughout the process. You evaluate your strategy for pricing from the beginning, throughout the proposal development, and even after you submit the bid. You're probably going to get evaluation notices, questions, discussions, and you're probably going to be asked for best and final or a final pricing revision. You even want to evaluate it after you've won: "Wow, what did we do right?" Or if you've lost: "What did we do wrong?" Or when you win: "Oh, by the way, there's something you did wrong." It's not always good news when you win; you need to be evaluating your strategy and your price all along because you need to be refining it. You need to be refining it with more price-to-win activities and the competitive analysis that you'll talk about with some other folks. And you need to be refining it throughout so that you can say "Wait a minute. What we decided a month ago is no longer valid because we now have different information." And if information changes, how will you go about revising your strategy to win?

Stephan Help me understand, because I'm facing my own situation. I've done a lot of research on the way pricing looks in the B2G world, and many of the vendors don't have dedicated pricing roles. They give the responsibility to different functions: a little bit to bidding, a little bit to capture, a little bit to costing. So how can you do what you're saying without having dedicated pricing people?

Marsha Often, you don't have dedicated pricing people unless you have a larger organization that can afford them. We get called on all the time to do strategic pricing for contractors. We can augment everything from working the strategy and letting some of their own talent do the actual pricing, to being hands-on throughout the whole process, including the pricing. It depends on the level of talent inside the contractor. I will say that estimating can and should be done by the technical people, always. It shouldn't be done by pricing people, as they have little or no knowledge of the technical solution. So that work should be done by the technical team. The actual costing and pricing, and the strategy that goes into the pricing, shouldn't be done by the technical team, nor should it be done by the business development or capture team. Too often we have to follow somebody who thinks it ought to be sold at some level and then we find out it's at a different level completely. That's because they have no idea what it really costs to do the job or what it takes to actually carry forth that capture plan into a proposal plan.

Stephan In one of your blogs, you mentioned the importance of teaming very quickly. Can you explain what you mean by teaming?

Marsha Teaming means going out and finding another contractor or more to fulfill the roles that are required. Sometimes if you're a prime contractor and you're going after the bid, you may not have all the talent technically in-house to do the job and you need to find other contractors who can round out your talent. Now here's the rub. Too often subcontractors get called in to make a team without having a discussion of what the strategy is for achieving the pricing. In return, they throw an uneducated pricing over the fence, which makes the bid very non-competitive. Teammates can be the one area that will make you lose a bid.

Stephan Good. Let's switch gears. What are the three to five great qualities of a communicated pricing strategy in a proposal? What would you say is super impactful?

Marsha First and foremost, there must be an executive summary. I am adamant about this. I know people will argue with me about this all day long. There should be an executive summary in the front of the business or price volume that's maybe a page, two pages that highlight the real importance of the value you're bringing to the table as a responsive contractor. Along with that is a value proposition to convey to your customer the value that you're bringing in your price. Those two must be paramount. Third, and equally important: there must be a basis of estimate. Whether you are requested to give it or required to give it or not, you should always have a basis of estimate. In other words, you should have the detail of what makes up your pricing from the technical people so that you can price through what is it they say the requirements are. Here we have the technical people knowing what they put in the technical proposal, and sometimes that never gets conveyed to the pricing people. Imagine that! And that's where the government will find out, in reviewing the technical and the business or price volume, that they don't match. That must be the third most important thing: they have to match and alongside that have a basis of estimate, whether it's required or not. I could write a whole book on that topic!

Stephan   For a company seeking to diversify in a B2G world, what are the three key success factors in getting started in B2G pricing?

Marsha   Generally what I see is the contractor with a B2B core trying to force-fit what they did in the B2B world into the government. But it doesn't fit because the government tends to look at cost-based information, and that's unlikely how you as a contractor have ever accumulated or looked at your costs. It's important to get some advice about that. Often people ask their bookkeepers or their CPA to do it, and if they don't know the government world, I can't tell you how often they fail. They may get a contract but fall flat because they're not making money and they don't know why. And if that person advising them doesn't know about the government world, then they may be leaving out some costs that are important to include in the bid. I would say that if you're going to go into the government world, get some really good advice from someone who understands government pricing before you dive into it. If you're going into government contracting, you need to start keeping your books as if you were a big company. People say to me, "Well, Marsha, I don't have to; I don't have a requirement to do all of that that you're talking about." And I say, "You're right, you don't; but someday you're going to grow up and be a bigger company. And if you do it the way a bigger company does it, it can be fairly simple. And if you keep your books and follow policies and processes that adhere to the way a big company does, you'll be compliant from the get-go."

Stephan You can't take just a plain process of B2B and think it's going to work out for B2G. You may have to do some adapting, right?

Marsha Yes. Now, some clients come to me who are currently operating with a commercial mentality. And that may sell very nicely in the government, if they stay with commercial pricing. But if you're dealing with a government customer who only understands cost, you'll have to get your act together first.

Stephan Another question is about the no-nos. What would you say the top three no-nos are in government pricing?

Marsha The biggest no-no is waiting until the last minute; I mean, it's just huge. The sooner, the better. Begin early with your pricing and strategy discussions. But the other part that to me is a big no-no is trying to force-fit the shoes you're wearing in the commercial world into the government world. In other words, trying to do business the way you're doing business in other sectors and getting someone who doesn't understand government contracting to do the pricing for you. You could be missing a lot of costs. I think the calls I get every year that make me really cry are the contractors who say, "I have a government contract and I don't understand why I'm not making money." And part of it is that they asked, like I said, their bookkeeper or their CPA to put together their costs for them, and they eliminated, not intentionally, but just because they didn't know, all the things they should and need to put into their bid. The other big no-no is getting teammates to work with you who haven't got a clue about what it takes to win, and who aren't in the same boat as you, with respect to their mentality about winning in terms of price. If they just want to throw their price together at the last minute without regard to this being part of a strategy, then you won't win.

Stephan   It seems that many of your blogs are about winning and putting together a strategy to win. Do you think it's forgotten a lot in the B2G world?

Marsha   I don't want to say it's forgotten. What I think is that people don't realize the importance of designing a winning strategy, which includes pricing. Some teammates might not be wired to win it with the price. They're not interested in rolling through the pricing a number of times early on to see whether they'll be competitive or not. If your teammates aren't competitive with their pricing mindset, you won't win, either. And if you don't win, why bother?

Stephan   I'm going to stop here. Marsha, I appreciate all the valuable insights. I recommend all readers to read Marsha's blog and to check out her website listed in her bio. Thanks again.

The author

Marsha Lindquist is an experienced price proposal manager and contracts professional. She is an expert in cost proposal management, development, and pricing strategy. Marsha has built a tradition of quality consulting to government contractors for over 30 years. She has wide-ranging experience with government contracting firms—mostly scientific and high-technology companies. Marsha dedicates her business expertise to providing inventive solutions designed specifically for each of her clients regardless of their size. Granite Leadership Strategies specializes in comprehensive consulting services for government contracting clients ranging from small startup companies poised to grow through Fortune 500 companies interested in continuing their successes. What distinguishes Marsha from others is her ability to provide innovative solutions to problems you face in today's dynamic business environment. This capability enables her to quickly gain an in-depth understanding of your business needs and to become an integral advisor to your management team.

Marsha is adept in persuasive pricing that wins and is masterful in authoring customer-focused winning pricing strategies. Marsha works with her clients on concepts that help people cut through the irrelevant, zero in on the things that distinguish, and create value. She is described by clients as tenacious and a true pro. She has achieved the distinguished titles of NCMA Fellow, APMP Fellow, and APMP Practitioner. She serves at the APMP Valley of the Sun Chapter's program chair. Marsha can be often seen hiking with her dog Ziva—a young Australian Shepherd with lots of energy. Marsha can be found in LinkedIn at www.linkedin.com/in/marshalindquist1/

Website: www.GraniteLeadershipStrategies.com
Email: Marsha@GraniteLeadershipStrategies.com
Telephone: 480-513-1132

Key Notes

_____

_____

_____

_____

_____

_____

Key Actions

_____

_____

_____

_____

_____

_____

5

Messaging in the Proposal Cost Volume—It's More Than Numbers

Dennis Berg, Shipley Associates

Introduction

MOTIVATE GOVERNMENT EVALUATORS TO recommend your proposed solution and question competing proposals from a cost and pricing perspective. Government evaluators are interested in more than the "numbers" in the cost volume. They want to be confident that they can "trust" your numbers and that the government is receiving value for the price proposed in order to recommend your proposal for selection. To this end, your pricing must align with other proposal volumes and be understandable by non-costing-experts.

Winning proposals incorporate consistent, aligned, and convincing messaging in all proposal volumes, including the cost volume. These messages respond to the interests and concerns of the cost volume evaluators that go beyond simply obtaining the lowest price. While some acquisitions for simple or straightforward products and/or services are designed to select the lowest-priced technically acceptable (LPTA) proposal, acquisitions for more complex solutions often use "best value" as the basis for award. Authors of winning cost volumes recognize that best value is in the eyes of the customer, not in the eyes of the bidder. Weave a descriptive narrative throughout your cost volume to help cost volume evaluators recommend and justify your solution as offering the best value.

Motivate the government buyer to choose your offer by communicating a compelling best-value "story." Make that story clear, persuasive, and easy to understand.

This chapter describes six focus areas to help you conceive and convincingly communicate your best-value story:

- Understand what cost proposal evaluators are seeking.
- Establish clear value propositions and strategic themes underlying your pricing.
- Broaden evaluators' vision of "cost" beyond the numbers.
- Demonstrate that your pricing is fair, reasonable, and realistic.
- Address risks within the cost volume—both yours and competitors'.
- Organize a "traceable" cost volume with summaries, introductions, visuals, and narrative that convince evaluators that your cost volume is compliant, clear, and compelling.

These focus areas include strategic thinking and tactical activities required before the proposal is written and during proposal development to distinguish your cost volume from the competition. By following this guidance, your proposal will clearly convey the specific pricing proposed, the rationale for that pricing, compelling reasons for selection, and reasons for discomfort with potentially lower-priced proposals.

Focus areas

Understand what cost proposal evaluators are seeking
Multiple individuals in key roles influence a customer's buying decision. A key focus when planning to write a winning cost volume must be to identify, understand, and influence those individuals. Financial buyers, users, and owners have different sets of issues and different views of the costs of those issues. Before the government issues a solicitation, plan and conduct customer-focused pricing activities to identify customer interests, issues, and priorities that will influence how evaluators assess your cost volume. Conducting these activities provides vital insights to help you develop a winning cost volume and gain a head start before a solicitation is issued. After the solicitation is issued, use the question period and other available means to clarify potential conflicts or uncertainties about the government's price evaluation approach.

Customer engagement and relationship-building activities help you connect with a range of government stakeholders. Conduct these activities during the capture and pre-solicitation phases of your business development process. Once the government issues the solicitation, unlike many commercial organizations, government agencies usually restrict direct communication with individual bidders to avoid giving any bidder an unfair advantage and risking a protest. Begin as soon as your company has made an opportunity pursuit decision, which might be months or years before the government issues a final solicitation.

Identify the significant individuals in your customer's buying process, their roles, interests, and concerns about the pricing. Cost volume evaluators are almost entirely distinct from the evaluators of other proposal volumes. They might include professional proposal cost analysts, accounting staff who conduct field audits, and technical staff / subject-matter experts who assist other evaluators.

Attend pre-proposal conferences when possible, and seek one-on-one customer meetings to establish a direct, personal relationship. Seek answers to the following questions:

- **Budget.** What is the government's budget for the product and/or services being solicited? Does the budget represent full or partial funding? When is full funding anticipated, and what is the probability of receiving less than full funding? What is the budget timing for a multiyear acquisition? What types of funds are budgeted: capital investment, maintenance funds, operating funds, or fee-based funds?

- **General issues and concerns.** What issues or concerns does the government have about price proposals in general? What pricing risks do they see in evaluating the proposals and in contract execution? Which cost elements are of greatest concern, such as quantities of labor or materials or unit prices? To what extent is the government concerned about unrealistically low price proposals? To what extent is the government concerned about unreasonably high price proposals? Some concerns may be obvious and some may be hidden and require exploration. Identify the basis of all concerns so you can address them in your cost volume.

- **Cost volume assessment.** To what extent will the government develop independent cost estimates to assess the realism and reasonableness of bidders' prices? What are their sources of information? Sources might include commercial product price lists, prior purchases, and published salary surveys for applicable geographic markets.

- **Issues and concerns about your offer.** If you're able to share information about your potential proposed solution and gain customer feedback, what pricing concerns do government individuals have about your solution? Note each concern and address them in your cost volume. What additional value does the government perceive in your solution? Emphasize that value in your discussions, and collaboratively try to quantify that value with your customer.

- **Incentives.** What incentives are valued by the government in your pricing? For example, is the government seeking contractor cost sharing, discounts from published prices, and/or discounts for increased purchase quantities? Does the government expect your final price in the initial cost volume submittal, or does the government anticipate requesting final proposal revisions that could include price reductions and other proposal refinements?

Much of the information you seek may not be available by direct contact with customer stakeholders. Direct contact is often limited—especially if you don't have an established customer relationship. Research each customer's purchasing trends or patterns during the pre-solicitation period:

- **Identify relevant solicitation trends or patterns.** Relevance includes the types of products or services, contracting office/authority, and timeframe.
  - Pricing type: cost-based (with fixed fee [CPFF], incentive fee [CPIF], or award fee [CPAF]), firm fixed price (FFP), time and materials (T&M), or hybrid combinations for different work scope elements.

- Basis of award—lowest price technically acceptable (LPTA), best value, best value with tradeoff.
- How cost proposal will be evaluated.
- Multistep source selection processes.
- Recency of purchase and similar budget and economic conditions.

- **Research award patterns.** To what extent do awards go to the same or to a limited number of companies? Research competitors' pricing practices to identify patterns. Since cost volume details are often redacted, consider using external consultants who have or can develop insights into competitor pricing.

The final solicitation will specify the information the government seeks in your cost volume. Read and analyze the cost volume instructions and evaluation factors and subfactors carefully. Your cost volume must comply with the requirements and address how the government will evaluate your proposal. Comply with all cost volume instructions, including the information required and sequence of presentation. Use the government-provided templates, such as pricing spreadsheets, without modification. Note how to handle any exceptions or deviations, if allowed.

Failure to follow instructions can result in disqualification for noncompliance. Submit questions during the question and answer (Q&A) period to clarify cost volume instructions and to avoid noncompliance. Don't use questions to explore pricing alternatives or strategies. Doing so might disclose important information to competitors and diminish your competitive position. Instead, address pricing alternatives prior to solicitation issuance.

Clarify cost volume evaluation ambiguities before developing your pricing approach in order to focus your narrative and maximize your cost volume rating.

Establish the value propositions and strategic themes underlying your pricing

In winning proposals, the proposed solution incorporates tradeoffs that bidders considered in order to meet and possibly exceed customer requirements, respond to key customer issues (or "hot buttons"), and deliver superior customer value. Although government organizations focus on proposed costs, that does not necessarily eliminate value as a consideration. As in the B2B world, as the perception of the product or service being acquired shifts from "commodity" to "custom" or "unique," value becomes a greater potential government consideration.

Use the cost volume to explain the rationale for your proposed solution and pricing, emphasizing customer value. Go beyond explaining the basis for the proposed costs. Unless explicitly stated in the evaluation criteria, the government might or might not acknowledge value that exceeds requirements. Assess the value you wish to deliver and clearly communicate that value in the cost volume as well as in other proposal volumes.

Determine the value you intend to offer as a critical element of the cost volume based on customer issues and concerns as described earlier in this chapter. Consider the value that your company (or team) can deliver that can't be matched by other bidders. Use opportunity capture activities to determine the "values" that are most preferred by the customer. Also use capture activities to vet with the customer potential means to deliver that value, identify potential customer concerns and perceived risks, and conceive the most viable and cost-effective solutions.

As you develop pricing, develop a storyboard for the cost volume, with emphasis on customer value. Customer value, or benefits, can be characterized as one of three types:

- Improved performance in terms of quality delivered or mission accomplished.
- Improved schedule (often accelerated, but a faster schedule is not always desired by the customer).
- Reduced cost, which supports budget savings or reallocation of "savings" to other priorities.

The *Shipley Proposal Guide* describes the storyboard process and provides a proposal development worksheet template to support this activity. Align the content of this storyboard with the solution and messaging content developed for the technical and management volumes that address your approach.

Call attention to where your solution offers the potential to deliver additional value that goes beyond the immediate scope of the proposed effort. This scenario, and guidance for addressing this additional value, are described below.

Broaden evaluators' vision of "cost" beyond the numbers

Cost proposals typically focus only on pricing proposed work under the contract. However, the work can directly impact costs outside the specific contract. The products or services may have multiple downstream cost impacts, often within the same program budget. For example, the quality of contract services to provide acquisition support or program management can directly impact the cost of other contracts, programs, and projects touched by those services. Similarly, for product-focused solicitations, higher-quality products with longer life spans and lower failure rates can postpone and/or reduce the costs for downstream product replacement.

For each solicitation, determine during your capture planning activities whether the products and/or services could save the government money or enable reallocation of saved budget due to specific capabilities and benefits of your offer. Preview these potential savings or reallocations with the customer to determine the extent to which they are valued. If you discern substantial interest, suggest that the customer include such savings in their proposal evaluation approach.

Use the cost volume to highlight these savings. Be prepared to cite specific quantified savings or a range of savings, and clear and compelling justifications for those savings. Cite technical and management approaches proposed in other proposal volumes to achieve these savings. Include as much past-performance detail as possible about previously delivered savings as justification. Also note assumptions that show the applicability of your prior experience to the current solicitation to help make your savings estimates believable. Describe areas of uncertainty honestly so that your proposal doesn't appear deceptive. Such honesty could refreshingly stand out from other bidders and help motivate the evaluators to select your bid.

To get maximum consideration of these cost savings, cultivate support from one or more individuals in the purchasing organization to advocate for these cost savings and the advantages to the government by selecting your company.

Discuss higher-cost approaches that might be proposed by competitors and that you rejected, and why these approaches could impose substantial additional costs on the government. These approaches might include the following:

- Proposing lower up-front product costs due to inferior designs, materials quality, assembly techniques, quality control processes, and so forth—that result in higher maintenance costs and/or shorter life.

- Proposing lower-cost labor categories in service contracts that lead to lower-quality service delivery and higher cost to the government outside the immediate contract.
- Proposing lower-cost approaches that appear to meet minimum requirements but reduce mission readiness and/or capability.

Demonstrate that your pricing is fair, reasonable, and realistic

In most cases, government evaluation of cost or price is independent of technical and past-performance evaluation. The focus is to ensure that costs or prices considered are fair and reasonable. On cost-reimbursable contracts, the Federal Acquisition Regulations (FAR) also requires cost realism to be determined, taking into account the work to be performed and the unique methods and materials proposed. Under limited circumstances, realism also must be determined for fixed-price offers.

Cost evaluators may determine that a reasonable, realistic cost or price is different from an offeror's proposed figure. On fixed-price contracts, such assessments influence evaluations of risk but do not affect evaluated price except through negotiations held as part of discussions. On cost-reimbursable contracts, they may result in the government arriving at an evaluated cost that is higher or lower than stated in a proposal.

To demonstrate that your pricing is fair, reasonable, and realistic, explain the basis for all pricing, including all direct cost elements, labor overhead, general and administrative expense, and fees (where applicable). Include the details. The government usually allows unlimited page count in the cost volume.

- For direct costs, cite the basis of estimate for resource quantities and the details and sources for unit pricing of those resources. Explain all direct pricing elements. In addition to labor and materials, these elements could include travel, equipment, licensing fees, and other direct costs.

- In your direct cost basis of estimate, explain the method used to determine the quantities proposed, emphasizing why the quantities are sufficient to deliver the contracted work and not excessive. Include a work-breakdown structure (WBS) to lay out the full scope of work, and a WBS dictionary to provide a framework for tracking program costs, schedules, and program performance. A well-prepared WBS and WBS dictionary give government evaluators validation and confidence in your calculations. Cite where that methodology has been used and evidence of its accuracy. Include clear evidence to justify all claimed efficiencies. A weak basis of estimate will undermine the government's confidence in your pricing.

- For unit prices, describe specific methods and information sources used to develop the prices, showing how the proposed prices are neither understated nor excessive. For each source, explain why or how the source is qualified and reasonable. Where possible, use recognized external sources to price common elements, such as published salary surveys for labor resources and published vendor price lists for parts and supplies. To enhance your pricing credibility, use capture activities to discover pricing sources that are most trusted by government.

Address risks within the cost volume

Government evaluators seek to minimize pricing risk when evaluating the cost volume. This is particularly applicable to cost-based and T&M contracts where the government is obligated to pay for additional effort beyond the proposed price. Cost-based contracts also pose the risk of higher actual unit prices than those proposed.

Winning cost volumes anticipate and address the risks that concern the government, giving greater confidence in the proposed prices. Government cost evaluators may "plus-up" your proposed price to account for risk. To cultivate greater confidence in your proposed price with minimal pricing risk, consider risk elements that could impact your proposed pricing. Technical performance risks often have a price risk. For example, schedule delays, defective parts or products, labor shortages, equipment outages, and other adverse events impact work activities and often increase actual costs. For contracts with uncertain workloads, increased workload demands will increase contract costs above the proposed price.

Address each risk element in your technical approach, management approach, and basis of estimate where applicable, and cross-reference these (or repeat them!) in your cost volume. Align your cost volume with all other proposal volumes to capture any and all assumptions made about contract workloads and performance that could impact the quantity and/or pricing of all cost elements. As you identify new assumptions when developing your proposed pricing, include them in the assumptions for other proposal volumes. Misaligned assumptions across proposal volumes prompt the government to lose confidence in your pricing.

As part of the risk discussion, identify from a technical perspective what could go wrong or contingencies that could occur for your contract. Explain how you've built these considerations into your technical approach and your pricing to minimize adverse impacts and save the government money. Indicate elements of your technical or management approach that may be unique and not proposed by competitors—elements that could add performance risk and cost risk to the government if they select a competitor.

Organize the cost volume to be compliant,
clear, and compelling

The cost volume merits the same attention as all other sections of the proposal. Too often, the cost volume contents are not completed until late in the proposal development process, leaving limited time for refinement and delivery of a compelling volume. Reduce the time pressure after RFP solicitation release to develop a compliant, clear, and *compelling* cost volume by applying these best practices:

- Begin drafting a cost volume executive summary as early as possible. Use this cost volume summary to guide pricing team efforts. This practice parallels the development of the overall executive summary early in the proposal planning and development process.
- Determine the cost volume portions that can be developed (i.e., planned and written in draft form) before the government issues the solicitation. These portions may include descriptions of financial and accounting systems, assumptions that will be used for pricing development, and first drafts of the basis of estimate and bill of materials.
- Begin key inputs to pricing before the solicitation release, and build/refine the necessary internal tools. These tools include pricing tables, alternate scenario tables, financial analysis spreadsheets, and templates for the WBS, bill of materials, and other cost categories. Refine these templates as needed once the government issues the final solicitation.
- Establish a pricing development and review schedule in line with the rest of the proposal development schedule. Avoid

pressures to let the pricing team work in isolation from the other proposal development volume teams.

From a cost volume organization and content perspective, apply these best practices:

- To achieve full compliance, create and use a detailed compliance matrix as described in the *Shipley Proposal Guide* to map all the cost volume requirements and confirm that they are addressed.
- Develop and use an outline that follows the required cost volume organization.
- Use the spreadsheets and other tools provided and required by the solicitation. Don't alter them unless allowed by the solicitation.
- Create subsections within the required outline that include the detailed explanations described in this chapter. Work within the government's sections wherever possible so that your expanded narrative will be read and not skipped.
- Include a cost volume executive summary unless precluded by the solicitation instructions.
- Confirm that all cost details are traceable and trackable. Cross-reference where an item summarized at a higher level is supported by details at a lower level.
- Mimic RFP terminology, numbering systems, and headings to facilitate evaluation and compliance with the RFP.
- Make your cost volume compelling by using effective, best practice, emphasis techniques—theme statements, callouts or focus boxes, benefits/features tables, informative titles, and action captions for all visuals such as tables and diagrams. Craft phrasing that evaluators can copy and paste into their evaluation forms to justify a high rating and low pricing risk.

- Use theme statements at the beginning of each subsection to highlight key benefits and supporting features as a preview of the subsection content. The most powerful themes contain the most important benefits and, where applicable, discriminators, something the customer wants that other bidders can't offer.
- Use callouts or focus boxes to direct the evaluator's attention to a key message that you want to stand out from the narrative text.
- For every table, diagram, chart, or other visual element, use an informative title to introduce a brief message, followed by an action caption to convey a complete thought that you want to the evaluator to associate with that visual element. For example, rather than providing a table titled "<Company Name> Staffing Hours," instead consider titling the table "<Company Name> Experience-Based Staffing Hours," followed by a caption such as "<Customer Name is supported by a staffing plan that uses a labor mix and assigned hours that reflects the same principles applied on <Customer Name>'s six recent programs that consistently receive Outstanding customer ratings for performance and cost efficiency."
- Use a consistent system for page layout, including headings, themes, action captions, lists, tables, callouts, and other page design features.
  - Use color and white space to direct evaluators to key points.
  - Avoid overusing emphasis devices such as bolding, colored narrative, and underlining.
  - Use flush-left text with a ragged right margin to enhance the readability of text and tables.

Conclusion

Proposal cost volumes are more than pricing summaries and detailed backups. The cost volume must tell a story, and that story must align with, and ideally surpass, government client expectations. Address all the government requirements. Provide a compelling story about why your price is fair and realistic. Where possible, use risk discussions to cast doubt on the reasonableness of competitors' pricing. Stress the value delivered by your offer, and how that value impacts the true "cost" to the government beyond the purchase price. Construct your price volume to be compliant by addressing all requirements, to be easy to navigate and evaluate, and to provide a clear and obvious story that helps evaluators rate your cost volume highly and recommend your proposal for award.

Implications for B2G pricing

Winning cost volumes in B2G proposals are the product of the following best practices:

- Begin pricing activities early, months before the expected release of the final solicitation. Directly engage government customer stakeholders, including the contracting officer / administrative officer, as early as possible.
- Determine the issues and concerns that the government evaluators will have about the proposal pricing in general and the pricing of your offering in particular. Address all issues and concerns to give your proposed price strong credibility and avoid a cost *plus-up* for perceived risk.
- Understand what the government will value and clearly delineate the value that will be delivered by your proposed offering. Emphasize the quantified value of a government direct cost

saving or a budget reallocation opportunity. Quantify that value with credible proof points to enable the government to assess these cost effects and "bottom line" price.

- Include detailed descriptions and substantiation of all cost elements, including basis of estimate, unit prices, pricing-related assumptions, and any proposed budget savings or reallocations.
- Design and deliver a cost volume that's compliant, that's easy to navigate, that clearly communicates the key reasons to select your solution, and that ghosts potential concerns about the pricing of competing proposals.

The author

Dennis Berg is a Senior Consultant with Shipley Associates. He has 40+ years of government program delivery and BD experience as a consultant, trainer, and coach. He has supported development and refinement of Shipley's proposal writing, proposal management, and capture planning best-practices workshops for responding to government procurements, and he has trained over 900 professionals with consistently high ratings. He has led and won a broad range of proposals to state agencies and to federal defense, civilian, homeland security, and intelligence government agencies for new business and recompletes, products and services, IDIQ contracts, task orders, and definite quantity contracts. These proposals encompass complex solutions exceeding $5 billion to smaller procurements valued at several hundred thousand. Prior to joining Shipley Associates, he served as Director of Capture Support and Proposals at Acquisition Solutions Inc. / ASI Government, and as Director of BD Practices and Deputy Risk Manager at American Management Systems, Inc.'s, Public Sector business area. Mr. Berg holds a BS in Economics and an MBA, both from the Wharton Business School at the University of Pennsylvania.

Key Notes

_____

_____

_____

_____

_____

_____

Key Actions

_____

_____

_____

_____

_____

_____

6

Government Requests for Proposals in the Digital Era: Win Tactics

Scott D. Miller, Miller Advisors

SELLING SOFTWARE AND SOFTWARE-ENABLED systems to government entities differs substantially from selling to the private sector. The rules of engagement will differ. The degree of scrutiny around evaluating and selecting vendors will differ. And the sales and bid submission process requires a unique skill set for sales and product teams to navigate through government procurement documents and processes that are "dense, confusing, and filled with bureaucratic speak and legal language" (2020 Vet Logistics Solutions, 2019). Some software firms avoid selling to government entities entirely because of this high level of complexity as well as the erroneous perception that there are minimal opportunities to earn profits; this alone can be based on the "governments only sell to the lowest bidder" mindset that is further reinforced by contractual clauses that mandate a lowest price to government (such as the "most-favored customer" [MFC] clause). But those companies that establish the right government-centric business model coupled with the right pricing, product, and sales tactics not only sell successfully within this more complex procurement environment but do so sustainably and profitably.

The changing landscape of government procurement for commercial software

The digital government landscape is continuously changing to reflect how governments are trying to find innovative digital solutions to social, economic, political, and other pressures, and how they transform themselves in the process (Janowski, 2015). For software companies, this has created a growing demand for commercial solutions that help governments drive to more modernized delivery of services, improve their operational efficiencies to make better use of government funds and resources, and, from a federal military perspective, drive an ongoing competitive advantage.

For software and software-enabled system vendors, this has provided an opportunity to deliver value-based solutions in what has traditionally been a cost-focused segment. Although they have been slow to adapt, many government procurement arms are now shifting how they go about purchasing software that includes new government funding mechanisms to better accommodate the recurring value and subscription pricing aspect of SaaS. "Software Is Never Done" was the title of a recent US Department of Defense Software Acquisition and Practices (SWAP) study: "Hardware can be developed, procured, maintained in linear fashion. Software is an enduring capability that must be supported and continuously improved throughout its lifecycle" (McQuade et al., 2019). Even France's procurement office, DGA, has recently undergone a major transformation to improve how they partner with the industry and improve procedures around both acquisition and delivery of software and innovation (Tran, 2018).

What this means for software and software-enabled system vendors is that there's no better time than now to be selling to government entities: the advantages of modernization are too big to ignore, and the expertise of the commercial sector enables vendors to become trusted advisors and major contributors to the development of the digital government.

Request-for-proposals (RFPs): Win tactics

For both government and commercial sectors, larger opportunities that involve software or software-enabled systems will typically go through the RFP bid process, whereby an RFP is a document that solicits a proposal through a bidding process by an agency or company interested in procuring a solution to potential suppliers to submit business proposals. For software vendors, a minimum set of technical requirements is often needed to qualify as a vendor candidate alongside a well-documented solution design, implementation plan, change management approach, staffing of resources, and training.

Although government RFPs may be more cumbersome than those from the private sector, there are some advantages that include greater transparency and accountability around how government selection committees evaluate vendors and award contracts. Understanding various nuances of government RFPs and applying certain response tactics can help an organization not only improve their competitive positioning during the evaluation process but also ensure that they're optimally priced.

These 10 B2G win tactics reflect best practices used by market leaders to drive ongoing favorable RFP outcomes:

1 **Develop a "bid/no-bid decision" evaluation process.** Every vendor needs to ensure that company resources are well used to drive the most favorable bid outcomes. In this case, not every deal is necessarily a good deal to pursue; government bids often involve a lengthy sales cycle, and if a vendor continuously pursues every opportunity, resources could be diverted from spending better-quality time on managing and developing better sales leads as well as focusing on more-profitable and higher-likelihood wins that are a more favorable fit for their organization.

   Best-in-class organizations will develop a *bid/no-bid scorecard* that typically addresses three to eight key questions for each of the following categories: the solicitation (e.g., What are the evaluation criteria?), the solicitor (e.g., What is our relationship?), the competition (e.g., Is there an incumbent? Who are the competitors?), our organization (e.g., Do we have resources to respond?), our solution (e.g., Degree of fit with solicitor requirements and objectives?), our strategic objectives (e.g., Is this bid aligned with our core objectives?), risks (e.g., Risks of winning? Penalties for nonperformance?), finances (e.g., Do we have the budget to respond?), and partners (e.g., Do we need to partner? Is the partner available to assist?). Using a standardized bid/no-bid process ensures that your teams are better aligned on how to best make use of company resources and maximize time well-spent.

2 **Know thy bid type—and understand how each impacts your bid-response strategy.** Governments typically issue three types of bid proposals with respect to software and software-enabled systems. It will be important

to understand what type of bid has been issued in order to determine how to best respond from a solution design (value) and pricing perspective. Two official (Watson, 2015) and one unofficial bid type are depicted in figure 6.1.

As mentioned above, software and software-enabled systems are helping to drive new and ongoing innovation for the

	Official Bid Types		Unoffical Bid Type
	Lowest Price Technically Acceptable (LPTA) Bid	Best Value Trade-Off Bid	Best Value Trade-Off Bid...but designed like an LPTA
Decision Driver	Cost	Value and Cost	Cost
Description	Requirements are well defined and participants in the evaluation have sufficient knowledge to confidently choose a technically acceptable proposal.	Evaluators are not as certain about the requirements and utilize non-cost factors to negotiate with offerors.	Intention is to be a best value bid, though the evaluation scoring is poorly designed and does not allow for sufficient value differentiation between vendors ("everyone meets the checkboxes"). Cost, by default, becomes the decision crtieria.
Tactics	1 Lowest bidder wins 2 Meet the minimum requirement; nothing more, nothing less	1 Premium price when value advantaged relative to known competitors 2 Price more aggressively when value disadvantaged relative to known competitors	1 Work with selector earlier in the process to improve bid design 2 Continue to push for value differentiation in selector discussions 3 Worst case could involve a bid protest

Figure 6.1. Government bid types.

digital government. In these cases, *best-value tradeoff bids* are a common type of bid for more complex solutions involving software. Optimizing pricing for these bids requires a sound understanding of the scoring criteria and how one's solution is value-positioned relative to competitors, influencing the potential to be premium priced (as in figure 6.2) or, alternatively, a need to be more price competitive.

I highlighted a more detailed price and scoring approach in chapter 20 in this volume.

3 **Influence RFP design early in the process—create the competitive advantage.** Request for information (RFI) and solicitor Q&A provide an opportunity to "inject" one's solution design advantages and differentiation within the evaluation scoring criteria; this provides an edge over competitors that may lack many of these advantages. As well, for larger, more established software firms, influencing the technical and company background requirements can also help "thin the herd" of potential new entrant competitors

	Price	Value	Price Score	Value Score	Total Score
Software Company A	$1,530,000	Good	6.2	6.4	6.3
Software Company B	$1,210,000	Acceptable	6.7	5.0	5.5
Software Company C	$943,000	Marginal	7.5	4.8	5.6
Software Company D	$2,450,000	Outstanding	5.2	6.9	6.4

RFP Award

Figure 6.2. Best-value tradeoff bids: Premium pricing opportunities.

that are unable to meet such minimum requirements. Alternatively, for newer entrants, it will be important to ensure that requirements are not overly stringent, thereby disqualifying them for consideration—many new software vendors, in particular SaaS-based B2G vendors, can be more adaptive and efficient at delivering new innovations and upgrades than legacy on-premise vendors. In this case, newer SaaS entrants should influence RFPs to include future upgrade-cost considerations as part of the RFP's price-cost assessment to work in their favor against higher future upgrade costs from legacy on-premise vendors.

4 **Become the trusted advisor rather than the vendor looking from the "outside in."** Influencing early in the RFP design process is an opportunity to work closely with the government team to build the best possible solution that addresses their current and future needs. "All we know is what we know" reflects buyer uncertainty around requirements and potential lack of awareness of new market trends and new innovation. Software vendors can strengthen their relationship by bringing in this industry expertise and best practices to help develop ideal (best-value tradeoff bid) requirements that help clients achieve their digital government objectives— all the while becoming a trusted advisor. In many cases, the evaluation committees will include scoring mechanisms with respect to a vendor's level of expertise, relationship, and partnership potential, as well as sales team service—in this case, an organization does not want to become the one vendor looking from the "outside in" throughout the RFP process.

5 **Gain access to the evaluation factors for award (scoring mechanisms)—and conduct internal mock score assessments.** Governments are much more transparent in their bid process compared with the private sector,

and each vendor should request and have in hand the planned scoring criteria that will be used by the selection committee. From the highest level, this should include the decision weighting between price and value, signaling the degree of price sensitivity. Subcategories of value have additional scoring criteria that will typically focus on technical merit (e.g., solution design, implementation, servicing) and oral/demo presentation (ability to meet business requirements and satisfy workflow scenarios). See also figure 20.5 in chapter 20 in this volume for a detailed software value scorecard.

A product team's internal mock RFP scoring should also include assessments of the most likely competitors—understand where your offering is value advantaged and disadvantaged and determine how your value position relative to competition will impact your RFP pricing response.

Best-in-class B2G vendors are well tuned to these scorecards and ensure that heavily weighted decision drivers are closely linked to ongoing improvements within their roadmap. Client value perceptions are also routinely validated with market research, user groups, and win-loss analysis.

6 **Consider partnerships within your solution ecosystem—enhance value, overcome short-term value gaps, and create competitive advantages.** For many vendors, the increasing complexity of solution requirements to meet the digital government is an opportunity to expand their portfolio to create a much larger, and more monetizable, ecosystem of working parts. For others, this can begin to create potential gaps in their solution offering—gaps that would typically be addressed as product "catch-up" in future roadmap development. But there could also be considerations to partner with other software firms as a means to enhance value or address these potential value gaps. For example, a

more mature software vendor could partner with, and integrate with, smaller niche best-in-breed software/app vendors (e.g., chatbot software), allowing their own developers to remain focused on improvements related to their core product offering.

Partnerships can also be used by smaller and newer software firms to establish an "in" with government entities under the umbrella of a more well-established software firm. For example, would a chatbot software vendor be more successful selling directly to government as a standalone offer, or would it be more successful integrating as a third-party application with a major government enterprise resource planning (ERP) software vendor?

Ultimately, partnerships are part of the strategic question "build, buy, or partner?" with an overall goal of enhancing the value of the broader solution for the purpose of overcoming value gaps and/or developing a monetizable competitive advantage in RFPs.

7 **Avoid ad-hoc pricing for every deal—create an ongoing structure around your software pricing models.** As I discuss in chapter 20 of this volume, there's a process for developing value-based pricing structures for software that address different needs for different client segments. Even for those software companies that have a limited number of RFPs per year, a rigorous *offer design* evaluation of pricing ensures that the pricing conversation (and RFP response) is strongly linked to the product value story—as well as to understanding how this value positioning changes with competition. Teams with internal price structures spend less time negotiating internally and more time developing solution designs that will win an RFP. Alternatively, those companies lacking a dependable pricing structure are less confident around how their

pricing is linked to the solution "value story"—more often than not, this results in teams underpricing the full potential of the software. These teams can also spend considerably more time building ad-hoc price structures for each deal at the expense of time better spent developing winnable solution designs.

Structured pricing strategies also help simplify the internal price conversation around "who gets what price, and why" and, when integrated with price discounting policies, ensure a compliant process that satisfies internal audit requirements as well as any government-mandated pricing obligations (e.g., MFC).

8 **Take advantage of post-RFP win-loss analysis— apply these outcomes to adjust your pricing and product strategy.** One advantage with many government procurement processes is the inclusion of post-RFP follow-ups to all parties that participated in the RFP. Depending on the degree of unredacted detail, these follow-up reports can provide a wealth of information about why one's organization was, or wasn't, awarded a contract. Direct quotes from those on the selection committee, for example, can help one better understand qualitative value perceptions. Quantitative scores in the assessment can help improve a company's understanding where they are value advantaged, disadvantaged, underpriced, or overpriced. Modeling these scoring results can also allow a product team to conduct what-if scenarios around both price ("Could we have been 10 percent higher in price and still win?") and value ("What if we invested more in the ease-of-use value category to drive a score of 8 instead of a 4?")

Surprisingly, many software firms pay minimal attention to these reports. But these *voice-of-the-client* insights are a major input to help drive awareness and improvements around one's overall price strategy and value positioning.

9 **Become a master of the demo—create the "wow" factor and address highest-weighted scoring criteria.** Product demonstrations to government selection committees and potential users can make, or break, an RFP win. This is where a company needs to bring in their "A team," validate what was provided in the written proposal (or overcome potential concerns), and build strong confidence that their overall solution, team, and implementation approach meets and exceeds both current and future expectations. This is the opportunity to stand out among the competition—the "wow" factor that hits home for them how your offering is a best fit for delivering their desired core objectives.

Prior to conducting demos, teams should ensure that they're fully refamiliarized with the scoring assessment mechanisms—and address those value categories that are most heavily weighted in the assessment team's scoring decisions; a "point here and there" can mean the difference between winning and losing a contract award.

10 **Celebrate team successes (and take the time to learn from losses).** Government RFPs—from date of issuance, to solution design and costing analysis, to written proposals, to oral presentations, to product demonstrations, to the final contract award—can be a lengthy process requiring considerable time, effort, and skill sets from countless individuals across the organization. The dependency on a strong, cohesive, and talented team to deliver winning solutions can never be understated—take in those moments of success, celebrate, and reward those who helped make the company's journey to contract awards possible.

Even RFP losses provide an opportunity to celebrate a team's effort—this enables various contributors a time to reflect, learn, and restrategize to drive more favorable outcomes in the future.

Ultimately, those organizations that build a winning combination of high-value solutions alongside high-impact product, sales, and delivery teams will dominate in this era of digital transformation.

References

2020 Vet Logistics Solutions. (2019). *Sections of an RFP: An easy guide to complex proposals.* Retrieved from https://cdn.ymaws.com/www.wipp.org/resource/resmgr /gm5_podcasts_rev/RFP_Help.pdf

Janowski, T. (2015). Digital government evolution: From transformation to contextualization. *Government Information Quarterly, 32*(3), 221–236.

McQuade, J. M., Murray, R. M., Louie, G., Medin, M., Pahlka, J., & Stephens, T. (2019). *Software is never done: Refactoring the acquisition code for competitive advantage.* Department of Defense, Defense Innovation Board. Retrieved from https://media.defense.gov/2019 /Mar/26/2002105909/-1/-1/0/SWAP.REPORT_MAIN .BODY.3.21.19.PDF

Tran, P. (2018). French procurement office to undergo transformation. *DefenseNews,* July 6. Retrieved from https://www.defensenews.com/global/europe/2018/07/06 /french-procurement-office-to-undergo-transformation/

Watson, K. (2015). *LPTA versus tradeoff: How procurement methods can impact contract performance.* Monterey, CA: Naval Postgraduate School.

The author

Scott Miller is the founder of Miller Advisors (https://www.miller-advisors.com), a pricing, monetization, and offer-design consulting firm with a specialty in B2B and B2G software. He is also a speaker and instructor on best pricing practices with the Professional Pricing Society (PPS) and the International Software Product Management Association (ISPMA), bringing over 15 years of experience from a variety of consulting and global corporate pricing roles. Scott is also a Chartered Professional Accountant (CPA) and a Certified Management Accountant (CMA).

Key Notes

_____

_____

_____

_____

_____

_____

Key Actions

_____

_____

_____

_____

_____

_____

Section 2

VALUE-BASED PRICING

7

Value-Based Pricing in the B2G World

I COULD WRITE A WHOLE book about how to conduct value-based pricing (VBP) in the public sector. Some say it's impossible, but I reject this argument. First, VBP is a methodology that can be applied anywhere and everywhere. Some of the steps might be different, but whether you sell toothpaste or missile systems, the principles of VBP apply. Second, VBP is already used in many sectors of the B2G world, especially when dealing with advanced technologies and science. It might be called something else, but the principles are well accepted (examples are software for education or pharmaceuticals). Third, VBP is not for everyone or for every market. For pure commodities such as paperclips or bottled water, there might be value in the services or supply chain for these good, but the product itself will be a commodity and might be best suited for a best-value analysis. In this chapter, I give a basic introduction to VBP without getting into too many details.

There are excellent books dedicated to the topic, and I encourage you to read. This section of the book also focuses on critical aspects of the methodology. After introducing VBP, I focus on three important dimensions of VBP in the B2G world: how to perform it in a profit-controlled environment; how to apply it to solutions and systems; and how to prepare for internal and external objections to VBP.

The six steps of VBP:
Introducing a formal methodology

VBP is a challenging methodology to design and deploy in any organization. But the result is straightforward. It allows you to do simple messaging in front of the customer, but it takes a lot of work to get to those simple messages that you can communicate with pride and defend with confidence. If you want to charge a premium, you proudly acknowledge that you're more expensive, but then you must justify that premium with your quantified value proposition, which in turn derives directly from your value drivers and your value modeling. Or you can argue that you're less expensive than the competition because of the value you add and how you express it to gain an advantage. You use rational arguments and tangible evidence expressed in dollars and cents, not wishful thinking and pie-in-the-sky selling messages. You rely on your value drivers and your value proposition, and your value-in-use financial analysis. Don't buy into the T-shirts with the fancy slogans or read the books proclaiming that VBP is something you just do quickly with little ramp-up time. You don't drop what you're doing, turn on a dime, and begin focusing intensely on your customers to the exclusion of costs and competition. That's the wrong answer to the wrong question. Here are some of the "right" questions you need to answer first for your customers:

- How much can I shorten your time to market?
- How long can I extend the life of your equipment?
- How can I make your mission more productive?
- How much downtime can I prevent?
- How much money can I save you?
- How much additional revenue and profit can I generate for you?

No matter the question, you need to express the answer, the value, in hard and defensible dollars and cents. How well can you answer these questions right now? Keep them in mind.

Figure 7.1 shows the six steps that will lead you to VBP in your organization. You'll immediately see that this isn't a light switch, a magic potion, or a silver bullet. It involves a journey of discovery about your market and the value you add to it. These are the six steps that I train managers to take in their own firms, after I give them a readiness assessment.

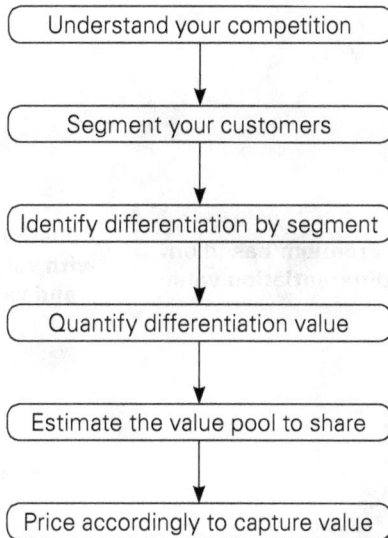

Understand your competition

↓

Segment your customers

↓

Identify differentiation by segment

↓

Quantify differentiation value

↓

Estimate the value pool to share

↓

Price accordingly to capture value

Figure 7.1. The six steps of value-based pricing.

To understand this process, you must understand the definition of customer value, customer needs, and customer hot buttons. More precisely, you must understand the definition of differentiation value. VBP is about not the *highest* price you can achieve but rather the *right* price for the value delivered versus your competitors. Right now, without the customer perspective, you can be totally underpriced or overpriced. That's the risk that consultants and scholars often cite when they criticize a focus on cost-based or competition-based pricing at the expense of customer-based pricing. But you need to consider all three. The only way to judge whether you're properly priced is to know the value you deliver to your customers and how to share that value. Figure 7.2 provides an overview of this concept.

Value can be anywhere nowadays. It often lies far beyond what you immediately perceive. Look for it! As companies innovate and add complexity, it's up to the marketers to find the tangible and intangible pockets of customer value that these companies

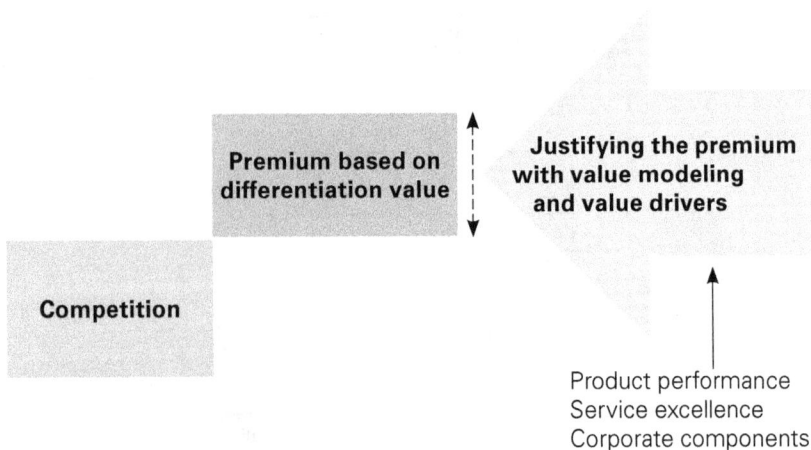

Premium based on differentiation value

Justifying the premium with value modeling and value drivers

Competition

Product performance
Service excellence
Corporate components

Figure 7.2. The key phrase is differentiation value. How high is yours?

create. That's the mission of marketing, its way of contributing to a company's success. It's also why getting to VBP is not a copy-and-paste exercise or a silver-bullet one. While it's possible to learn from what others have accomplished, each company's value and each company's desire to share it is unique to that company. Each situation is unique. There's no copy-and-paste. Nor are there any guarantees of success. I often begin the process of identifying and dollarizing differentiation with a specific customer, only to demonstrate that their differentiation level for some products is weak or even negative. For other products or services, that differentiation is much more positive. Until you begin this process, everything's theoretical. You won't know your differentiation value until you get into the details of the customer's perceived value and then start building these models.

VBP for solutions and systems

Solutions and bundles present a more complicated challenge when you're trying to understand the value they provide and then dollarize it. The more complex the system, the more complex the VBP analysis. When you have systems of systems, the work takes a long time. In my short experience in B2G, we've attempted to conduct such deep value analysis, and we weren't as successful as I'd have hoped. This approach requires patience, expertise, and deep understanding of the value of system engineering. More often than not, we would not go the whole nine yards to dollarize the value of the gel of the system. This is where all the differentiation resides. Good system integrators understand the value of their services and what they tangibly provide their customers.

The sticking point here is that many companies try to do this exercise holistically rather than breaking the solution or the bundle into its components. The trick is to follow the path you took when you looked at the value of an individual product, that is, you understand your customer's needs and capabilities, and your competitors' ability to provide solutions. With solutions and systems, as with services, you also need to consider "do it yourself" as a viable alternative.

You perform your value modeling analysis on each individual component of the system, then look at the value of overall solutions based on combinations of these components. Factors such as goodwill, brand, management quality, integration, design, testing, communication, and reputation also matter at this stage. This process gives you the basis for defining a value pool for the solution or system and for making the same kinds of value-sharing decisions. The process is summarized in figure 7.3. This is advanced modeling, and I could write an entire book on how to dollarize complex systems. You know customer dynamics and know who the direct and indirect competitors for each component are and do the value map for each component. This debundling, rebundling, and understanding influencers each step of the way is the process you need to follow for very complex products such as battleships, complex IT infrastructure, security systems, power plants, or other complex, multimillion-dollar installations. A fighter jet isn't a product in the strict sense. It's a system.

VBP in a profit-controlled environment under government acquisition processes

Some governments require signature of cost and profit principles, limiting the profit margin that vendors can achieve. Costs are transparent, and projects can be audited by government entities. This is highly probable in sole-source contracts. While it is difficult to achieve greater levels of gross margin and profit in these

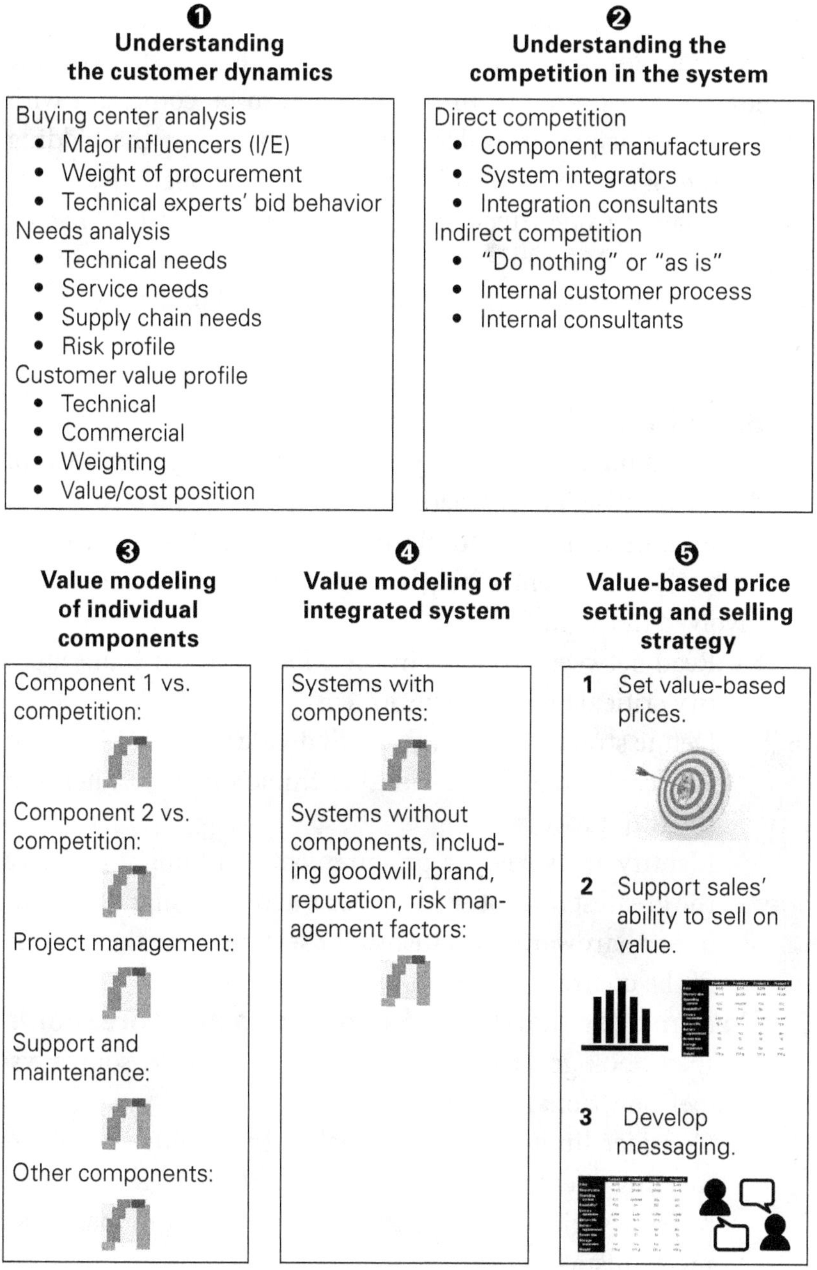

❶
**Understanding
the customer dynamics**

Buying center analysis
- Major influencers (I/E)
- Weight of procurement
- Technical experts' bid behavior

Needs analysis
- Technical needs
- Service needs
- Supply chain needs
- Risk profile

Customer value profile
- Technical
- Commercial
- Weighting
- Value/cost position

❷
**Understanding the
competition in the system**

Direct competition
- Component manufacturers
- System integrators
- Integration consultants

Indirect competition
- "Do nothing" or "as is"
- Internal customer process
- Internal consultants

❸
**Value modeling
of individual
components**

Component 1 vs.
competition:

Component 2 vs.
competition:

Project management:

Support and
maintenance:

Other components:

❹
**Value modeling of
integrated system**

Systems with
components:

Systems without
components, includ-
ing goodwill, brand,
reputation, risk man-
agement factors:

❺
**Value-based price
setting and selling
strategy**

1   Set value-based
    prices.

2   Support sales'
    ability to sell on
    value.

3   Develop
    messaging.

Figure 7.3. Dollarizing the value of systems and solutions.

situations, there are mechanisms that bid and financial managers can consider for extracting incremental value in their bids. The foundation of working in this situation is to be compliant with cost/profit principles in order to be able to stay in the bidding game. The objective is to find pockets of positional advantages we may have through technology or expertise and to ethically respond to RFI/RFP while extracting more value. Here are 10 tips to defend your higher margin in open-book and profit-controlled situations:

1 **Spend time studying the RFP in detail** and linking it to the customer knowledge you might have: customer areas of deep expertise, areas where the customer might focus heavily, level of sensitivity to big-ticket items in the offer, sensitivity of buying-center stakeholders, knowledge of individuals involved in the RFP.
   - Read between the lines in the RFP documents and identify critical areas of focus for cost.
   - Define strategy for how you will divide your time between "benchmarkable" and "non-benchmarkable" cost items in the RFP process.
   - Identify areas where a procurement team might not have the greatest level of expertise or interest. It might be product or hardware costs instead of services over the lifetime of the contract, for example.

2 **Have a clear mapping of conditions and thresholds** of open-book/government-audit situations (sole source vs. competition, dollar thresholds).
   - Consider limiting offer size below thresholds and piece-mealing offer to generate revenues at a later stage (tranches, phases, variations, adjustments, and/or additional tasks mechanisms).

- Maximize profitability of rate cards and markups for future quoting of tasks or variations (often rate cards are not the primary concerns of evaluations during acquisition contracts, contrary to services or panel contracts).

3 **Understand some critical primary drivers** that could justify being outside standard parameters and limitations:
- Safety of troops or end users.
- Sustainability and carbon footprint in a very sensitive area.
- Survivability of troops.
- Major capability being potentially compromised (fleet, ship, deployed troops, operational capability).
- Critical national capability availability.
- Reputation and credibility of military around the world.
- Prestige in accessing modern technology or participating in coalitions.

4 **When possible, and for specific opportunities, change the operational performance specifications and criteria** in the response to the RFP. This is obviously somewhat risky but is manageable when a vendor has a high level of capability uniqueness. This is best done, of course, when engaging with the customer early in the capture process.

5 **Respond with an alternative offer or two separate offers** to highlight something the government entity may have missed in the RFP process. Keep the base offer compliant and adjust the alternative offer. The key is to be compliant in order to stay in the bidding game.

6 **Profit being a function of risk, the risk argumentation is key,** and there are definite opportunities to argue a high level of risk provisions due to criticality, development and customization, high complexity, and levels of requirements.

This "sold" level of risk can be higher than effective assessed risks of the program.

7 Defend market price when possible, arguing that it's the price on the market for a product that is publicly available or at least known to government bodies.

8 Defend scarcity of some capability or resources (e.g., cyber security, AI, expert engineers, software, type of skills) where price might be better than the competition but attracting higher margins. This is also where positional advantage might be a key factor in promoting a premium.

9 Ensure that you show value/price control in your procurement offering, but keep the final negotiation phase to extract more savings at later stages of bid or contract negotiations when there is open book on supplier prices (stage the procurement cycle between bid post contract signature). It's also essential to understand the service life cycle of your offers. Services might be required toward the middle or the end of the contract, giving an opportunity for the customer to upsell higher-value parts and services.

10 Know your cost well and be conservative in estimates! Prepare for the worst-case scenario under the RFP guidelines and hope for the best in delivering the acquired technology. Keep in mind that in a controlled profit environment, most competitors know how to maneuver around all these considerations. This is also a competitive advantage.

Bottom line, when profit is controlled, it's essential to execute well on programs and to manage costs with excellence. Therefore, doing a deep segmentation analysis is important, and knowing the customer bidding behavior is essential. There are ways to apply best-value principles in an environment that's acting more like best-price compliant!

Standard objections for VBP in B2G

In the B2G world, most people believe that VBP is more appropriate for the B2C and B2B worlds. In a way, I agree with their view, but I also disagree that VBP cannot work well in the B2G world. I often hear the following objections:

1 **VBP isn't used in the B2G world.** I disagree. VBP is a methodology that can be applied everywhere. It's a matter of adapting it for the B2G world. For example, total cost of ownership is a form of VBP that has been used for decades in the public sector.

2 **B2G customers are far too cost-driven to focus on value.** It's true that most governments focus more on costs and less on value. However, for complex and innovative offers, focus is increasingly being given to customer value.

3 **B2G customers often don't understand what value means.** Value means different things to different people. It's the vendor's responsibility to educate customers early and often during the capture process. Some of the buying centers I've worked with in the public space can be very complex, with sometimes conflicting views of what value is. You need a highly skilled strategic account manager who can understand complex organizations and navigate government formal and informal networks.

4 **B2G customers aren't that sophisticated.** This is too advanced: it depends on the agency you're dealing with. Governments around the world are growing more sophisticated.

They hire highly professional consulting to design and execute better procurement methods. They recruit professionals from the B2B world. Because technologies are becoming more prevalent in the government business, they also must learn them quickly and understand price/quality tradeoffs. I believe that the government business will be more sophisticated and cost-driven for commodities while being more selective and value-driven for specialties.

5 **VBP will never work for our markets.** This is a way of saying "I'm unwilling to make an effort to give it a try." VBP requires a growth mindset. There's no doubt about this. I wouldn't say that it's not for every market. I would say that VBP doesn't work for people with a fixed mindset!

6 **It's impossible to make decent profit for a LPTA contract.** This is of course not the easiest situation, but there are things you can control. First, you need to be compliant. Second, you need to give your customer the right-engineered technology or solutions for the exact LPTA they're insisting on receiving. Don't overdesign. Focus on making productivity and efficient gains so that you can compete better with lower pricing and optimized margins. Make sure you bring up and document all the non-cost-related investments to do in your project to delight the customer and make them operational. Finally, as mentioned above, be smart in your risk management approach and in what you can integrate and improve on. So, there's being competitive and there's improving margins. Under a LPTA process, you must focus on both.

Implications for B2G pricing

You can do VBP in the B2G world. Chances are it will look different from a traditional B2B VBP process. When you're responding to a best-value contract or RFP, this is a necessary exercise. Request-for-offer evaluators will look for technical versus price advantage to score your proposal and select a winner. You need to conduct the same internal scoring process. That's VBP! In the context of an LPTA contract or RFP, the focus needs to move to right engineering, cost excellence, and truly understanding risk and the contract life cycle. In this situation, you'll face strict cost guidance and transparency. But you'll also face an internal lack of confidence to focus on extracting greater margin over the duration of the contract. Teams tend to "give up" and focus on cost 100 percent. There are things that can be done to position an offer in a way that's price-compliant but also focused on the long-term value that can be extracted. In this situation, the bid manager, the capture leader, and the pricing manager must focus on the internal bid positioning to convince top management to adopt a long-term value approach while being LPTA- compliant.

This was a short introduction for this section of the book focused on VBP. In the rest of the section, we review the six steps of VBP in the context of B2B. Particular attention is given to customer segmentation, competitive analysis, and customer-value quantification or dollarization. This is an essential section of the book because the topic of VBP in the B2G world has never received much attention. I'm trying to gain more attention from practitioners on the topic so that we can begin the conversation.

Key Notes

_____

_____

_____

_____

_____

_____

Key Actions

_____

_____

_____

_____

_____

_____

8

B2G Pricing Begins with an Intense Focus on Customer Value

Katie Ashton, CGI

WE ALL KNOW THAT pricing isn't easy. This book emphasizes that B2G pricing can be complex and requires different attention. And it's even more complex as products become more sophisticated, advanced technologies are adopted more widely in the public space, and public sectors become more professional in their procurement approaches. It's a real challenge to introduce changes in pricing strategies for very successful and protected core businesses. At the same time, we must brace for a digital tsunami and be ready to value-price disruptive data-driven offers offered to public entities. I often say that one way to get started is to begin doing progressive and value-based pricing in the innovation process and in the early capture phases, that is, during business development. We dare to say that paying attention to pricing at the front end of customer interactions makes pricing a bit easier and customer-centric at the back end of the same processes, when products and services are launched in the market. So, the sooner you can begin with the customer needs, the customer hot buttons, and the value analysis and pricing hypotheses, the better! In the IT world, this is called shifting left, which means interacting sooner with users and testing things faster in the design process. In the B2G world, this can be defined as interacting sooner with customers and truly understanding their needs and requirements to test concepts and hypotheses before R&D spends any cash.

A holistic process for managing customer value

First, it's imperative to connect all critical functions of the go-to-market process and to include customers as the heart of it. This can begin early in the innovation process when customers express a need or when an unmet need is identified. Your innovation team plays a key role. This is assuming that you have an innovation process and/or function. It might also work for research and development or research and technology functions, although it's more challenging.

The goal of interacting with the customer at the beginning of their need definition is to focus on creating value for customers and relevant partners of the ecosystem you live in. And that value comes from a front end of innovation (FEI) that's dedicated to solving customer problems and that responds to these problems in a compelling and differentiated fashion. I posit that the heart of innovation must be to create differentiation and to focus on the "WOW" differentiators that will shape marketing and pricing later in the process. One way to do this is to beef up the strength of innovation councils by adding representatives of the selling, marketing, and pricing teams. Multifunctional teams can inter-act in such councils to gauge how compelling and value-creating FEI ideas might be. The sooner this is done, the better it is for the rest of the value management process. And the more unfeasible or difficult the new idea is, the more disruptive and value creating it might be!

An intense focus on the customer

Obviously, having innovation and business development processes connected to marketing, pricing, and selling is a great first step for managing customer value. But it's not enough. The value-based go-to-market process must be extremely customer-centric, and it must focus on customer problems, on needs, and eventually on solutions, as shown in figure 8.1. I propose that the greater the focus on customer pains and gains, on customer needs, and on developing differentiated customer solutions, the greater the pric-ing power when new offers are launched in the market.

Easier said than done! Focusing on these three components requires skills, processes, and investments. This requires access to the customer's information and deep customer intimacy, and it explains why I distinguish between innovation and R&D. These are two different functions and activities. If R&D is done without an intense customer focus, you might get lucky once or twice with successful products, but it will most likely result in a techno-push to the market. Innovation suggests a connection to the customer base and a strong collaboration with marketing, sales, and pricing.

Traditional customer-insight methods aren't enough

Uncovering and understanding customer needs early in the inter-action and innovation phase is the name of the game. B2G vendors

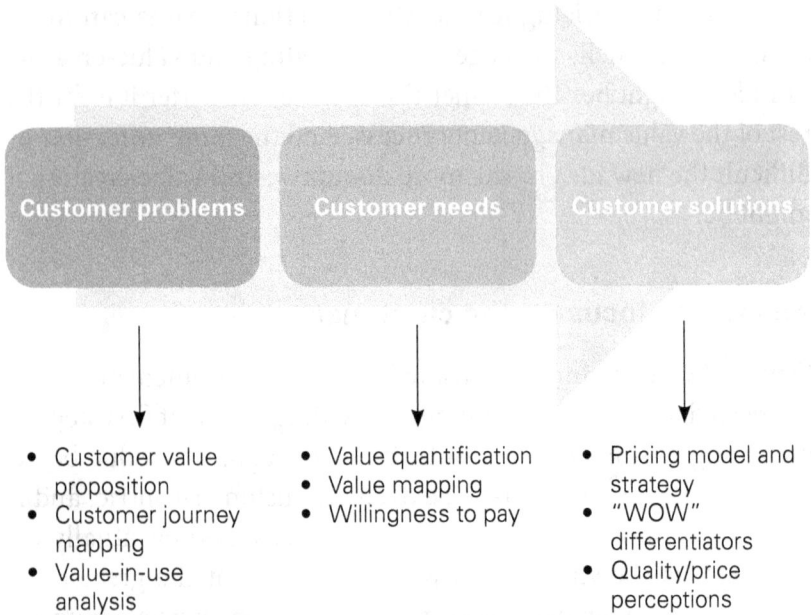

Figure 8.1. The customer is the priority in the process of creating a superior solution.

must focus intensively on customers and on the various stake-holders involved in the need's definition. For this, a vendor must realize one important thing: customer value begins with deep customer insights. The deeper you can go into discovering true unmet and unexplored customer pains or problems, the greater the probability of designing a compelling and differentiated value proposition that the customer's willing to pay for. The key here is a willingness to go deep and to use the best customer-insight tools available. I list a few in figure 8.2.

We can no longer explore customer needs through focus groups, customer visits, and expert interviews. Your competitors can also do that. I recommend graduating from traditional techniques to

Digital innovation starts with customer insights

- Lead user meetings, panels, and councils
- Customer observations and ethnographic research
- Customer advisory boards
- Customer co-creation/experimentation sessions
- Deep value-in-use analysis
- Community of enthusiasts and brand evangelists
- Market and technology radars
- Signal analysis from near and far industries
- Customer journey mapping and process blueprinting
- Brainstorming sessions: day in the life of a customer / staple yourself to an order

Figure 8.2. List of customer insight tools.

focus on value-in-use analysis, customer journey mapping, and customer observations. To do this, your account management, innovation, and business development teams must develop strong research muscles and have a way to collect, connect, and mine all the identified customer nuggets. It also means that every function involved in the go-to-market process and the capture process must get out of the building and spend over 50 percent of their time in the market. Little will be found in your building! These teams will also be the ones making sense of what was discovered from customer interviews, mapping activities, and customer process observations. Interpreting, refining, testing, and validating customer pains and gains remain the most intricate and valuable parts of the process.

All these activities are ongoing. They can't be done just for a large pursuit or a specific bid. Value selling and shifting left is a state of mind that is continuous and deep. Information collected well before the capture process is initiated can then be fed into the early capture discussion in Gate 0 or before. This in turn will accelerate the design of customer-centric offers and value propositions.

The use of canvases to help frame the B2G opportunities

Early in the process of understanding and framing customer need, go-to-market teams must embrace the right methods, processes, and canvases. They must embrace design principles to systematize and industrialize customer-need discovery and offer shaping. This begin very early in the process, and the focus must be on all customer activities and sections. The rest of the canvas can be filled out later, when customer needs and requirements are shaped and validated. To do this, they must choose right canvases and techniques, using the following criteria:

- Credibility of the creator(s) in the relevant subject matter
- Degree of adoption in the B2G ecosystem
- Simplicity of canvas design and execution
- Complementarity of the canvases (avoiding overlap or repetition)
- Availability of content (paid or free) to raise skill levels

A business model canvas is defined in Wikipedia (2020) as "a strategic management and lean startup template for developing new or documenting existing business models. It is a visual chart with elements describing a firm's or product's value proposition, infrastructure, customers, and finances."

The Lean Canvas (n.d.) is "a 1-page business plan template created by Ash Maurya that helps you deconstruct your idea into its key assumptions. It is extremely customer-focused and can be used for a simple offer or an advanced innovative value proposition. It is adapted from Alex Osterwalder's Business

Model Canvas and replaces elaborate business plans with a single page business model." The Lean Startup canvas was created to give innovators a tool for applying the Lean Startup principles. The Lean Startup process, developed by Eric Ries, is a "scientific approach to creating and managing startups and get[ting] a desired product to customers' hands faster. The Lean Startup (n.d.) method teaches you how to drive a startup—how to steer, when to turn, and when to persevere—and grow a business with maximum acceleration. It is a principled approach to new product development."

The Strategyzer business model canvas (2020) combines value proposition and business model canvases to better inform innovation and digital decisions. It's "a global standard used by millions of people in companies of all sizes. You can use the canvas to describe, design, challenge, and pivot your business model. It works in conjunction with the Value Proposition Canvas and other strategic management and execution tools and processes." The customer-value proposition can be used to map customer jobs to be done, pains, and gains. It can also be applied to several stakeholders of a single public agency. The right side of the business model canvas is focused on the customer segment, the customer needs, and the customer experience. Both canvases can be used and applied for a large capture opportunity or for a specific product.

The Pricing Model Innovation Canvas (PMIC) was developed by Stephan Liozu, the founder of Value Innoruption Advisors, to deep dive into the revenue model block of Osterwalder's Business Model Canvas. The PMIC focuses on the three C's of pricing (cost, competition, and customer value) and a fourth C related to change management to support the design and execution of pricing models. The canvas describes the various methods, analyses, and outcomes of the four C's. It helps users select the proper pricing model(s) and the relevant pricing test plan and make better-informed pricing decisions. This canvas is often used in B2G sectors to frame pricing decisions for large deals or bids, especially those using advanced technologies.

So there are plenty of other designing-thinking techniques that can also be used to uncover customer needs and map their current processes: process mapping, blueprinting, customer journey mapping, affinity mapping, concept mapping, data visualization, heuristic evaluation, mental modeling, stakeholder mapping, and storyboarding. What are the benefits of using canvases as part of the B2G early capture framing?

- They promote convergence early in the customer analysis for various actors in the organization.
- They provide structure to teams who may be multifunctional and who might lack basic knowledge about go-to-market strategies.
- They help you focus on the most critical elements of your offers: Strategyzer focuses on critical partnerships and the types of customer relationships needed. The Lean Canvas zeroes in on the WOW differentiators and unfair advantages. The PMIC zooms in on the four C's of pricing.
- They remind you of the important dimensions of the business model: framing an offer requires discipline and comprehensive customer analysis. There should be no omissions or cutting of corners.
- They include a strong testing dimension: Strategyzer proposes testing of viability, feasibility, and desirability. The PMIC discusses pricing research to test willingness-to-pay, pricing model(s) options, and pricing levels. Testing begins early in the customer analysis process.
- They help bridge several businesses or components that may be involved in a large B2G opportunity (product,

software, services, spare parts): all canvases allow for more collaborative discussions, brainstorming blitzes, and strong alignment.
- They help frame the story: they don't replace a deep project plan or strategic capture plan, but they help elevate the story to a higher level.

Remember, a canvas is just a canvas. Nothing will get done without research, curiosity, energy, coaching, and great facilitation. Having a good canvas customer lead is as important as having a canvas.

Implications for B2G pricing

Good pricing begins early in the capture process. The sooner you can get to the heart of the customer's pains, the sooner you have a chance to identify pockets of value to be quantified and extracted through price. It's common sense to think that the more painful the customer's problem, the greater the customer's willingness-to-pay, and the higher the price premium might be versus competitors. This is of course assuming it's all done well! Remember that your competitors might be performing the same analysis. The amount of investments you make in your customer-insight process; the level of collaboration between your account management, business development, and pricing teams; and the unique research capabilities you develop are three critical components of your future pricing power. If your company's focus is purely on R&D, chances are that you're not a customer-centric innovation company. Learn from the best-in-class and begin shifting left toward a true ongoing customer-centric strategy. You'll see an amazing impact of your pricing power and ultimately your performance level.

References

Business model canvas. (2020). *Wikipedia*. Retrieved January 21, 2020, from https://en.wikipedia.org/wiki /Business_Model_Canvas

The Lean canvas. (n.d.). Retrieved January 21, 2020, from https://leanstack.com/leancanvas

The Lean startup methodology. (n.d.). Retrieved January 21, 2020, from http://theleanstartup.com/principles

The business model canvas. (2020). Retrieved January 21, 2020, from https://strategyzer.com/canvas /business-model-canvas

Value Innoruption. (n.d.). Retrieved January 21, 2020, from www.valueinnoruption.com

The author

Katie Ashton is Director of Consulting, Strategy Consulting at CGI. She is responsible for industry, market, competitive and comparable research for the US manufacturing industry as part of CGI's Emerging Technology Practice. In her role, Katie is responsible for the strategy, business development, and thought leadership for the US manufacturing segment. She drives innovation workshops and the market design, development, and commercialization of strategic products. Katie joined CGI in 2018 with 20+ years in manufacturing, including the Industrial Internet of Things, as a strategy, business development, program management, and solution architect. Her educational background includes a BS in Accounting from Duquesne University and a master's in Technology Entrepreneurship from the University of Maryland.

Key Notes

Key Actions

_____

_____

_____

_____

_____

_____

_____

_____

_____

_____

_____

_____

9

Five Key Considerations about B2G Customer Segmentation

CUSTOMER SEGMENTATION IS AT the heart of marketing. It's one of the most essential steps in progressive marketing management, and also one of the most neglected in the B2B and the B2G worlds. By neglected, I mean it's either not performed at all, designed in a very traditional fashion using demographics or firmographics parameters, or designed and not operationalized. Over the last decade, the science and art of segmentation has evolved. Best-in-class B2C organizations have embraced the scientific data revolution and have begun to design both qualitative and quantitative segmentation processes that leverage their rich data.

In both B2C and B2B markets, best-in-class organizations have quickly realized that the one-size-fits-all approach is no longer relevant. Progress in the science of segmentation and the availability of data allow marketers to become more refined in their segmentation depth. In the B2G sector, because of the nature and dynamics of markets in any specific region, customer segmentation is rarely conducted. Often, vendors in the B2G space conduct market or account segmentation to prioritize their market verticals and to classify their existing accounts. They rarely conduct real pricing or customer segmentation.

I could write a whole book on segmentation types and techniques. A number have already been published on the subject. But this isn't why I'm writing this small essay. I've conducted dozens of quantitative and qualitative customer segmentation projects, and I find that the segmentation science is hard to grasp. Each project is different and encounters unique challenges. In the spirit of sharing some of the best practices, I focus on five considerations that are essential to successful customer segmentation: leveraging customer data, conducting segmentation with qualitative information, positioning segmentation as a cost optimization program to improve adoption, operationalizing segmentation in a business, and specific considerations for the B2G world. Let's get started!

1. Segmentation is at the heart of customer data analytics

The use of big data in marketing and sales allows for micro-segmentation and more relevant one-on-one marketing. You might not realize it, but you already have all of the data required to conduct a basic segmentation analysis: survey data, quality data, transactional data, website traffic data, performance data, software usage data, and so forth. The data might be fragmented rather than located in a centralized place, but with a bit of intention and focus, it can quickly be assembled and mined to begin the segmentation process. You might also consider conducting additional surveys to collect need-based customer preferences, but beginning with the data you already have is a good first step (figure 9.1).

The primary objective of segmentation through data analytics is to identify the profile of your most successful and profitable existing customers. Your salesforce might think they know who they are, but they'll mostly rely on intuition and experience. By adding the data analytics dimension to the identification process, you can validate some of these impressions and accelerate the process. The next step is identifying similar profiles in the market: customers who formerly bought from you and no longer do, and prospects who might have similar characteristics. You're equipping your salesforce with better sales intelligence so they can better qualify prospects, find greater revenue opportunities with ideal clients, and focus time on those customers who have the greatest potential

Data for Segmentation

Transactional data
(sales, pricing, volume, discounts, rebates, returns, supply chain data)

Customer survey data
(satisfaction, positioning, demographics, behavioral, share of wallet)

Marketing data
(web traffic data, net promoter scores, loyalty score, market share data)

Quality data
(customer scorecards, quality data, internal performance data)

Figure 9.1. Data for segmentation.

and/or who understand the concepts of value. When lead generation and sales effectiveness increase, you allocate your efforts at the right time with the most-profitable accounts.

Successful segmentation allows for a scientifically based deployment of sales resources that leads to expense optimization with your existing assets. Finally, your marketing and sales efforts will be targeted to the right customers with the right messaging. Guess what? That makes customers happy, and their loyalty level increases. You get the picture. Segmentation isn't easy and requires skills and science. When done right, it delivers tremendous benefits for you and your customers.

That's the theory, of course. In practice, there are many possible complications in running data-based customer segmentation: incomplete data, biased data, fragmented data in different formats and languages, sampling errors in customer surveys, inconclusive data analysis, lack of integrated systems, and lack of readily available pricing data. I could have mentioned many other issues, but let's stick with these. The reality is that we have data but we're missing many of the cylinders needed to get the segmentation engine running. Early in my career, I was a consultant in B2B marketing research, and running cluster analysis was one of the most complex statistical analyses, along with conjoint analysis.

Books on quantitative customer segmentation often omit the fact that a good segmentation analysis begins with a qualitative segmentation process. This is what I call *integrative customer segmentation,* which includes qualitative segmentation, validated with quantitative segmentation, and then tied to transactional data. Integrating the three components allows you to operationalize your segmentation. That works well in the retail world or the B2C sector, when you have many customers to research. It's harder to do in the B2B and industrial worlds. This leads to my second consideration.

2. Customer segmentation using qualitative data

Sometimes a B2B, B2G, or industrial customer population might have only a dozen global accounts. In some business-to-defense (B2D) markets, there are just one or two accounts! So what do you do? Give up and not do any segmentation? This is where it gets complicated, and for two reasons. First, go-to-market professionals with engineering and analytical mindsets struggle with the notion of qualitative work. They want hard facts derived from statistics. Second, your customer segmentation may end up having two or three segments with a few customers in each. That leads to a lack of confidence in the process and a quick return to a traditional firmographics or product-based segmentation process (figure 9.2).

Most of the successful B2B and B2G customer segmentation projects I've conducted used qualitative information. In general, they

Figure 9.2. Qualitative data.

are global projects with customer populations ranging from 50 to 200 in B2B or B2G environments. These qualitative projects took three to six months and required intense deep dives into accounts as well as multiple working sessions with multifunctional groups. I'll begin by saying that you cannot run a qualitative customer segmentation project without the deep involvement of the salesforce and account managers. It's not going to happen. So one of my basic rules of engagement is the presence and active support of the commercial teams. Without that, I won't begin such a project. Below I propose six more best practices for conducting qualitative customer segmentation.

1 **Train and experiment in parallel.** You must give your team the fundamentals on the topic of segmentation. I usually spend about two hours training on the differences between strategic, market, product, customer, and pricing segmentations. Then I show many examples of how well-done companies have performed it. The key is to also conduct some easy exercises to get the multifunctional group warmed up. So it's a half-day of training and short exercises leading into the first steps of the process.

2 **Focus on information depth.** Because the process is qualitative, I get groups to focus on all customers in the population (prospects, lost accounts, new accounts, legacy accounts, etc.) but also on listing all the potential critical classification criteria that will be used later to segment the customer population in question. It's not unusual to end up with up to 50 to 60 classification criteria. These classification criteria focus on firmographics, product purchases, usage of products or services, buying behaviors, nature of the customer organization, customer culture, and more. This exercise typically energizes the

working group because they realize that there's lots of information to capture and later analyze.

3 **Run multiple iterations of the analysis.** Qualitative segmentation requires several iterations with learning in between. The segments that emerge at the end of the first workshop are not what will be used ultimately. Although the working group might feel good after the first workshop, more work is needed. The number of iterations will be based on the level of discrimination between the identified segmentation. Are the segments significantly different, or is there too much overlap? Another key question is whether you can put all relevant customers in the buckets you've identified. Remember that in this qualitative process, the sales team is actively involved, so you have to make sure they understand the process and when it's done.

4 **Consider multiple dimensions.** The complexity of qualitative segmentation is that you need to identify discriminant classification criteria qualitatively. A computer won't do statistical testing for significance. You're doing this for the group. Generally, you can consider three or four such criteria at the same time. These criteria come from the list of 50 or 60 criteria you've identified in the initial workshop, as explained in point 2. The reason you must iterate is that you might have to change one or two of these discriminant criteria and start over. Some of the most common B2G discriminant criteria are value/price buyers, service-requirements intensity, technical maturity level, outsourcing philosophy, and propensity to accept partnership.

5 **Generate trust in the process through validation.** To build adoption of the segmentation process and acceptance for the qualitative process, you must ensure that the work is validated by the salesforce multiple times. Your project team

will include up to 50 percent of sellers, and they will represent the entire salesforce. One of the projects I conducted had 12 people in the core team, including six sales managers from around the world. We then validated the work twice, with up to 75 sales representatives, using Excel and a short survey. Remember that you must keep it simple for them. You also need to give them a reason and time to respond.

6 **Rationalize by focusing on customers and not the process.** Your project team will also include product managers, technical managers, and pricing managers who will fight your qualitative process until the last minute! So you need to focus on the customers and not the process. Make sure the team enters into many exchanges about customer names, customer data, and examples of customer transactions. You'll get pushback because the process is fuzzy and incomplete. It's not rational enough. If you have 50 customers in your population, make sure you review all of them!

Qualitative customer segmentation works well. But many forces could derail it. One of these is the desire to test the results of the qualitative work using statistics. I've seen this many times: some geek proposes to use Excel or another software package to mine collected qualitative data so that they can be validated. That's the kiss of death.

3. Segmentation is about optimizing costs without cutting costs

If you tell financial executives that you want to conduct a customer segmentation project to better market your offerings, you might get some attention. If you tell them that it will help cut costs and improve asset use, they will be all ears. That's the reality of change management! The choice of words matters. In general, conducting a thorough and scientific segmentation analysis offers compelling benefits. When designed and operationalized well, B2G customer segmentation can become a game changer in go-to-market strategies. It allows you to better leverage existing assets while optimizing sales and marketing expenses. Most of all, segmentation done well can positively impact customer satisfaction and loyalty (figure 9.3).

Scientific segmentation offers numerous advantages for businesses in search of margin improvements. And these improvements can be made in a matter of weeks following the discovery of customer segments and the operationalization of dedicated segment activities. This can have a significant short-term impact on the bottom line.

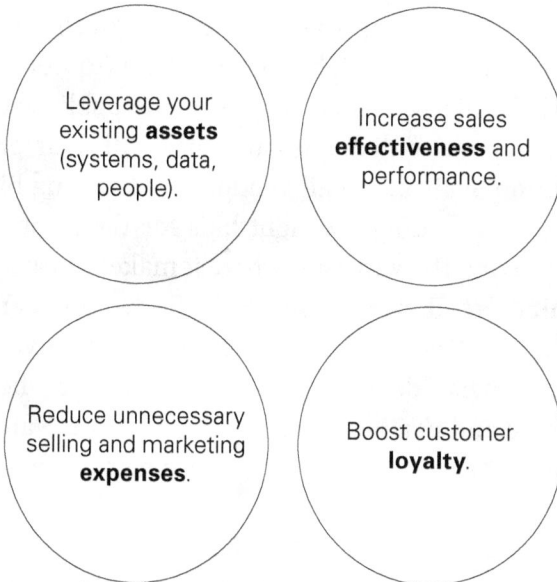

Figure 9.3. The benefits of segmentation.

Segmentation allows organizations to optimize cost and resource allocation without necessarily engaging in painful cost-cutting activities. Resources can be reallocated swiftly to engage more-profitable customer segments or to right-size a suite of product and service offerings. In the B2G world specifically, a good customer segmentation can help reduce bid costs in general by providing better guidance on how to bid, where to bid, and when not to bid!

There are seven ways that segmentation can help businesses optimize their costs. There may be more, but let's focus on these seven and discuss them in detail.

1 **Optimize bid costs.** Conducting customer segmentation at the global level for categories of customers (navies, transport authorities, equipment integrators, etc.) helps define better bidding guidelines by prioritizing the bid costs and allocation of resources. Knowing that a potential government agency is a pure price buyer might trigger a team to not pursue the next bid. Similarly, power players in the public sectors tend to run competitive dialogues and make all their proprietary information available to all vendors. Optimizing bid costs is achieved by pursuing the right bids for the right customers and improving the win ratio where it makes sense.

2 **Optimize R&D costs.** Similarly, R&D costs can be optimized by selecting the right project in which to invest with the right customers. Identifying the B2G customer who wants to collaborate and partner in exchange for greater value capture should lead to greater R&D ROI. It also helps a vendor achieve the right balance between project and product orientation.

3 **Optimize sales expenses.** Get your salesforce in front of the right account and the prospects with the highest potential. Your sales revenues per sales rep and per customer will

significantly increase. Thus, your selling expenses for each sales dollar that's uncovered should decrease. An existing better-equipped salesforce in front of the right clients at the right time and with the right offer should boost your growth rate as well.

4 **Optimize marketing resources.** And because your segments will be clearly defined and their needs better understood, your marketing efforts will be better focused to respond to these needs. In the end, it becomes a matter of the quality of marketing, not the quantity. Moving away from a one-size-fits-all marketing approach will improve your conversion rate and boost the ROI of your marketing investments. In other words, customers who aren't interested in your glossy brochures or your latest branded polo shirts shouldn't receive them. That money can be used to better satisfy your core customer target segments.

5 **Reduce customer cost-to-serve.** The combination of cost-to-serve analysis from your pricing analytics solutions and of segmentation will allow you to refine the pricing and service conditions that are offered to distinct segments. For example, your "value" customers will be offered higher service levels that they're willing to pay for. For your sophisticated technology-driven buyers, a technology-based supply-chain approach might resonate better.

6 **Improve product mix.** Scientific segmentation also allows you to right-size your product offering to specific segments of the markets. It also allows you to create unique offerings such as product bundles and product/service packages. You might realize, for example, that a large portion of your accounts don't care for the extra performance of your product and won't pay for it. This may trigger a category management discussion with R&D and marketing that leads to right-sized products being offered. That implies savings in raw materials, in engineering, and in manufacturing of advanced product and technologies.

7 **Versioning of offerings.** Combine points 1 through 4, and you can imagine the possibilities. Scientific segmentation allows versioning business offerings to respond to specific customer needs. While it might create a bit of complexity, it also allows customizing your business models to your customer segments. The savings will be immediate!

Whether qualitative or quantitative, B2G customer segmentation generates powerful benefits. So why is the process so neglected in many organizations? The data are there. There is software to help. There are books written on the topic. That's the topic of our fourth consideration.

4. Without operationalizing it, customer segmentation is just a theory

I posit that the main issue with customer segmentation relates to the difficulty in operationalizing the outcome of the segmentation analysis. Moving from one type of segmentation approach to another might require turning the organization upside down. And that's not going to work. So the key is to focus on designing a hybrid segmentation process that takes into account organizational constraints (regions, legal entity, asset locations) while embracing the go-to-market approach as shown in figure 9.4. Then you have to be good at executing the whole thing.

Now you can see the complexity of running and deploying a thorough customer segmentation process. How do you organize for it? How do you change the internal structure to organize around the customers? Who does what, and who has the authority to allocate funds to customer-segment programs? In figure 9.5, I

Internal organizational dimensions
(divisions, territories)

Execution discipline

- Marketing programs
- Value management
- Commercial excellence
- SAM process

Customer behavior dimensions
(usage, buying behaviors, needs)

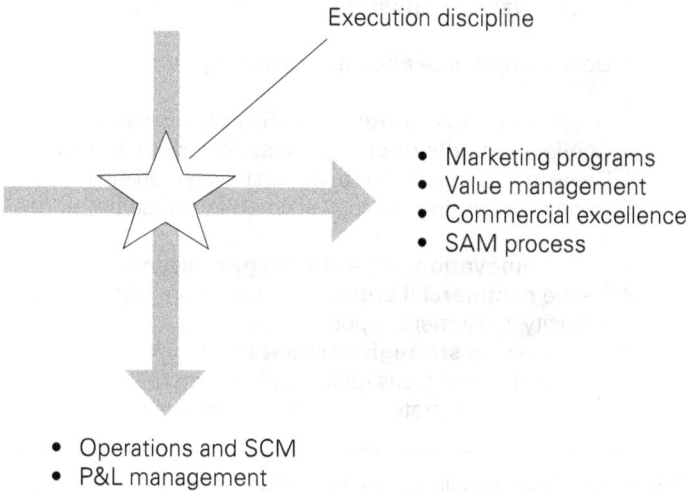

- Operations and SCM
- P&L management

Figure 9.4. Execution discipline.

propose 10 activities that are essential in deploying and executing a customer segmentation outcome while working within organizational constraints.

These 10 points are directly related to a business' go-to-market approach and/or marketing plan. Remember that segmentation comes before the four P's of marketing and then leads to the proper selling strategy. Some of the most successful B2B and to B2G segmentation projects I've conducted led to the development of business models and marketing plans for each customer segment. In these projects, I had the marketing and sales executives very involved and aligned on what to do next. The three of us proposed new business models, action plans, and resource plans to the top executives in the business. It was a winning play for the business that was truly customer focused. These executives

---

Operationalizing Segmentation

1 Prepare **value proposition** and **business model** by customer segment.
2 Define a **resource allocation strategy** by segment (HR, Capex, R&T).
3 Develop **modular product platform** to overlap across segments.
4 Configure **bundle offers** (product, service, data, etc.).
5 Develop a **good/better/best** versioning marketing strategy.
6 Define a **branding** strategy adapted to a good/better/best approach.
7 Define **innovation** rate and strategy by segment.
8 Define **commercial approach** by segment (nature, engagement, intensity, customer support resources).
9 Organize with **strategic account team** by key accounts that are empowered and focus on integrated customer needs.
10 Adapt **bidding** strategy and process to segment behavior.

Figure 9.5. Operationalizing segmentation.

had the courage to propose these drastic changes in their go-to-market approach. They had no choice in the end. The market had changed dramatically.

5. Specific segmentation considerations for B2G markets

Below are some specific considerations to keep in mind when conducting customer segmentation in the B2G world.

1 **Elevate the scope at the global level.** You need some type of a population to segment in the first place. You might have 45 radar integrators, 75 navies, 100 national health agencies, and so forth. The population becomes workable for segmentation when you reach 50 or more. In some public spaces,

you might have hundreds of customers, which is very appropriate for running statistical analyses if you have available data.

2 **Focus on your addressable market.** The total population size might not be the addressable market size. For example, if you want to sell equipment to navy forces around the world, you might have 100 or more national navies, only 25 of which are very active and have budget to spend. So, although it might be a good theoretical process to segment the 100 navies, only 25 might be relevant. This raises the question of whether to include existing customers, prospects, active or nonactive customers, and so forth.

3 **Identify the right classification criteria.** Whether you're segmenting global education agencies or air forces, you'll need to use very specific classification criteria. Some might be the same, but in my experience it's best to start from scratch and find the right criteria.

4 **Focus on depth of the analysis.** When it isn't possible to run a global customer segmentation process, go deep at the customer level by conducting the required analysis: buying-center analysis, stakeholder mapping, relationship mapping, customer-value proposition, and so on.

5 **Don't succumb to the pressure of running statistical analyses.** In the B2G world, many marketing activities are greatly influenced by engineering and science. Product managers might be tempted to run a cluster analysis or a principal component analysis on 30 accounts. This might work after massaging the data, but it's not realistic. I strongly encourage teams to move to qualitative analysis, which can yield practical and executable results.

Final thoughts

In times of soul searching, many businesses will race to cut costs without deeply exploring their customer segmentation process. Cost-cutting is a short-term process that reaps short-term gains. Scientific qualitative and/or quantitative segmentation can achieve the same optimization of cost and resource allocation, but it also allows redesigning a firm's offerings and positioning for the long term. The effect of such a scientific exploration can revolutionize a go-to-market strategy while minimizing the incremental costs needed to better serve market segments. Segmentation isn't new. It's been around for decades. It remains one of the most difficult marketing concepts to explore and execute. The five considerations I listed in this chapter might help you get started. To succeed, put the customer first, and then adopt an agile and hybrid process—not the other way around.

Key Notes

Key Actions

_____

_____

_____

_____

_____

_____

_____

_____

_____

_____

_____

_____

_____

10

Competitive Intelligence for Value-Based Pricing and EVE

THREE PRIMARY PRICING ORIENTATIONS are used to set prices: customer, cost, and competition (the three C's). Most scholars, consultants, and practitioners agree that pricing based on customer value is the orientation most preferred for fully capturing the value from markets. The reality is that you need to inform your pricing decisions with information from the three C's. These orientations are not mutually exclusive, and all require equal amounts of analytics and high-quality data. The connection between customer value and competition is probably the most critical. Because customer value is relative and competitive advantage is reference-based, I often state that value-based pricing (VBP) can't be done without a deep understanding of your competition.

I'm not recommending an obsession with competition. I'm advocating a deep focus on understanding the competition—their

"Value-based pricing
requires an in-depth
understanding of your
competitors, their
offering, & pricing!"

Stephan Liozu, Ph.D.
Agent of Disruption
Pricing Thought Leader

offering, behaviors, and pricing approach—to support the analysis of competitive advantage and the quantification of customer value. I posit that in order to design and deploy value-based strategies, including VBP, firms must be equally obsessed with obtaining deep customer insights and deep competitive information. These two dimensions are the anchors of the VBP analysis and are part of the initial steps of VBP focusing on customer segmentation and competitive analysis. A firm's ability to deploy a VBP program depends on the level of maturity on these two dimensions, as depicted in the matrix in figure 10.1.

If maturity is low on both dimensions, the priority is to build a strong knowledge foundation on how to do VBP, how to conduct competitive analysis, and how to collect customer and competitive intelligence (CI). At this stage, it's essential to integrate the process of collecting, connecting, and mining customer and competitive information into all go-to-market processes in the firm. Everyone in the go-to-market community needs to be responsible

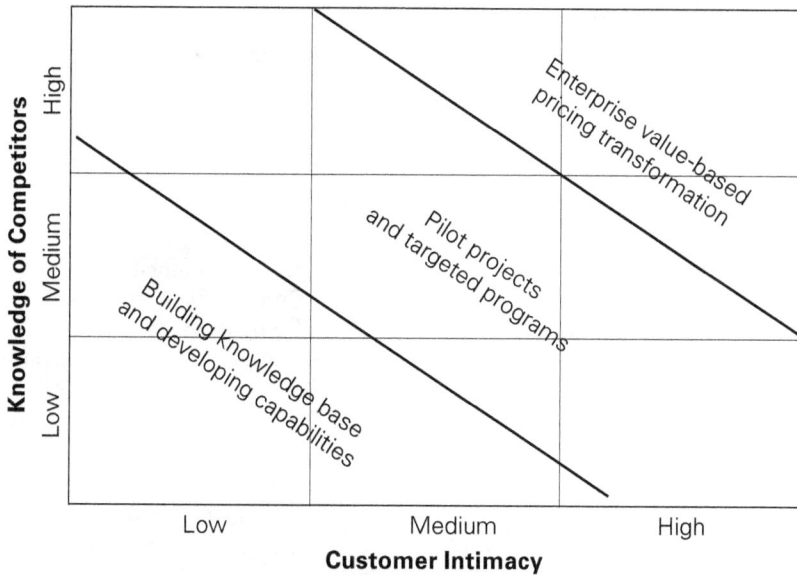

Figure 10.1. Two dimensions of value-based-pricing maturity.

for this process. It's unrealistic to think that the CI and customer research teams are solely responsible for this. Even though they manage the process and have expertise in the science, they need data from the business side to feed the process engine. It's a true team sport. Only when this is done systematically and deeply can a firm move along the maturity spectrum and eventually be able to think about an enterprise-wide value-based-pricing deployment.

VBP requires CI. Let's now explore the VBP process in detail and see what's needed, and at what step.

CI in the VBP methodology

VBP is a six-step methodology. At each of the steps, there are competitive analyses or competition-based activities to perform (see figure 10.2).

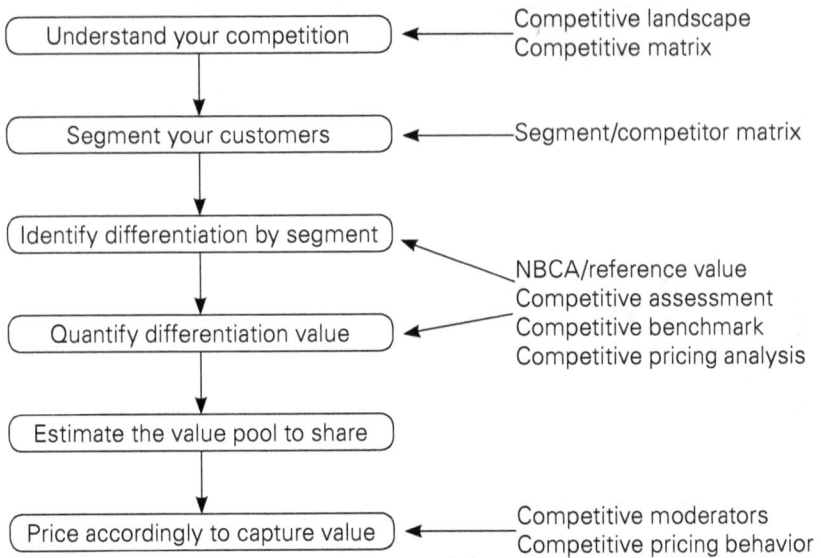

Figure 10.2. Competitive activities by value-based-pricing step.

Step 1 is about mapping your competitive landscape and understanding all competitors using some critical descriptive variables. A competitive landscape is usually the first visual to begin with. Positioning and value maps are also useful for clustering your competitors in terms of value and price. You might also consider preparing a competitive matrix, another tool for rating and ranking competitors. Examples of these tools are readily available via a Google search!

Step 2 focuses on customer segmentation and how competitors play in each segment. For this step, I typically recommend preparing a segment/competitor matrix, which is a list of competitors (direct, indirect, secondary, future) by customer segment. This helps identify differences in competitive intensity and competitors' ranking by segment. It's also pre-work to list possible next best competitive alternatives (NBCAs) by segment.

Step 3 focuses on extracting true differentiation, and step 4 is all about quantifying the impact of differentiation in terms of your customer's financial benefits. This is the heavy-duty part of CI. To extract true differentiation and to quantify customer differentiation value, you must perform deep and advanced CI activities. We explore some of these below, but they include selecting the right NBCA, conducting competitive benchmarks and assessments, and finding competitive pricing levels. These are must-do to perform EVE (economic value estimation framework, as depicted in figure 10.3) and get to the heart of VBP. If detailed, granular information about your competition is unavailable, the customer-value analysis won't lead to anything you can use in the price-setting or the value-based-selling processes.

Customer Value Modeling
Economic Value Estimation (EVE®) Framework

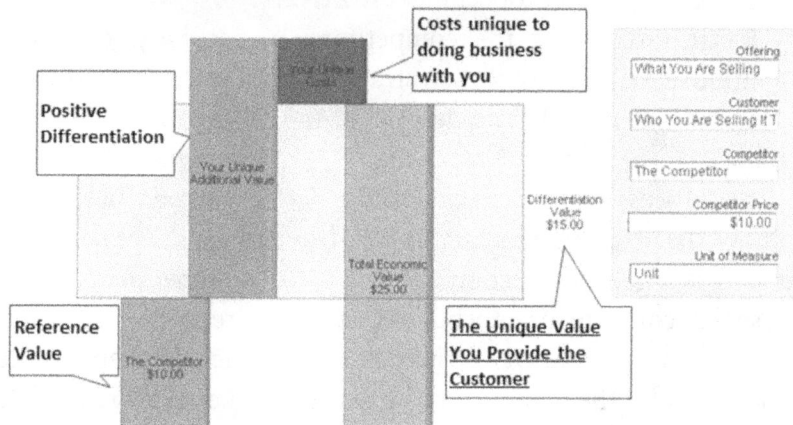

Figure 10.3. The EVE framework.

Steps 5 and 6 focus on sharing the value pool and eventual pricing setting within the value pool. Here, too, some CI is needed. I focus on the positive and negative pricing moderators that might influence the value pool sharing as well as the understanding of your competitors' pricing behaviors.

Selecting the right NBCAs

Depending on your competitive analysis, and for any relevant offer within a particular segment, you might have three, five, or 10 competitors to consider for the reference value. This is why I recommend that you rate and rank your potential reference values using a selected list of criteria. The goal is to derive the top three NBCAs so that you can begin your EVE analysis. Selecting the right reference is often challenging. The following short process offers an opportunity for rational preparations.

1 Prepare a competitive landscape **mapping** direct global, direct local, indirect, partial, and future competitors.
2 Prepare a competitor/segment **matrix**.
3 **Rate and rank** the competitors: by intensity, customer mindshare, share of wallet, strategic suppliers, and so forth.
4 Run **multiple** EVE models (NBCAs 1, 2, and 3).

This process won't deliver you *the* perfect answer, but it will remove the anxiety of having to pick from a long list of competitors. I often get the question about "partial" competitors, that is, those that compete directly but not on the entire scope of the offer under consideration. My answer is simple. Include them in the process, and if they make it to the top list, make sure you include the right differentiation comparing partial and full integrated offers. A one-stop shop brings value!

Selecting the right reference value (NBCA)

Another challenge is finding the competitor's pricing level. It's easier in B2C but more complicated in B2B to reach a final net price for a specific product, service, or offer. There are four possible situations with respect to the reference value:

1 **You have the competitors' pricing levels.** You can therefore run a traditional EVE model.
2 **You have a range of competitive price levels.** You can use the range as a reference value knowing that, traditionally, this competitor prices within this range. This works well for large offers, complex offers, and bundled solutions.
3 **You have a market price for a similar offer.** If you can't find the detailed pricing reference value, you might switch the scope of your value model and focus on an industry or market average price. This isn't ideal, but it's better than nothing. The key is to get going while collecting more competitive information.
4 **You have no information.** This is obviously what happens when there's no process for gathering credible competitive pricing information. In this case, I recommend doing the value model against what's called "doing nothing." This assumes that there are no competitors in play and that the customer hasn't begun the process of gathering competitive alternatives. This is highly unlikely, but, again, the key is to get started.

Depending on where you stand on the customer/competitor maturity matrix above, you might get stuck because of the lack of competitive information. I recommend that you get unstuck quickly and get your teams to learn the EVE process, even if the information's imperfect. Pick an initial model that you can run for which information is more readily available. The key is to get started! If you wait for perfect customer and competitive information, you might never begin.

Competitive moderators in value pool sharing

An additional key consideration in the EVE framework is identifying the relevant competitive moderators to define the best way to share the value pool and to avoid the traditional 50/50 split. Some of the moderators are "positive," which means they might allow you to capture more of the value pool, whereas others are negative. I list a few below, but this list isn't exhaustive.

- **Response behavior.** What's the typical response of specific competitors? Will they respond aggressively and perceive that you've attacked them frontally?
- **Industry structure.** What does the Porter model tell us about the nature and strengths of the competitive landscape?
- **Number of competitors.** Are there five or 50 competitors sharing the industry pie?
- **Competitive intensity.** Are all competitors acting aggressively, or is there relative order in the industry?
- **Competitive entrenchment.** How deeply is the NBCA entrenched in the customer or segment that we are conducting the EVE model for? Will it be easy to dislodge and replace the NBCA?
- **Customer relationships with competitors.** What are the relationship maps between a customer's accounts and specific competitors? Are some relationships stronger than others?
- **Propensity to enter pricing wars.** Will competitors feel attacked and declare a price war in our core business? Should we price cautiously in the value pool to avoid a frontal attack?

- **Competitors' sensitivity to market share.** How obsessed are competitors with market share in their communication? Should we first focus on small accounts under the radar at a higher price?

Remember that pricing moderators aren't negative differentiators. These are two different things. If you have a negative differentiator, you'll have to quantify the cost to the customer and deduct this from the total positive differentiation value. Moderators don't address differentiation. This is done early in the value-based-pricing process. The moderators allow you to set the price in the value pool.

Methodologies for conducting CI

There are six techniques or methodologies that I recommend when conducting CI, as shown in figure 10.4. If course, there are more! But six is a good start. These require training, capabilities, and sometimes the appropriate tools. Let's review them at a high level.

1 Competitive reviews, black hat review, war games. These techniques allow teams to put themselves inside the skin

> 1 Competitive reviews, black hat review, war games
> 2 Competitive profile matrix & value maps
> 3 Detailed technical & product benchmarks
> 4 Price-to-win analysis
> 5 Competitors' pricing behavior analysis
> 6 General competency inventory

Figure 10.4. Six methodologies for conducting competitive analysis.

of competitors and role play for a day or two. These sessions can be conducted for large strategic bids or for long-term-contract preparation. The key is to find people who know enough about the specific competitors and who understand their culture. These techniques are well structured and managed by a professional coach and/or facilitator. The real value comes at the end of the session, when the debrief is conducted in front of leadership and the capture leader.

2 **Competitive profile matrix and value maps.** These tools are used in the early stage of the value-based-pricing process when marketers study their competitive landscape in preparation for the next steps. Both require some type of ratings of us-versus-competition so that a relative value score can be computed. The value is in giving clear competitive positioning and in having a high-level view of the most dangerous competitors.

3 **Detailed technical and product benchmarks.** These provide deep and thorough analysis of competitive offers, technology, and products. They require a granular review of competitive functionalities, attributes, and technology components. Traditionally, product-line managers and technical managers might work jointly to conduct these. The value of these assessments is in their identification of product or service differentiators that can be used in the EVE framework among other differentiators. Often, consulting companies are used to conduct reverse-engineering of competitive offers.

4 **Price-to-win analysis.** This methodology is most likely used in the B2G sector because part of the overall capture process is both a process and a result. Price-to-win can be best defined as the cost-capability tradeoff that embodies a firm's strategy. Price-to-win, the process, identifies the position that a firm needs to achieve to meet its business goals and

objectives. The price-to-win analysis output is a window-to-win map plotting the customer's budget considerations, the competitors' capabilities, and price levels.

5 **Competitors' pricing behavior analysis.** This simple PowerPoint template lists 10 pricing dimensions profiling the pricing approach of each competitor. These include pricing behaviors in the market, propensity to enter into price wars, declared pricing strategy, and others. Profiles can be added to the outcome of the overall competitive analysis.

6 **General competency inventory.** The most complex competitive analysis involves conducting a competence and/or capability assessment for each competitor or specific area of interest. This is needed when studying technical capabilities, service competencies, or corporate strengths. This type of analysis includes asset inventory, factory functional and technological capabilities, laboratory capabilities, service personnel credentials and accreditation, and corporate financial relationships.

These are some of the most commonly used techniques. They require working in teams with marketers, market research teams, consultants, and your internal CI team. They require budgets and resources as well as a detailed CI roadmap.

Ninety-day process for collecting and connecting competitive pricing information

You'll need to find competitive pricing intelligence (CPI). In B2B and B2G, reaching a net price that's precise and credible is a challenge. The collection of CPI needs to be ongoing as part of the business mindset. Most firms lack a formal process for CPI collection, connection, and mining. Instead, this work is done

informally under the impetus and drive of business individuals in the marketing, sales ops, or pricing team. If your firm has not yet begun to gather CPI, I propose the approach below. This can be initiated and fully operating in 90 days.

1 **Assemble and launch a CPI task force.** This task force can meet once a month to share CPI and ensure that it's exploited in the day-to-day business via the sales ops plan and the pricing council. The task force must include sales, marketing, business development, CI, and pricing. Other functions can join as needed.

2 **Assign responsibility and accountability.** Someone needs to lead this effort. I recommend someone on the pricing team, joined at the hip with the CI expert.

3 **Conduct an internal evaluation of what CPI is already readily available.** People gather CPI but don't share it. Others have knowledge in their heads and keep it

there. Industry and marketing reports might contain relevant CPI information. By conducting an internal inventory of what's available, you'll see the gaps and set priorities for what's needed.

4 **Conduct gap analysis, CPI data needs, and tracker.** This is ground zero. It's the start of the process, and the role of the task force is to fill in the gaps and begin connecting and mining information.

5 **Launch formal mechanism to systematically collect CPI.** The task force needs to reach out to their communities and begin gathering all CPI entering the organization through multiple entry points. This includes ensuring that you're aware of what's being gathered. The big challenge is to know when information is available. People need to know that the process exists and that CPI is being collected.

6 **Track progress of CPI collection in task force and pricing council.** You'll be surprised to learn what can be collected with attention and intention in the first 45 days. We often think that we have no CPI until we begin paying attention to what's being collected. The process then needs to move into proactive mode. Data are being caught coming into the organization. But the task force can also request specific information that's missing and critical to the organization. It can also task consultants with conducting CPI research.

7 **Integrate relevant and credible CPI into the pricing decision process.** No data will be useful until it's being used in the price-setting process. This includes the value-based-pricing process, the price-to-win process, and the EVE framework. These are essential best practices to keep in mind when using and sharing CPI. The data need to be accurate and credible enough to generate confidence in the pricing decision-making process.

8 Design tools and technology to automate the CPI process. After 90 days it might be time to think about the future and consider automating the process. Of course, there's software that can help you manage CPI. Beginning with a simple CPI database that's connected to your pricing software might be a good middle step. The priority is the quality and currency of your CPI.

Collecting CPI is both a science and an art. The key is credibility and confidence in the data. For that, the CPI must be triangulated. Having just one data point for estimating competitive pricing levels won't cut it. You need multiple data points to come up with a pricing range or a credible competitive price point (see figure 10.5). There's no way around it. You also need to document the sources of information and gauge their credibility.

Implications for B2G pricing

This chapter highlights the need to develop strong capabilities in CI to support B2G pricing excellence and the deployment of VBP. The responsibility is shared among go-to-market functions:

Key success factors in collecting competitive pricing intelligence (CPI):
1 Conduct specific competitive pricing research
2 Combine internal and external sources of CPI data
3 Collect multiple pricing data points from various sources
4 Triangulate competitive pricing data for credibility
5 Refine data accuracy and validate to increase confidence
6 Make collection of competitive pricing data systematic
7 Connect all CPI data to customer and cost data
8 Leverage technology to manage CPI data

Figure 10.5. Key success factors in collecting competitive pricing information.

product management, sales management, bid management, capture leadership, marketing, technology, and so forth. Your firm might have a CI or business intelligence function. That's very helpful. CI is a profession. There are professional organizations in the field, and I highly recommend that you visit the website of the Society of Competitive Intelligence Professionals (www.scip .org), the Academy of Competitive Intelligence (www.academyci .com), or the Institute of Competitive Intelligence (www .institute-for-competitive-intelligence.com). ACI offers a certification called CIP™ that I highly recommend for any pricing professionals wishing to go deeper into the value-based-pricing domain. A certification in CI can be a good complement to your Certified Pricing Professional (CPP) certification from PPS.

Certification and training are important. CI is one of the strategic skills that any pricing professional needs to have. You cannot perform truly competitive-based pricing and VBP without deep knowledge of the competition. Doing CI in the B2G world is not straightforward. There are many situations where competitors collaborate one day and compete the next. There are many opportunities to work with prime contractors who are competitors but also customers. Competitors might have joint ventures in some countries and compete head-to-head in other regions. The CI methods and concepts need to enter your pricing process in the same way that pricing analytics and pricing tactics do. CI is part of the job description, roles, and responsibilities. These are also shared with marketing managers, product managers, and key account managers with excellent process guidance from your CI team. The functional experts and the consumers of competitive information share the responsibility.

Key Notes

_____

_____

_____

_____

_____

Key Actions

_____

_____

_____

_____

_____

_____

11

Black Hat Best Practice— How to Black Hat

Chris Street, Thales UK

Introduction

SUN TZU WROTE, "If you know the enemy and know your-self, you need not fear the result of a hundred battles. If you know yourself but not the enemy, for every victory gained you will also suffer a defeat. If you know neither the enemy nor yourself, you will succumb in every battle."

While Sun Tzu might have been imagining a more life-limit-ing consequence of losing 100 battles, his advice still holds true for the commercial battles you face. To understand the differen-tiated value that your offer brings to the customer, it's critical to understand how you stack up against the competition and how they might behave in a particular procurement.

There are a number of routes you could choose to collect basic competitor information. For example, you may conduct some internet research or visit your competitor's stand at a trade show. The challenge comes when trying to predict how your competitors will behave in a given procurement scenario: for example, is this a critical bid? How do they behave when trying to dislodge an incumbent? This is the scenario that a black hat review was designed for, taking basic competitive information and adding a layer or multiple layers of intelligence to create a dynamic view.

Why the Black Hat?

The key to a winning bid is not donning your best trilby. A black hat is called a black hat because you adopt your competitor's persona to identify weaknesses in your own strategy and how best to attack theirs.

So what does a black hat look like? Essentially, it involves creating a simulated bid strategy. This is achieved by bringing together a group of people with knowledge of the competition or the customer. Ideally the people you use will have either previously worked for the competitor or competed against them a number of times. The review usually takes place over the course of a day and seeks to answer such questions as how important this is to the competitor, what their unique decimators are, and what their technical and commercial offer looks like. It's important to bring in the customer's view, again by using people who have previously been the customer or have worked with the customer for some time. This allows the simulated competitor offer to be shaped to hit the customer's hot buttons and to create an additional level of insight. Ideally you will split your participants into teams to work on a competitor that best fits their experience, and provide them a set of templates to fill in, which standardizes the output you get back.

Hitting the spot:
What do we mean by customer hot buttons?

Customer hot buttons are the key concerns of the customer, the things that keep them awake at night. They're the key factors influencing the buying decision. Ensuring that you understand those is critical to understanding how you and your competitors stack up against each other.

However, you can use black hats for more than just procurement bids. For example, you could use one to test how your competitor would respond to your cutting prices or introducing a new product to the market. Ultimately the purpose of a black hat is to bring color to your competitive intelligence, to move the view you have from static two-dimensional data to a three-dimensional scenario.

Once you've decided on the value that a black hat will bring to your project, how do you ensure its success? The answer is preparation. We've identified the following areas to be the most critical to holding a successful review.

Preparation for the event

What's the objective?

This might seem obvious, but if I had a dollar for every time a capture lead has said to me "We need to have a black hat" and my response of "What are you trying to achieve?" is met by either silence or "Well, the process says we need one," then I'd be a very rich man. You need to identify what sort of output you'd like to achieve and how this will shape your bid strategy. As an example: do you want a full simulated bid strategy with an approach to a technical and commercial solution, or are you trying to answer a single question, such as "How will our competitors respond if we team with X?" Identifying the objective early will allow you to be more efficient in the other preparation activities outlined below. You also need to decide at this point how many competitors you will workshop. In general, any more than three or four becomes difficult to manage, so identify which competitors are most important for you to understand.

People

A black hat will stand or fall depending on the quality of the people you include in the review. You need people who truly understand how the competitor thinks and acts, which usually means former employees who now work for your company. As a note, before we go any further, you need to take care to not infringe on any nondisclosure agreements or other binding commercial agreements when you invite someone to a black hat. Assuming that you're commercially sound, then having former employees at your review will bring great value. You also need to ensure that the people you invite are not too entrenched in your own way of company thinking. If you end up with participants saying things like "Our competitor couldn't do that because we can't," then they're probably the wrong type of person to be at the review. It's true that you need a certain level of realism, but this needs to be tempered by the understanding that sometimes our competitors do things differently—and sometimes better, too! Once you've identified the people and then get those invites out, you need to maximize your attendance, so giving people plenty of notice, especially if it's an all-day meeting, is critical. You'll also want to start building a picture of who'll go into which competitor team, assuming there's more than one, to ensure a good level of experience in each. As a guide, we try to have four to six people in each team—any more than that becomes unwieldy and any fewer means running the risk of having too few people if anyone drops out at the last minute.

Facilities and catering

It may seem a small detail, but the quality of the facilities and catering that you use can make a big difference in the success of your review and in subsequent reviews. It might seem odd that catering and facilities can affect future events, but, as previously stated, the success or failure of a black hat depends on the quality of the people attending. If you arrange the event at an appropriate location and feed and water attendees well, they're more likely to feel appreciated and to attend another review in the future. In a tactical sense, people don't tend to operate well when they are hungry and thirsty, so to maximize the output on the day, keep them well fed and watered. Finally, you might want to consider taking your event offsite. Doing so might cost a little more, but the benefit is that participants won't be drawn back into the day job, especially if you can find somewhere with a poor mobile / cell phone signal! The other benefit of heading offsite is that your participants are more likely to be able to remove themselves from your company's thinking. If you're looking at multiple competitors, then it's best to have individual syndicate rooms for them to break out to. The teams need to immerse themselves in the competitor, and this is more difficult to do when you're fighting to be heard above the other teams.

Identify the questions you want to answer

To make the black hat review a success, it's vital to identify what you want to get out of it. Some obvious topics include the following:

- How important is the outcome to our competitor(s)?

- What pricing strategy will they adopt? Bait and hook? Low risk versus high risk? Will they invest? And so forth.
- Will they try to introduce a new business model, such as leasing or availability services?
- What does their solution look like?
- What are their key weaknesses that we should focus on?
- What are their key strengths that we need to mitigate?

Pre-reading

Once you've identified the question you need to answer, it's time to begin preparing the pre-reading. The idea here is to produce a document that provides the participants relevant information on the opportunity and the competitor(s). Ideally you will want a few pages on what the opportunity is, the trade space, and any hard customer requirements. On the competitor front, you might include details of relevant capabilities and any primary intelligence you've picked up to date. Ideally, you're providing enough information to bring everyone up to the same level of understanding, but not so much that it shapes the review output with any bias or view that you already hold. You want to get this to your participants a week or two ahead of the review to give them plenty of time to read it and ideally undertake some of their own research. You only want to send information that's relevant to the individual participant. So if you have multiple competitor teams, make sure you send the participants their relevant competitor pack only.

Templates

Ideally you will want to ensure that you capture a minimum level of output from the teams. In our experience, if you don't provide templates, you will get wildly varying levels of output, from a team that produces 100 slides to a team that captures four hours of discussion on one slide. To maximize the value of the session, we suggest providing a set of templates that helps answer your original question. You can make these as prescriptive or as free-form as you feel comfortable with. Another important role here is assigning the right person to fill in the slides. There are a number of approaches you can take here, either by bringing in a team of graduates and putting one in each team with this responsibility or by identifying a suitable person in the team already. Whoever you pick, this person needs to be comfortable populating the templates, with good PowerPoint skills and an ability to take input from multiple people to answer the questions. Equally, you don't want someone who gets bogged down in detail and fails to progress from the first template.

Once you've completed all the preparation, it's important to continue to monitor the competitive environment and to add additional primary or secondary intelligence to the packs for inclusion on the day. You'll also need to keep an eye on attendance numbers, as it's not uncommon for people to drop out as you get closer to the event.

Dropouts

Unfortunately people dropping out, even on the day, is common for any large meeting. This can be particularly difficult to mitigate and also extremely disruptive to your review planning. Some of the techniques that we've found to reduce the dropout rate include these:

- Individually calling potential attendees. This builds a personal relationship and allows you to ask for their full commitment.
- Holding a pre-call a week before the event to remind everyone that it's happening and to check that they've received the pre-reading.

- Sending the pre-reading at least a week in advance to keep up the drumbeat of communication.
- Having a senior sponsor who should be contacted should any participant wish to withdraw.

These ideas aren't perfect and won't work all the time. Things will always crop up that result in dropouts. What you're trying to do is show that this review is critical to business-winning activities and should not be seen as something that can be deprioritized without consequence.

The big day

The big day has arrived, the culmination of the diary organizing, location selection, and pre-reading creation. It's worse than planning a wedding! You're almost there but you're not done yet. On the day, the facilitator plays an important role in ensuring that participants remain in character, keep to time, and maximize the collective experience in the room. There are loads of great guides and training on how to be an effective facilitator, so there's little value in repeating that information here. The key thing is to weed out any preconceived bias and to keep the teams focused on thinking like the competitor. There are a few things you can do to help this process and raise a smile at the same time.

Be as one with your competitor

A great indicator that your black hat will succeed is hearing participants using the term *we* in relation to the competitor that they're role-playing rather than the company you work for. There are a number of actions you can take to encourage this mindset.

- Brief at the start of the day that it's essential that participants leave company mindset at the door. If appropriate, ask them to remove their lanyards or company IDs.
- Set up the "war room" with company posters, strategy documents, and so forth. If you're heading to a trade show soon, pick up some pens and notepads from your competitor's stands, and task your colleagues with doing the same.
- Facilitators need to stamp out any "company chat" as soon as they hear it. Sometimes participants don't even realize they're doing it.

Taking these steps won't guarantee that your participants completely "become the competitor," but doing so will help create the right environment.

The pre-brief

A great way to kick off the review is to ask the capture lead to deliver a program brief. Ask them to deliver an objective view of the program that doesn't include details of your company's solution; you don't want to taint your competitor team view of the opportunity with internal thinking. Once complete, set aside some time for Q&A to allow the teams to ask any questions that will help shape their solution. Just before sending the teams off to their rooms to undertake the key part of the day, walk them through the templates you want them to fill in to ensure a level of consistency when they are completed.

Back brief

In your agenda you'll want to ensure that you leave time at the end of the day for each of the teams to brief back. This is an important part of the day, as it allows you and the capture team to ask clarification questions to ensure that the output is understood. It also allows participants who might have knowledge of a competitor to contribute further insight if they were placed in another competitor's team. The back brief is your final opportunity on the day to dig out those nuggets of competitive insight, so leave plenty of time to make the most of it. The back brief is also the time to remind participants that now that they understand the competition and the opportunity, they are critical to collecting intelligence in the future, and highlight who they should send it to, ensuring that nothing falls through the cracks.

After the review

After the event, it's critical that you collect all the output and format it in a way that's easily consumable by the capture team. All the effort you've devoted to organizing and running the review will be wasted if the capture team put the output on the shelf and forget about it. It's often worth formulating some actions with the capture team that identify additional intelligence requirements and actions that the team need to undertake to develop your solution. Don't forget that you have a wide network of participants to reach out to when trying to fill intelligence gaps. It's also critical to keep the capture team informed of any changes that you identify in the competitive environment going forward. It's also best practice to re-run the black hat if there's a change in the competitive or customer environment. Many opportunities have been lost because a company failed to react to a change in the customer or competitive environment.

Wrap-up

This short guide draws upon the collective experience of a number of practitioners, but there's no substitute for learning what works for you. It's important to ask for feedback at the end of the events from both the capture lead and the participants to understand how you can improve in the future. It's also critical that you share the key successes of the event through the appropriate channels to ensure continued support from both participants and your leadership team.

Good luck!

The author

Chris Street has been supporting business-winning activities in the B2G environment for over 10 years. He graduated from the University of Brighton in 2006 with a 2:1 in Business Studies and immediately joined Lockheed Martin to deliver black hat and position-to-win activities. In 2009 Chris joined Thales UK, where he has held a variety of business-winning support roles across a wide range of sectors, from Avionics to Unmanned Systems and Land Vehicles to Electronic Warfare.

Chris is now Head of Value Marketing for Thales UK, where he leads on position-to-win and value-based pricing. A key part of this role is ensuring that the black hat and position-to-win processes deliver impactful output to help shape winning propositions. He can be reached via LinkedIn at www.linkedin.com/in/chris-street-7134bab/.

Key Notes

_____

_____

_____

_____

_____

_____

Key Actions

_____

_____

_____

_____

_____

_____

12

Best Practices for Customer-Value Quantification in B2G Markets

M OST OF THE LITERATURE discussing customer value and value quantification is focused on the B2C and B2B worlds. There's very little discussion of these in the B2G literature related to the capture process and price-to-win. In this chapter, I cover the basic concepts of customer-value quantification, also known as dollarization, the golden nuggets of performing good customer-value analysis, and 10 best practices for applying the knowledge to B2G offers. There's no magic trick or silver bullet to becoming good at dollarizing differentiation value. It requires deep customer intimacy and a deep understanding of competitors. You could say that these also apply to price-to-win analysis. Exactly! That's my point. But it's customer and competitor intimacy on steroids! Let's get into the key topics.

Essentials of value quantification and dollarization

In the B2B and the B2G worlds, value is relative and not an absolute. Unless you have radical disruptive innovation and no reference value or alternatives, what matters when you sell to your customers is not how much value you deliver but how much more value you bring versus the competition. This differential represents your true value, your differentiated value, which becomes the basis for your pricing strategy. So customer value is always a number. You need a rational story about how much economic or financial value you bring to the customer and the relevant stakeholders, and that rational story must include dollars. Saying you offer 20 percent more reliability than competitors is a nice benefit, but that benefit closes sales only when you express it in terms of cost savings, revenue potential, or an emotional benefit, as shown in the value triad in figure 12.1.

The language in figure 12.1 is plain and straightforward. You're reducing cost or providing savings. On the cost reduction side,

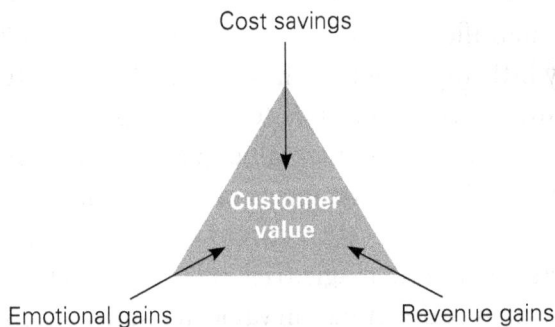

Figure 12.1. The value triad describes benefits from the customer's perspectives.

perhaps your product offers lower weight, greater efficiency, or better coverage. Perhaps the benefit you provide helps customers grow their revenue, potentially by charging higher prices. You can also provide a benefit through an emotional contribution: reassurance, confidence, lower risk, better relationships, long-term sustainability, resilience.

The value triad also shows where total cost of ownership (TCO) differs from value-based pricing (VBP). TCO is focused on cost improvement. Customers can improve their margins in only one way with that. The other way for your customers to improve margins is higher revenues through higher prices. In this case, you've enhanced the value of your customer's products to such an extent that they now have higher differentiated value. TCO is evolving into a concept called TBO, or total benefits of ownership, which encompasses savings and gains. VBP is still different from TBO, though, because it takes the emotional component (e.g., intangible benefits) into account. TCO and TBO are two techniques commonly used in the B2B world. There are generally six of these techniques readily available, as shown in figure 12.2.

TCO Total cost of ownership
TBO Total benefit of ownership
EVE® or **CVM®** models
LCC Life cycle costing analysis
LTV Customer lifetime value analysis
ROI Customer ROI calculation

EVE is a registered trademark of Monitor Company Group Limited Partnership. CVM is a registered trademark of Value Innoruption Advisors LLC.

Figure 12.2. Techniques for dollarizing customer value.

When a discussion begins about turning benefits into money, someone will inevitably use the word *monetization*. I need to make an important distinction here between monetization and dollarization. Many people use the terms interchangeably, but they're distinct, as I show in figure 12.3. Monetization can mean many things, from turning something illiquid into something liquid, to any number of methods for converting an asset into money.

Monetization is the conversion of something into a stream of something else. It's a very general term. *Dollarization* is much more precise. You translate something specific (a customer benefit) into its equivalent impact in dollars and cents. It expresses in monetary terms the extent to which your products and services improve a customer's situation. Dollarization goes much further in depth than monetization. Dollarization forces you to create hard facts. The secret to dollarization is to translate an attribute or product feature into a benefit and then to create a fact or a ratio or a number for how you can change it or improve it. Let's say that figure is a 20 percent improvement in efficiency. Dollarization turns that 20 percent efficiency into $1 million.

Dollarization	≠	Monetization
Dollarization is translating the benefits that a product or service delivers to a customer into the actual dollars-and-cents impact.		Monetization is the conversion of an asset into money or the establishment of something as a medium of exchange. It can refer to methods utilized to generate profit, and it also can mean the conversion of an asset literally into money.

Figure 12.3. The important difference between dollarization and monetization.

I've been dollarizing customer value for nearly 10 years. Many times, I've taken teams through the process successfully. Other times, I've failed to do so. There's no perfect way to quantify customer value. It's both a science and an art. There are different techniques, as shown earlier. The process needs teamwork and collective interpretation. In the end, I'm not in love with a process or a technique. I've used life-cycle costing (LCC) to dollarize customer value for very large transportation systems for municipal authorities. I've created EVE models for laser-guided-missile targeting systems for a national air force. I've applied TCO for a service outsourcing calculation for military missions in emerging countries. Each technique works. What's needed for all dollarization techniques is deep customer intimacy and very good knowledge about the competition or the alternative solutions. For some very large pursuits, I've worked with teams in mapping customer needs and requirements and reverse-engineering the potential solutions coming from a frontal competition. In the end, we decided to use EVE to map out the incremental customer value versus the competitors. The EVE methodology was created in the very early days of the development of VBP, in the early 1990s, by some of the pricing pioneers (Tom Nagle, to drop a name!). Since then, it's become the most widely used dollarization technique in companies that are designing and deploying value-based strategies. In companies more traditionally focused on cost management and operational excellence, TCO might be the most widely accepted technique. For the rest of this chapter, I focus on the EVE methodology. If you're unfamiliar with this concept, I encourage you to search for it on Google documents; you'll find many examples and papers on the subject. My book *Dollarizing Differentiation Value* is focused on VBP and explains how to build EVE models.

Golden rules of customer-value quantification

In 2008 I read Jeff Fox's book *The Dollarization Discipline*. This was my introduction to the science and art of dollarizing competitive advantage and differentiation. At that time, I was well versed in marketing and strategy and had basic knowledge of pricing. Reading this book opened my mind to the science of VBP, value quantification, and dollarization. It was the beginning of a journey that has lasted 11 years so far. During this decade, I studied and researched VBP inside and out and was deeply involved in designing hundreds of quantified customer-value models, or EVEs, across various industries and regions. The purpose of this short chapter is to share best practices with the pricing and marketing communities on the best practices for EVE models. I call them my golden rules. These are the 10 principles that I frequently advise people to keep in mind when we dollarize and brainstorm on specific value drivers. This list is my list based on 11 years of experience in dollarizing. It's by no means exhaustive, but it's a good start!

1 **Contextualize your value model and quantify within the context.** The context of your EVE sets the frame for the quantification work. That includes the customer, the customer segment, the geography, and the offer under consideration. Groups often diverge and end up mixing up contexts across different value drivers within the same EVE model. So, from one value driver to another, the context changes. I often remind them to go back to page 1 of the templates we use and to refocus. The most common situation is to begin the work with one customer in mind and to be stuck when extrapolating to all customers during the value-quantification process. Stick with that customer only or that one customer segment.

Extrapolation and generalization come later in the value management process.

2 **The unit of analysis and time of analysis need to match the customer's daily business.** On the same page 1 of the templates, we discuss the unit of analysis and the time of analysis for the EVE model. This is where it often gets complicated and groups have difficulty agreeing. Both components of the value model need to be set and kept the same across value drivers and for the duration of the group's work. The unit of analysis matches the customer's value metric: how do they measure their costs, profit, or the outcome of their business? So if a customer thinks in terms of vehicles produced, we cannot produce an EVE per tire. The same goes for the time of analysis. Some customers think in terms of three- or five-year increments. Others might think in terms of the lifetime of the product they buy. Both unit and time of analysis need to reflect the customer's way of doing business and vocabulary.

3 **Never dollarize a product feature—always dollarize a customer benefit.** I think I've repeated this golden rule a million times! The sequence is from product attribute or characteristic to customer benefits to formula to quantification. So, if an engine goes 2,500 RPM versus one that goes 2,000, we dollarize not the extra 500 RPM but the outcome benefits, which might be increased yield or greater productivity. In a product-centric and manufacturing environment, it's a hard habit to break. The translation of product competitive advantage to customer benefits is essential in customer-value modeling and EVE. This is a very challenging step for technically focused professionals.

4 **Dollarize three to five value drivers for a value proposition, not more.** Understanding and quantifying

customer value requires prioritizing what's essential for the customer's business. A good value proposition isn't a long and hypnotizing list of value drivers. It's a maximum of three to five value drivers that are carefully packaged in a well-delivered value story. The difficulty is in selecting the right value drivers. When I manage dollarization hackathons, we usually go through two rounds of discussion to prioritize and extract the right differentiators and customer benefits. First, we use the VRIO framework (valuable, rare, inimitable, organized for success) to select the three to five true differentiators. These get translated into customer benefits. We then use the 4C framework (customer-pain-centric, credible, commensurable, compelling) to select the most critical three to five customer benefits that will move on to be fully quantified. Remember that your customer wants to hear value propositions that are focused on their problem, that are very compelling, and that can save them money!

5 **Carefully select the order of your value drivers in your analysis and story delivery.** The 4C framework was also developed three years ago based on feedback from dozens of people who'd done dollarization exercises with me as a coach. The main issue is to figure out in which order to place the value drivers. My golden rule was created to ensure that the key customer benefits that are quantified have a highest score in the 4C framework, with a minimum of 9 out of 10 for the first C, which is focused on customer-pain-centricity. Again, teams struggle with the value-driver sequence and with which one to start in the delivery of the value proposition in front of customers. I always recommend starting with the big-bang value driver—the most resonating and compelling for them. I tell teams to revisit the value proposition they built for this segment or specific customer and to revisit the customer problem. Additionally, if the first value driver is powerful enough

to convince the customers to buy from you, you don't really need to spend too much time on value drivers 2 and 3. Simpler is often better. Some of the story can be delivered in writing and some during presentation. That's where value selling comes into play.

6 **Focus on the flow and credibility of your dollarized value proposition and on the sequence of the customer-value proposition delivery.** Value proposition design has much to do with the delivery of a great story. The same goes for an EVE model. It's nothing other than a quantified value story. The quantification part of the work is a bit messy and requires many iterations. That work in progress is never shown to sensitive internal stakeholders or to customers. During dollarization hackathons and EVE workshops, I ask teams to deliver a quantified storyline in three minutes. It's a difficult exercise. Some people like to spend time on the nitty-gritty details of the calculations. Others forget to contextualize the model and to explain the critical assumptions. Story delivery is part of the value modeling process!

7 **Price and costs never enter your EVE models.** The objective of performing an EVE is to derive the right price level. Therefore, the price of the offer we build the model for is not included in the model. The price of the alternative does, however, get factored in as the reference value. I often see confusion about negative differentiation as being the price of the offer. That's not the case. These are different concepts. Similarly, the cost of your offer does not play a role in the design of an EVE model. You should be able to build this model without cost information. When the price is set at the end of the price analysis, costs enter into the decision. Remember the three C's of price setting: customer, cost, and competition.

8 **Focus on both positive and negative differentiators and value drivers.** When conducting internal EVE and

dollarization workshops, it's necessary to study both positive and negative differentiators of your offer versus the alternatives. It's essential for teams to hold candid discussions about what makes their offer better and what makes it worse versus alternatives. That doesn't mean that we'd volunteer all negative differentiators in front of customers. But it's best to be ready in case educated customers bring these up. When selecting the offers to dollarize in groups, be mindful of selecting offers that are somewhat differentiated, meaning they have more positive differentiators than negative ones. Bottom line, it isn't realistic to present quantified value propositions to B2B or B2G customers without mentioning potential negative differentiators.

9   **Dollarize not to reach accuracy and perfection but to be credible and have a good story.** During working sessions, I often witness groups arguing about small numbers or decimals. The goal of dollarization sessions isn't to reach 100 percent accuracy. It's to reach agreement around a number range or a rounded number. Whether we save the customer $1,500 or $1,458.78 doesn't matter. What matters is that the customer acknowledges that there's value to be shared and that they want to investigate that with you. You do need to find and use the correct formula for the quantification exercises. So during EVE workshops, I remind participants to focus more on the logic and credibility of the value story and less on numeric accuracy. I recommend that when you reach greater maturity in value quantification, you should use detailed value calculators by end-use application or by customer segment. These ROI, value, or TCO calculators usually have greater levels of accuracy.

10 **Document your assumptions and hypotheses for internal discussions but also for external disclaimers.** This is a must-do activity during EVE workshops. I have

two extra pages that I always use in the dollarization template. One is for listing assumptions and hypotheses for the model and the value drivers. The second is for listing the actions that need to be taken to further develop the EVE model within 45 days. Running EVE models often requires putting your offer in customer situations or scenarios. In fact, you will dollarize for the most common customer applications or uses of the product or services. Your story will often list a set of very important assumptions. In some value-based marketing materials, we also list some disclaimers such as "calculations assume normal wear and tear in the application." When value models are worked in team, new members might come in and pick up the work where others left off. Assumptions and hypotheses are essential for continuity of work.

These 10 golden rules are the most common points that I emphasize and reinforce in training and workshop sessions. I wanted to document them for you so that you can also share them with your multifunctional teams when you begin your EVE activities. Remember that value quantification of dollarization is just one step in VBP. There are many additional golden rules to consider when we deploy the six steps of VBP for an offer. That's a topic for another time. In the meantime, you should practice, practice, and practice some more. That's the best way to get better at building EVE models.

10 best practices for dollarizing B2G offerings

So, what's different when quantifying and dollarizing customer value for B2G customers?

1 **Focus more on cost savings.** As you see from the value triad, you save customers money, you make them money, or

you create an emotional connection. In the B2G world, it's recommended to focus first on the low-hanging fruits, which typically are cost savings. These hard savings are tangible and much more relevant to procurement teams. I'm not saying that experiences and user emotions aren't critical. I'm saying that it's easier to push forward quantified value propositions when they focus first on cost savings and expense optimization.

2 **Carefully decide whether you can discuss head-count reduction and labor savings.** In the B2B and the private worlds, discussing head-count reductions and labor savings is straightforward and common. It is not in the public sectors. It might be a sensitive subject for some agencies where size does matter and where unions have a dominant position. For example, in the defense sector, military size is a signal of prestige. In other sectors, budgets are correlated to the number of employed public staff. Therefore, in these cases, one should refrain from dollarizing head-count reduction or focusing heavily on these value drivers.

3 **Make sure you select carefully what numbers are shown in dollars or euros instead of percentages.** Similarly, and in general, public employees are not fluent in the language of value and relevant financial savings. It might be surprising to them to discuss savings in terms of euros and cents. A better approach might be to discuss differentiation as percentage savings versus alternatives. In the medical technology and pharmaceutical worlds, discussing the value of a life or of life extension is commonly done. In the military world, discussing the value of a life in dollars and cents might be less acceptable.

4 **Understand the customer's definition of value and receptiveness to discussing value with you.** Government entities might be composed of several stakeholders and

a complicated buying center. Because of the fragmentation of the overall decision-making process, there might be various definitions of customer value as well as various levels of receptiveness to listening to a value story. So it's not as straightforward to influence the users with value numbers if they aren't used to hearing dollarized value propositions.

5 **Actively engage stakeholders in the buying center and reconcile the definition of value at the account level.** In analyzing the buying center, the strategic account manager will work closely with the capture leader for a specific large pursuit. They will map out a plan to deliver the right price for the opportunity and will anticipate the proposal evaluation process. The strategy for presenting and positioning dollarized value propositions will include all the required stakeholders. Evaluators will play a key role in understanding the dollarized value numbers.

6 **Develop the appropriate testing methods.** For customized, innovative, and complex offers, it's often impossible to calculate the delivered differentiation value, as test methods are often not available. This often makes calculating value difficult. There are three choices in this situation: (1) define new test methods and conduct internal tests to calculate incremental value, (2) work with university or other research entities to do so, or (3) create theoretical testing and embark on academic testing to validate testing methods. This takes time and resources. But it also creates competitive advantage when done well, as it sets benchmarks in the marketplace.

7 **Leverage the power of value simulators.** For very large offers, complex offers, and very long timespans, the use of value calculators can be powerful. Proprietary tools can be beneficial in calculating lifetime differential value, in

projecting TCO, and in educating customers on the drivers of value in new technology or complex offerings. I've used such very advanced models for the space business, where satellites, for example, are highly customized and in space for quite a long time.

8   **Study the RFP, the scoring criteria, and the evaluation formula.** Calculating TCO and designing EVE models are very useful for conducting price-to-win or position-to-win analyses. Calculating the differential performance in products or services helps model the scoring mechanism that customers use to evaluate competitors' proposals.

9   **Be ready to fail and to move on quickly.** I've conducted dollarization exercises for five years in the government space, and I've failed many times. So it doesn't work every time you try. Many times, the team I worked with stopped at the percentage level because it was impossible to dollarize. Other times, we lacked access to the customer's operational process or we lacked key information to dollarize. Finally, for many defense contracts, we lacked access to comparative testing information that customers often run independently to validate performance. The teams also didn't feel comfortable showing theoretical calculations. Bottom line, it doesn't work for every offer or for every customer.

10 **Understand the customer's perception of risk and how to manage liabilities.** Risk management and appetite for liabilities vary across government agencies. Dollarizing the risk of cybersecurity breach for the CIA is probably not the same as dollarizing the same risk for the Department of Agriculture. The dollarization process often includes risk mitigation. It's essential to understand the risk appetite of different agencies and to research how these agencies protect

themselves. This is a critical difference between the B2B and the B2G worlds.

Implications for B2G pricing

When responding to complex, differentiated, and best-value RFPs in the government space, dollarizing differentiation value is a requirement. There are different techniques available to conduct such analysis. Calculating the differentiation value fits well in the capture management process and helps drive the best pricing decision. There are many considerations to think about:

- What technique is the most appropriate for the opportunity?
- Who should oversee the dollarization process?
- How can the value analysis be validated?
- Do you have enough customer insights and knowledge of the operational process?
- How credible is the customer-value analysis?

Like anything, dollarization is a muscle that needs to be developed and strengthened over time. It's also a science and an art. It requires social intelligence and a great deal of collaboration.

I realize that this chapter provides a lot of information at once. It's advanced marketing and pricing. I encourage you to read more about value quantification. In 2016 I wrote a book on VBP called *Dollarizing Differentiation Value*. This book focuses on VBP for B2B companies and highlights in easy steps how to deploy the methodology, including dollarization techniques. Keep learning about the subject.

Key Notes

_____

_____

_____

_____

_____

_____

Key Actions

_____

_____

_____

_____

_____

_____

Section 3

PRICE-TO-WIN

13

Lightning Strike

Differences and Similarities between Price-to-Win and Value-Based Pricing

I N THE B2B WORLD, value-based pricing (VBP) is well known and deployed by roughly 20 percent of companies. In the B2G world, price-to-win is well accepted, and many consulting firms offer as part of their services such analysis. I'm often asked about the differences and similarities between the two methodologies. I thought I'd write a short chapter to provide definitions as well as the top five differences and top five similarities. Let's get started.

Some relevant definitions

Price-to-win is both a process and a result. Price-to-win is more than a number; it could be best defined as the cost-capability tradeoff that embodies your company's strategy. Price-to-win, the process, identifies the position your company needs to achieve to meet its business goals and objectives. The price-to-win analysis output is a window-to-win map plotting the customer's budget considerations, the supplier's capabilities, and price levels, as shown in figure 13.1.

VBP is a pricing strategy that sets prices primarily, but not exclusively, according to the perceived or estimated value of a product or service to the customer rather than according to the cost of the product or historical prices. VBP has six steps, as shown in figure 13.2.

Top five similarities between price-to-win and VBP

1 **Both methodologies use positioning maps.** This is very beneficial for users of both methodologies. Positioning maps help position all competitors in one simple visual to establish value and price relationships. VBP uses value maps

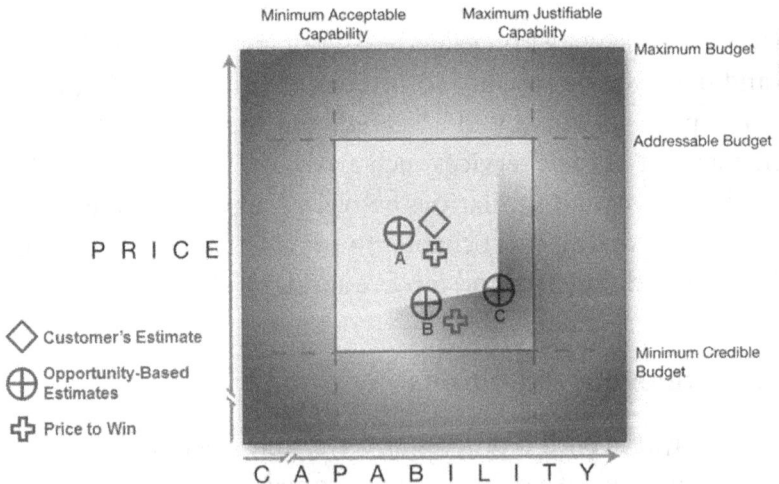

Figure 13.1. Price-to-win and the window-to-win.

```
        ┌   ┌─────────────────────────────────┐
        │   │  Understand your competition    │
        │   └─────────────────────────────────┘
        │                   │
        │                   ▼
        │   ┌─────────────────────────────────┐
        │   │   Segment your customers        │
        │   └─────────────────────────────────┘
        │                   │
Value  ⟨                    ▼
        │   ┌─────────────────────────────────┐
        │   │ Identify differentiation by segment │
        │   └─────────────────────────────────┘
        │                   │
        │                   ▼
        │   ┌─────────────────────────────────┐
        │   │  Quantify differentiation value │
        │   └─────────────────────────────────┘
        │                   │
        │                   ▼
        └   ┌─────────────────────────────────┐
            │  Estimate the value pool to share │
            └─────────────────────────────────┘
                            │
                            ▼
Price  {   ┌─────────────────────────────────┐
           │ Price accordingly to capture value │
           └─────────────────────────────────┘
```

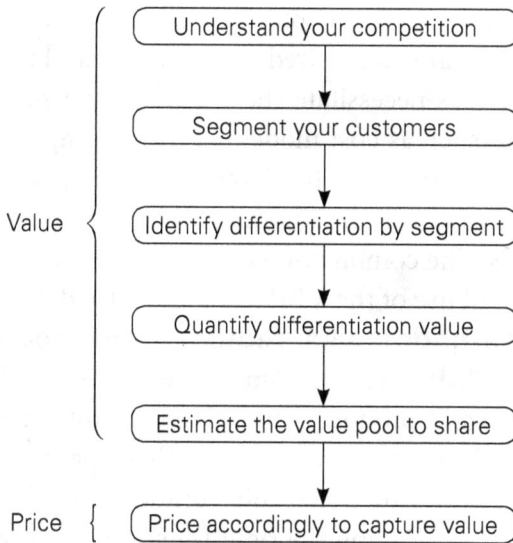

Figure 13.2. The steps of value-based pricing.

that position all competitors on a matrix using two axes: value score and price. Each competitor is represented by a bubble whose size is equivalent to their market share in volume. PTW uses the window-to-win to map competitors based on their capabilities and prices.

2 **Both methodologies are well documented and follow a process.** Both are well documented in process manuals and books. VBP is a bit more confusing, as consultants have yet to settle on one approach, and the pricing profession uses a variety of terms and approaches. PTW is much more standardized and does not suffer from the consulting bias.

3 **Both methodologies require granular data and analytical capabilities based on robust research.** Both require deep customer, competitor, and cost data. The "garbage in, garbage out" concept applies to both. Having data isn't enough. Someone needs to analyze, connect, and synthesize

all the data to reach the required outcome. This is why consulting firms are often hired. Besides data and research, both methodologies necessitate the use of off-the-shelf or proprietary tools such as cost modeling, reverse-engineering, value simulators, and so forth. Companies that perform VBP or PTW systematically end up industrializing their process with these tools. The combination of data, insights, and tools leads to successful use of the VBP or PTW methodologies.

4   **Both methodologies require multifunctional and active collaboration.** Someone working on their own in one office can't produce a useful and credible PTW or VBP analysis. It's essential to work on these processes in teams over time. Multifunctional collaboration is a requirement, not a nice-to-have. Having the right functions involved for must-win bids is paramount to creating alignment and credibility. This is often considered a luxury or an expensive process, as people must make themselves available and often must travel. But remember the "garbage in, garbage out" concept. So who should be involved? The usual suspects include sales, bid, capture, product, marketing, and finance professionals. Other functions might bring value as well: technical support, program management, and quality control, for example.

5   **Both methodologies require anticipation and continuous sensing.** Assembling multifunctional teams to work punctually on capture opportunities is a good start. But the commercial cycles in B2G are often very long. So the benefits of multifunctionality kick in when a team works together over time and learns more as they go. This is part of the left-shifting process for capture management that forces much anticipation and market-sensing skills. Key account managers and marketing managers have to become sensors of what's happening in the market as well as what might influence a large pursuit opportunity. They bring that the knowledge to

the team. As a result of this ongoing sensing, the approach to the bid might change, and additional information and activities might be required.

Top five differences between PTW and VBP

1 **PTW is not as customer-centric as VBP is.** PTW is very much focused on competitors' capabilities and costs. The methodologies require a deep dive into competitors' cost structures and cost levels. Costs are then applied based on anticipation of what they might propose in a response to an RFP. Customer information focuses on hot buttons and budget information. VBP is much more customer-centric. It begins with a deep segmentation process and an even deeper customer process analysis through the use of research techniques. So VBP is equally focused on customers' and competitors' information.

2 **PTW is strongly focused on cost. VBP is not.** VBP doesn't focus on internal cost information. In fact, cost information is never discussed until it's time to make a pricing decision based on the three C's of pricing. PTW is heavily cost-focused, as previously mentioned. PTW analysts need to research competitors' cost information. This is a real specialty, and it's why PTW consulting firms often hire highly skilled research analysts with years of experience.

3 **PTW is opportunity-focused. VBP can be done at the customer-segment level.** PTW is specific to a bid or an offer. The information might be reused for another bid, but the analysis will be redone. Each complex or technical solution will be different and will need to be reverse engineered. In VBP, the goal is to conduct analysis at the customer or market-segment level to avoid conducting customer-by-customer analysis. The customer-value quantification might

begin at the customer level, but it's essential to generalize at the segment level provided customer segmentation is conducted well. This is often an issue in the B2G world. Because most large and technically advanced contracts are different, vendors think and act like project companies. The goal of VBP is to move to pricing structures and VBP at the segment level in order to become much more product- or solution-oriented.

4 **PTW can be outsourced. VBP cannot.** Because of lack of skills, data, and analytical tools, B2G vendors will call on consultants for help. They might then outsource an entire PTW analysis; VBP cannot be outsourced in its entirety. Parts of VBP, such as customer segmentation, customer research, or competitive analysis, might be outsourced, but the integration and interpretation must stay inside. Generally speaking, marketing managers or value managers are in charge of the "art part" of VBP. This is where VBP gets a bit tricky! Information from customer research needs to be triangulated with internal existing information, and from gut-feeling impressions on the part of the salesforce. So, in a way, PTW is more rational and pragmatic than VBP.

5 **PTW is very tactical. VBP is both strategic and tactical.** Finally, PTW feeds into the pricing decisions. But VBP informs and directs the pricing strategy. VBP is a pricing and marketing strategy. In fact, it's more a way to go to market. I've written a lot about VBP, and the name is misleading. VBP is an approach and an orientation. It's much more strategic than tactical.

Combining the two methods into the position-to-win approach

So which approach is best to use? I could say both, but both are time-consuming and require resources. I strongly recommend taking the most important part of the two methodologies and making them your own. Some large B2G vendors have combined both to create what's called *position-to-win*. Position-to-win is an opportunity-based methodology that integrates the entire PTW methodology with the differentiation and dollarization analyses from VBP. The methodology looks at much more than technical and product capability by paying attention to intangible value drivers as well. The review of competitors' capabilities includes a dollarization process. So position-to-win integrates cost, customer, and competition in a single methodology without naming it VBP. See figure 13.3.

Because VBP is often related to B2B and little used in the B2G world, I believe it's a good way to make a change in the world of pricing for the public sector.

Implications for B2G pricing

For the past five years, I've worked on pricing opportunities for both the B2B and B2G sectors. I've promoted the three C's of pricing decisions day in and day out. Good pricing decisions are

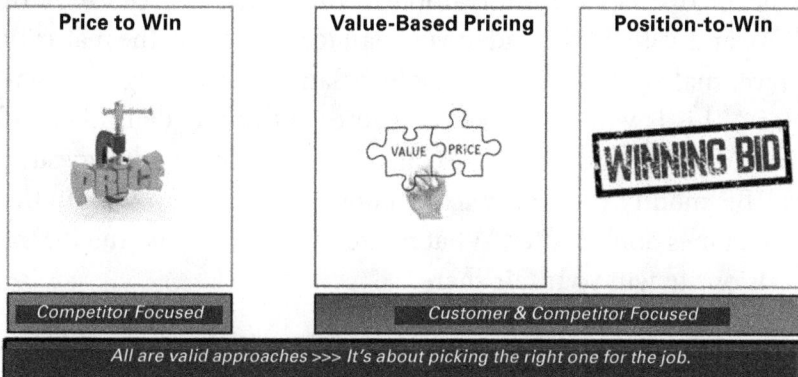

Figure 13.3. Comparing pricing-to-win, value-based-pricing, and position-to-win.

Customers
(segmentation, customer value proposition, customer value models, customer journey mapping, customer research)

Competition
(price-to-win, black hat, war games, strategic business intelligence, value map, performance benchmark, competency inventory)

Costs
(design-to-cost, should-cost, top-down/bottom-up, life-cycle costing)

Figure 13.4. The three C's of pricing and relevant methodologies.

informed by a balanced set of information from customers, costs, and competitors. For each of the C's, there are a series of techniques and analyses to be conducted, as shown in figure 13.4.

Most B2G vendors have a good level of maturity in cost and competition because they conduct PTW analysis. They lack knowledge of and experience in dealing with customer insights. When I promote the use of VBP in B2G, I don't ask them to forget about costs and competitors. I remind them of the need for that balance to make more intelligent decisions. Of course, nothing happens overnight. It's a real journey to reach maturity in both PTW and VBP. In the end, if you plan to move along the maturity curve, make sure to use the right balance and the right vocabulary. This is why I began this chapter with some definitions. If your company doesn't want to introduce a new methodology such as VBP, modify your PTW to be more like position-to-win. In the end, names don't matter. What matter are balance and intelligent decisions to win your fair share.

Key Notes

Key Actions

_____

_____

_____

_____

_____

_____

_____

_____

_____

_____

_____

_____

14

Price-to-Win: Bidding Smarter, Not Lower

Alex King, Amplio Services

How complex sales pricing differs

THERE IS A VACUUM of information around pricing complex sales. B2C pricing strategies can be national news, for example, when Apple releases a new phone or Sony releases a new gaming console. However, little attention is paid to B2G pricing in the news or even in academia. Even when government contracts are overspent, there is little attention given to or understanding of the original pricing. There appears to be an embedded assumption that the original price was reasonable and that the scope of work was well defined such that a reasonably competent contractor would be able to deliver it. The same logic that governs B2C pricing cannot simply be ported over to a B2G context. The fundamental difference is that complex sales separate buyers and users, whereas consumer buyers are also users. For example, you would normally pick the smartphone you want. You buy it, and then you use it. In a government context, there's usually a separate procurement division that buys what other divisions want to use. Not only are they separate entities in a B2G context; often they are committees rather than individuals. In complex sales, buyers don't use the product or service, and users don't buy it. There are other compounding factors, such as the relatively low-volume/high-value nature of government purchases. If your internal business case is based around selling millions of smart-phones, then the pricing can be adjusted over time depending on the market reaction. The product may even be redesigned to reduce its cost. However, if you build ships for a navy, then an order of five units would be a relatively large order! There is little, if any, opportunity to adjust the pricing after the deal is made, and the ships cannot be redesigned without the consent of the buyer. Against this background, price-to-win is a process specifically designed for complex sales to businesses and governments; it isn't designed for consumer sales. Price-to-win makes complex sales pricing a predictable, repeatable process that balances risk and reward.

The price-to-win process

Price-to-win is defined as the highest price at which your organization can bid and win for a given probability of winning (PWin). Sometimes, sales and bid professionals become overly fixated on win rates. Win rates alone are not a good measure for evaluating the job performance of sales and bid professionals. In January 2018 one of the largest UK government contractors went bankrupt. It was winning major contractors just months before it collapsed, and its sales were increasing year-on-year. Carillion didn't go bankrupt because its win rate wasn't high enough. However, a major factor in its bankruptcy was a lack of profitability on key contracts that it had won. So, there's always a need to balance the PWin and profitability of the opportunity.

Our definition of price-to-win does create a secondary question about what a "good" win rate is. To answer this properly, we must segment the answer between bids that have an incumbent and those that do not. Incumbents win so much that they distort the average. One self-reporting survey found that 59.8 percent of contracts were won by the incumbent bidder (Thacker, 2013), and another survey found nonincumbent win rates from 30 percent to just over 40 percent but incumbent win rates from 70 percent to 90 percent (Shipley Asia Pacific, 2013). These vary from industry to industry, and many people answering these surveys often boost their "win" rate by including noncompetitive contracts that were not "won" competitively. Most major government bids begin with at least three bidders, so many companies will have a win rate below 30 percent if they're not bidding selectively. An independent contractor can't tell a company what its win rate should be, but for nonincumbent bids, a long-term win rate above 70 percent is unlikely to be profitable. Likewise, a long-term win rate below 20 percent is unlikely to sustain the turnover of a significant government contractor.

Price-to-win is also a measure of the value your organization has created as part of the bidding process. This is because price-to-win treats price as the dependant variable in its equation. Price-to-win is a completely external view of pricing. It begins by analyzing and predicting competitors' price and technical score. The combination of the price (as a score) and the technical score is called the most economically advantageous tender (MEAT) score in Europe or value for money (VfM) in the US. Usually, the lowest price will get the top score for price, but there are many alternative ways of scoring price. The highest combined technical and price score of the competitors will become the benchmark score to beat.

Deducting our predicted technical score will give the required price, as a score, which is then reversed back to a currency value.

In this analysis, there is a 50 percent probability that our organization will win if we bid at $291 million. If we bid at $284 million, then the probability of winning improves to 70 percent. The graph in figure 14.1 can be produced for any bid; if we took 10 past bids where we had bid at the 70 percent PWin, then we would expect to have won seven of them and to have lost three. This assures us that our process works and our analysis is accurate. It's important to remember that our profitability is not the same at $284 million as it is at $291 million; specifically, it's better at $291 million. This means that the 90 percent PWin is not inherently a good point at which to bid. The organizational value of price-to-win as a process

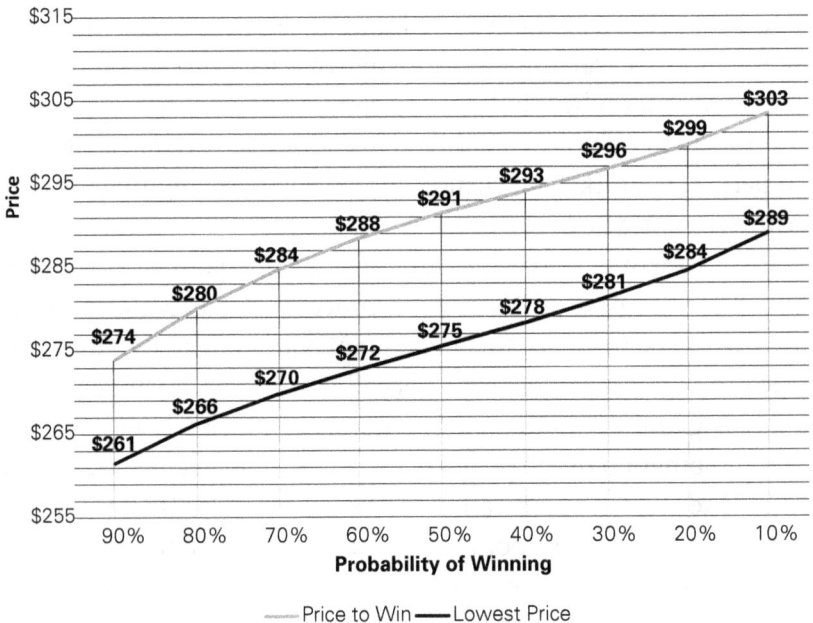

Figure 14.1. Example price-to-win analysis.

is in balancing the risk of losing the bid with the rewards from winning.

Figure 14.2 shows the inputs that created the previous graph. The inputs to the price-to-win are a three-point input of the competitor's price, technical scores, and a three-point estimate of our technical score. Since our technical score is better than the competitor's technical score, the price-to-win will be higher (i.e., more expensive) than the competitor's. That's why the light gray price-to-win line is higher than the dark gray line in figure 14.1.

If our competitor has a worse technical score, then their price will need to be lower than ours in order to compensate. This means that our most likely estimate is that $275 million will be the lowest price and therefore score 100 percent of the available price score, which is weighted by 40 percent. The 40 percent price score added to the 66.7 percent technical score weighted by 60 percent (40%) gives an overall MEAT/VfM score of 80 percent. Since our predicted technical score is 45 percent, we know that we need our price to score 35 percent and also to score 80 percent. Since we know that $275 million scores 40/40 and is the lowest price, we can find the point above $275 million that would score 35/40.

	Weighting	Minimum	Most Likely	Maximum
Strongest competitor price	40%	$250.00	$275.00	$300.00
Strongest competitor technical score	60%	62.5%	66.7%	75.0%
Strongest competitor MEAT score		77.5%	80.0%	85.0%
Our technical score		40.0%	45.0%	47.5%

Figure 14.2. Price-to-win inputs.

Price-to-win is never a single price; it's a price with a probability attached to it. We've discussed typical win rates, but what
about typical profitability? The average net profit margin of any
company, in any industry, is 8.3 percent (Damodaran, 2012).
This includes super-profitable industries like real estate investment trusts; therefore, government contractors tend to be lower
on average (e.g., 6.7% for defense). Thus, if we find a company
with an average win rate above 50 percent on competitive deals
for which they are not the incumbent and their net profit margin is above 8 percent, then they are doing something unique. It
could be that the company is very selective in its bidding and minimizing money spent on long-shot opportunities. However, this
is much harder for larger companies to achieve than for midsize
and smaller ones. When a company has a multibillion dollar turnover and has governments as its primary customers, then there
are only so many opportunities to chase. Typically bid costs are
1 to 3 percent of the potential contract value on larger deals and
up to 6 percent on small ones (Shipley, 2011). The win rate can be
improved by not bidding long-shot opportunities. However, it's
also a good idea to allocate larger bid budgets (as a percentage) to
the better opportunities. Even though this won't affect the overall
win rate, it will improve the profitability of the deals won.

Three-point estimates

The price-to-win inputs are the predicted technical scores of our
competitors and our own bid, plus a three-point estimate of their
price. Of these, prices are the harder estimates to produce. Usually
technical quality is scored on an absolute basis. That means that
the customer will usually define that a technical solution that does
x will score 6/10. A technical solution that does x and has proved it
in the field will score 8/10, and so on. In that sense, it's easier to be

objective and accurate about what difference technical solutions will score. Price is harder, although we do know that companies are in business to make profits. Actual instances of companies bidding below cost are rare, although people like to speculate that they're frequent. One concept key to better estimating prices is to use multiple estimating methods for the same work package, as shown in figure 14.3.

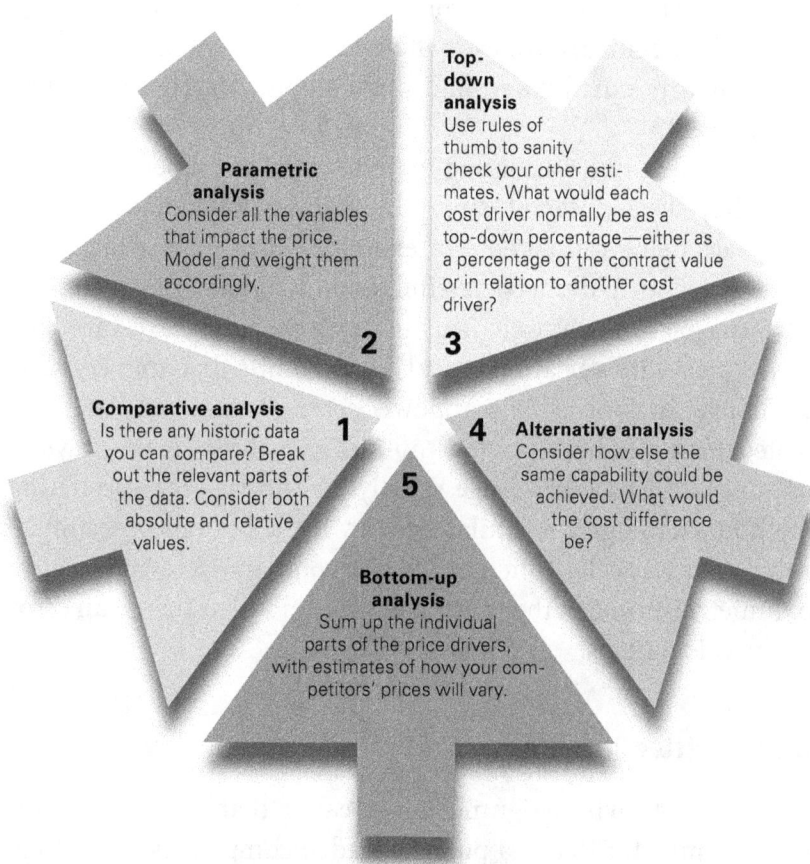

Parametric analysis
Consider all the variables that impact the price. Model and weight them accordingly.

Top-down analysis
Use rules of thumb to sanity check your other estimates. What would each cost driver normally be as a top-down percentage—either as a percentage of the contract value or in relation to another cost driver?

Comparative analysis
Is there any historic data you can compare? Break out the relevant parts of the data. Consider both absolute and relative values.

Alternative analysis
Consider how else the same capability could be achieved. What would the cost difference be?

Bottom-up analysis
Sum up the individual parts of the price drivers, with estimates of how your competitors' prices will vary.

Figure 14.3. Five difference-estimating methods. Image copyright Amplio Services, 2015.

Any individual estimate can contain mistakes. By producing and reconciling these independent estimating methods, we gain increasing confidence in our price-to-win after understanding any variances. For example, we might know from historical data that bottom-up estimates are 70 percent accurate. That means there's a 30 percent chance that the bottom-up estimate is wrong. But if we also have a parametric estimate showing a similar prediction, and we know that parametric estimates are 85 percent accurate, the combined accuracy is now 95.5 percent. Add a comparative estimate with 60 percent accuracy that also supports our answer, and our combined accuracy is now 98.2 percent.

It's not that one estimating method is always superior to others. They have different strengths and weaknesses depending on what's being estimated. For example, when estimating hardware products, parametric estimates and comparative estimates perform particularly well. This is partly because hardware correlates well with certain physical design limits that are very slow to change. In contrast, a manpower service might be better estimated with a bottom-up and top-down analysis, as the ways of offering services can change rapidly. In theory, each estimating method should give a similar answer. If the bottom-up estimate comes out radically different from a comparative estimate or a parametric estimate, the most likely reason is that there's an error in the calculations.

Competitive intelligence

Some price-to-win assignments are easier than others. Analyzing a competitor that is a publicly traded company is easier than analyzing a private one. But even if the competitor is small and obscure, there are techniques we can use to understand them. Michael Porter (2004) described three "generic strategies" that describe the fundamental ways in which companies can compete. Correspondingly, the *Shipley Capture Guide* (Newman, 2011) describes three customer "buying types." Now, the issue isn't whether there are really three types or four but a fundamental principle that some bidders come into particular bids better able to compete and therefore having a greater need to win. For example, some companies compete by developing technically superior products that sell at a premium price. The development costs for these products require a level of investment that is reflected in their labor rates. Depending on the industry, the opportunity to share some of these development costs with a customer are few and far between. This is the kind of logic that builds a picture of the bids that will be most critical for them to invest and win, as well as the constraints they will face.

This logic is summarized in a grid showing the logical, top-level strategy to win. Your company should fit into one of the generic strategies (horizontal). When selling to different customer types (vertical), some strategies are inherently better than others; examples are shown in figure 14.4.

Implications for B2G

The most common mistakes companies make in complex sales are these:

- Rewarding sales and bid professionals based on win rate without considering profitability.
- Chasing long-shot deals, for example "technical leadership" companies trying to sell to "capability satisfied" customers.
- Underfunding the bid budgets for their best opportunities, for example "technical leadership" companies trying to sell to "best value" customers. This usually happens because they've diluted the bid budgets to chase long-shot deals.

	Cost Leadership	Focus Strategy	Technical Leadership
Capability Satisfied	Supply early pricing information and create a compelling event to speed up the decision	Help your customer explain the key tradeoffs between extremely cheap or technical alternatives	No bid
Budget Limited	Highlight the risks of uncertain solutions to contrast with the certain benefits of low price	Explain "tipping points" and cost drivers so that the customer keeps their requirements moderate	Demonstrate the whole-life-cost argument (usually new products have cheaper support costs)
Best Value	Highlight the risks of uncertain solutions to contrast with the certain benefits of low price	Explain "tipping points" and cost drivers so that the customer keeps their requirements moderate	Highlight the "false economy" of locking yourself into the solutions of "yesterday," today

Figure 14.4. Generic influencing strategies.

Price-to-win is not about winning at zero margin, artificially lowering labor rates, or taking excessive risk. It's about creating value for the customer and competing with productivity. The creation of value means that the customer will set requirements and assign them technical scoring in a way that enables the technical score to offset a higher price in a MEAT/VfM calculation. Labor rates should be reasonable in relation to your competitors', but the real innovation comes from improvements in productivity. Productivity is the ratio of an input to an output. Usually that input is an hour of labor; there are too many outputs to name, but examples include software code produced per hour, number of assets maintained by a network, tonnes of steel welded per hour, and so on. Note that the output is never money; money is what the output is exchanged for. If your productivity is good and your labor rates are reasonable, then you can only really lose "bad business." Why not allow your competitors to win at zero margin and end up taking a loss when they inevitably can't deliver?

Conclusion

Pricing complex sales fundamentally differs to pricing consumer products. Reading about how Apple shocked the market for smartphones with the iPhone or how Sony entered and dominated the gaming console market is interesting, but the practical application for selling ships to a navy is limited. Price-to-win is a process specifically for the B2B and B2G sales process. The industry-wide fixation on win rates is fundamentally flawed if it doesn't also consider profitability. However, companies don't make this mistake out of stupidity. Instead, they're desperate to measure and quantify the complex sales process. Unfortunately, they're measuring the wrong thing. When a company implements a proper price-to-win process, the true measurement is whether it wins 6/10 of the bids that it bids at the 60 percent PWin. The share 5/10 isn't good enough, nor is 7/10. It takes time and expertise to develop this level of accuracy, but this process is ultimately the best way to balance the risk of losing with the profitability from winning. Most companies are perpetuating unsustainable tactics like slashing margins, taking arbitrary percentages out of their estimates, or setting unrealistic productivity targets for the workforce. These tactics can bring them down, even companies with turnovers in the billions. Ultimately, when the price-to-win looks unattractive, there are two good questions to discuss: "Can we create more value for the customer?" and "Can we be more productive?" While these can't always be achieved within the context and time scales of a specific bid, the conversation will usually happen between a bid team and an authorizing committee of senior management. This is the intersection where those companywide changes can at least begin. In short, price-to-win is a process with a language that pushes companies to increase customer value and productivity, not decrease profit margins. Profit margins should be encouraged because they are the reward for creating value and delivering good productivity.

The author

Alex King is a specialist in price-to-win and competitive intelligence. Alex has over 10 years' experience on multibillion-dollar deals in a variety of industries including defense and transport, telecoms, and software. Price-to-win is an external view of how to price a bid within a complex sales process. Alex works as an independent consultant with many of the largest companies in the defense industry on specific deals. He is based in the UK but has done deals around the world, including in Asia, Europe, and America. He is also a trainer in price-to-win for Shipley and has spoken about price-to-win at multiple conferences for the Association for Proposal Management Professionals (APMP). Alex holds an undergraduate degree from Cardiff University in Business Administration. He also has a master's in International Relations from Staffordshire University. To learn more, please visit https://amplioservices.com/ or contact Alex at alex.king@amplioservices.com.

References

Damodaran, A. (2012). *Margins by sector (US).*
Newman, L. (2011). *Shipley Capture Guide v3.0.* Kaysville, UT: Shipley.

Porter, M. (2004). *The competitive strategy: Techniques for analyzing industries and competitors.* New York, NY: Simon & Schuster.

Rebuilding Solutions. (2013). *Attitudes to incumbents: What procurement professionals really think about incumbents' performance at rebid.* Retrieved from https://rebidsolutions.co/the_rebid_survey.pdf

Shipley Asia Pacific. (2013). *Asia Pacific Business Development, Tender and Proposal Survey.*

Key Notes

_____

_____

_____

_____

_____

_____

Key Actions

_____

_____

_____

_____

_____

_____

15

The Secrets to Setting the Price-to-Win

Michael O'Guin and Kim Kelly, Knowledge Link[1]

RAYMOND COREY OF THE Harvard Business School said that "pricing is the moment of truth—all marketing comes into focus in the pricing decision." Bid price is paramount to success in competitions for major contracts. Outsourcing, digitalization, corporate consolidation, free trade, and even the internet are leveling technological advantages between competitors across the globe. This is reducing discrimination on technical capabilities between competitors on major bids. As discrimination between solutions decreases, the importance of price increases (see figure 15.1). However, that does not mean that the lowest price always wins—far from it. While your business may be different,

---

1   This chapter is reprinted with permission, with minor revisions for style, from Michael O'Guin and Kim Kelly, *Winning the Big Ones—How Teams Capture Large Contracts*. Copyright Michael O'Guin, 2012.

our analysis of 155 major contract awards (all over $40 million) found that the offeror with the lowest price won 54 percent of the time. Also, when examining the buying behavior of over 50 international customers, we found that more than 90 percent of customers have picked a higher-priced solution at one time or another. Therefore, determining the winning bid price is complicated at best.

Despite the importance of pricing, many companies allow their solution design to determine their pricing. They allow its costs, irrespective of competitive forces, to dictate pricing, as opposed to identifying the winning price and then ensuring that the solution design fits the price. Then, as the proposal submittal date nears, management often decides their price is too high and demands that it be slashed. Management usually bases the new price on conjecture rather than facts. To reach management's desired price, the company suddenly finds itself desperately scrambling to reduce costs and frequently jettisons the features and discriminators they'd spent weeks and months selling to the customer. This late price cut also forces management to make painful choices, including cutting profit margins, committing millions in R&D,

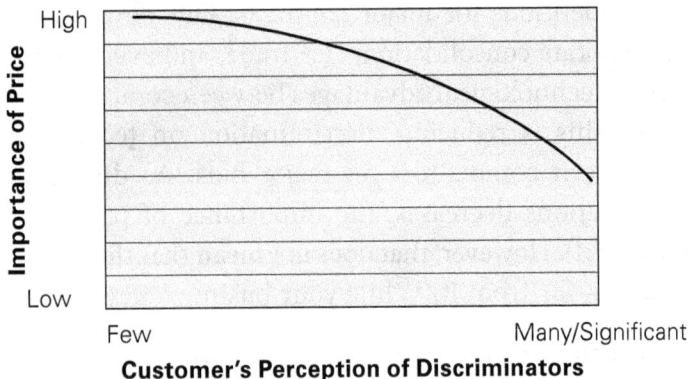

Figure 15.1. Decreasing discriminators versus importance of price.

and risking cost overruns, all of which jeopardize the win and future returns.

Executives from a construction company were delivering a proposal to the California Department of Transportation (Caltrans). This $650 million bid to expand and repair freeways across the state was critical to their business unit. As their car pulled into the Caltrans parking lot, one of the executive's cell phones rang. The construction company's president was on the line. The president knew Caltrans always went to the lowest price contractor, and he was concerned that their bid was too high. He told them to cut the bid price by $30 million. They changed the proposal's bid price in the Caltrans parking lot. They won. They had underbid every competitor by $70 million. This meant that the executive had forfeited $30 million in profit in 15 minutes on the phone in the parking lot without any competitive intelligence. Our analysis of 25 recent large pursuits found that winners significantly underbid one quarter of the time. In these cases, companies had significant cost advantages that would have allowed them to increase their bid price and still win. Because they did not know of their cost advantage versus their competitors', they failed to leverage their cost discriminators into a higher price. There is a better way to price bids.

Setting the "right" price

Developing a winning price, while upholding margins, is critical to victory and to increasing shareholder value. But determining the "winning" number is one of industry's most difficult challenges. For best-in-class companies, achieving the winning price, which is not always the lowest price, is not the result of luck. It is the result of a systematic and repeatable, yet rarely discussed process called *price-to-win* (PTW).

PTW is shaped by external factors—namely a customer and the competitors. The PTW has nothing to do with your ability to meet the price determined. A PTW analysis is a market-based analysis of an opportunity, conducted to identify the highest price that a company can bid and still win. As figure 15.2 shows, this formal process includes systematically analyzing the customer's buying patterns and evaluation process in order to predict the customer's likely source selection behavior. The analysis includes a top-down estimate of the competitor's likely bid price based strictly on their past bidding behavior. In parallel, a rigorous competitive analysis deciphers the competitor's offering from a bottom-up estimate of their costs and their likely bid price. An important component of the competitive cost analysis is comparing the competition's costs with a "should cost" analysis on the company's offering. A should cost is the company's current cost baseline minus cost inefficiencies, described in detail later in this chapter. Comparing these cost baselines allows the PTW analyst to identify and quantify differences between the company's offering and the competitors'. By estimating the competitor's bid and how the customer is likely to make their source selection, the PTW analyst identifies the highest possible winning bid price with the right balance of capabilities. This comprehensive analysis significantly increases a company's win probability by independently validating and refining the company's strategy.

Developing the PTW is a mix of art and science. It combines the science of cost engineering with the art of competitive analysis. The analyst must project the competitor's likely approach and bid aggressiveness, and deduce their solution architecture. They must overcome all of the ambiguity of the situation and make judgments about how the competitor will behave. Since large pursuits are complex, developing the diverse skills needed to accurately predict the competition's bid is challenging.

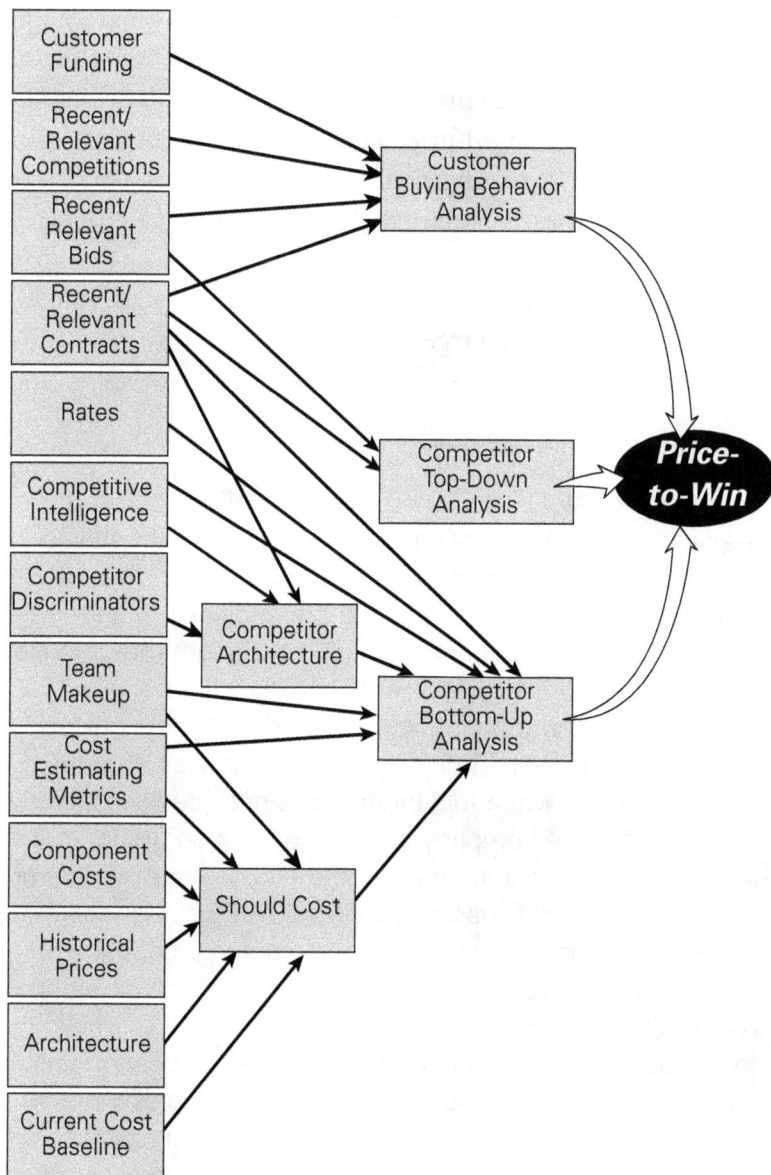

Figure 15.2. The price-to-win analysis process: Significant data, multiple approaches.

Some managers mistakenly believe that a PTW is merely a justification for slashing profit margins, but it's not. PTW is a process for managing costs while maximizing win probability. Establishing an early market-based price and subtracting out the desired profit margin allows management to set and deploy cost targets for the offering. These cost targets feed the design-to-cost (DTC) process. The technical team then develops a solution that meets a market-derived price. Starting early allows design teams to achieve challenging cost targets.

—Strategy in Action—

For example, Air Force General Merrill McPeak decided that the Joint Direct Attack Munitions (JDAM) contract should have an average unit price of under $40,000 per unit. He based this number not on an in-depth engineering analysis of the requirements but on how much he thought the defense budget could afford. Initially, McDonnell Douglas's JDAM engineering team thought no one could produce a guided weapon at that cost. Their original estimate was $68,000 each. However, when told by their business development manager that the company was going to "No Pursuit" if the engineers stuck to that position, the engineers reconsidered. McDonnell Douglas was motivated to win. Having recently lost a major competition for the sole-source production of the Tomahawk missile, they realized that if they wanted to remain in the precision-guided munitions business, they had to win JDAM. The design team committed to beating this challenging target. Eventually, McDonnell Douglas won the competition with a bid of $14,100 per unit. Their competitor was a mere $300 per unit higher. Setting an aggressive cost target forced the design teams of both companies to break paradigms and use innovative technologies and approaches to achieve their huge cost reductions. That is the power of setting early up-front cost targets.

Results in the space launch business between 2000 and 2002 clearly demonstrated the power of the Price-to-Win process.

—Strategy in Action—

In April 2000, one of the authors, Kim Kelly, transferred into Lockheed Martin's International Launch Services (ILS). He began implementing a PTW process for rocket-launch sales to commercial satellite companies around the world. By studying his competitor's bids, he was able to decode their pricing formulas. As ILS institutionalized the process over the next year and a half, ILS's pricing became more effective. They raised their win rate from 50 to 80 percent. ILS's market share increased to over 60 percent, and ILS became the market share leader for the first time in history. Their revenue increased by almost $500 million while profits skyrocketed. ILS's principle competitor, Arianespace, failed to respond and continued to lose sale after sale. Arianespace had no comparable Price-to-Win capability. They did not understand what was happening in their market. In 2002, while ILS's executives were receiving record bonuses, Arianespace's board of directors ousted their entire executive team.

Almost every large buying decision usually comes down to a group of key decision-makers selecting a winner. While in most cases the decision-makers can pick whoever they want, they must use the proposal and price evaluation to justify their decision. The way to ensure victory is to be the offering the key decision-makers want most *and* to "correctly" balance the proposal evaluation and price. By correctly balancing the proposal evaluation and price, you make it easy for the decision-makers to justify selecting you. What is "correct" depends on the customer and is discussed later in the chapter. The PTW process is how one determines the correct balance of evaluation score and price (see figure 15.3).

An important point to remember is that you'll have to take actions to achieve your price target and your desired proposal scoring. These actions must be consistent with your win strategy. That means that your win strategy tactics should not conflict with actions you employ when getting your price down to achieve your PTW; nor should they conflict with your approach to improving your evaluation scoring. In other words, don't jettison your discriminators to get your costs down, if jettisoning undermines your win strategy.

Figuring out how much the customer has to spend

The first step in conducting a PTW analysis is to determine how much money the customer has to spend on your work scope. This

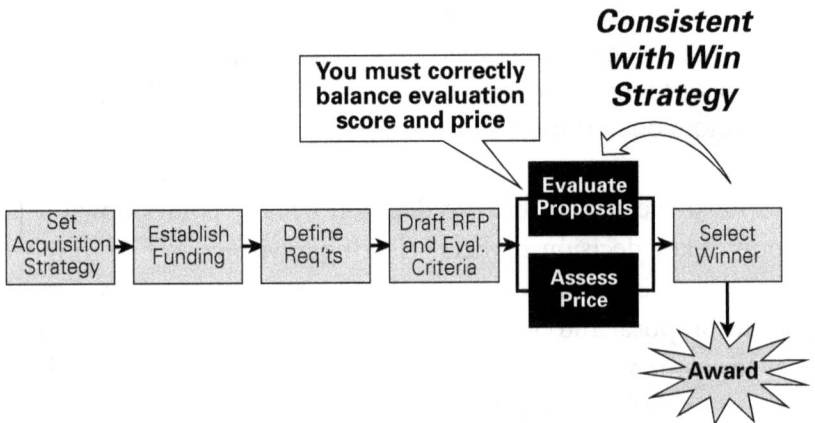

Figure 15.3. To win, you must correctly balance evaluation score and price.

customer funding analysis frames the competitive landscape and bounds all the solutions. It's no fun wasting time chasing an opportunity with a solution that the customer can't afford. Many governments publish their project funding, and commercial customers will often tell you how much money they have available. This forthright approach saves everyone time. However, many customers are not so enlightened, and in those cases, bidders have to figure it out. Someone in the customer's company has a specific dollar amount in mind, and it's best to find out who it is and what they know. The available funding will determine what requirements the customer can afford. It's also important to understand their funding expectations. The customer expectations can determine how open they are to different solutions, or to bidding lesser requirements, as well as whether the proposed project is realistic.

To identify available funding, a PTW analyst should try to determine what logic and data sources the customer used to estimate the project's budget:

- Is this a repeat buy?
- Did they conduct a market study?
- Did they receive any prior rough order of magnitude or unsolicited proposal prices?
- Did they use a comparable project as the basis?
- Did they request pricing in a request for information (RFI)?

Once you identify the sources, you need to ask yourself whether these estimates are comparable. More importantly, does the customer think they're comparable, and what adjustments did they make? You'll also need to examine the project's affordability within their overall budget. Can they afford the project as currently scoped? If not, the analyst needs to consider this as they develop their approach. When trying to project future funding, examine the organization's likely revenue growth. Within most bureaucracies, looking at a department's percentage of total funding works as a fair guide. Departments mightily resist any threat to their relative status, such as a reduction in their budget to increase that of another department, so an analyst should be skeptical if the customer is projecting that their department's funding is growing as a percentage of the customer's overall funding.

—Strategy in Action—

When strategizing about how to win an electronic archives program for the National Archives, architecting a solution around the available funding was very important. The National Archives was projecting the program budget to be $100 million per year for six years. Our experience told us that the National Archives' program manager would hold on to his belief until proved wrong, so he would stick to his assertions that the project would be fully funded. However, Congress has traditionally underfunded the agency and restrained budget growth. The National Archives would need an overall budget increase of 20 percent to fully fund their archives project. This seemed unlikely given the limited clout of their congressional oversight committee and the tight budget environment. Therefore, the analyst needed to design a solution that could satisfy a program with a $100 million/year budget but that could also be scalable to a project with half that amount, a target we estimated was more realistic. This scalable strategy provided a distinct advantage over the competition because the competitors believed the program manager. The competitors were then forced to slash their system's scope when Congress published the National Archives reduced budget.

When customers publish budgets, they don't always break out all of the other distributions that will come out of that budget. The analyst must sift out the management reserves that program managers bury in their budget numbers. Once the team has identified the actual project budget, they must understand how much of the budget is available for the contractor.

Surprisingly, we have seen many multibillion-dollar proposals submitted with bids over the customer's published available funding. This represents a complete failure of the company in their price-setting and cost management. *Never bid above the customer's available funding.* Customers cannot commit to a contract unless it's within their budget. And they rarely go back and try, much less successfully, to get more money. If a customer is ever presented with one bid over their available funding and another below it, they will always pick the competitor who came in within their funding.

If the project is commercially funded, then the availability of funding depends on the project's financing and the company's business case. Bidders will need to forecast the project's revenues and expenses. The business case needs to consider all of the project's risks, from receiving government approvals to avoiding labor problems and currency exchange fluctuations. Then they'll need to assess the eligibility of debt and equity financing to this customer to determine how big a budget the project will have.

Identifying the customer's buying behavior

The next step is for the PTW analyst to examine the customer's buying behavior. Procurement departments and executives usually follow the same formal procedures from one purchase to the next. Executives and contracting staff tend to have longevity, and organizations develop norms of behavior. As a result, customers usually have consistent buying behaviors over the years. For the PTW analysis, consistent means predictable. Identifying these behaviors is of strategic importance, yet few companies conduct even an elementary analysis of how their customers actually buy.

Examining a customer's buying patterns allows one to understand a customer's true value in the source selection decision—if, how much, and under what circumstances they are willing to pay a price premium. While the US Coast Guard claims to always buy "best value," a look at their buying history over the last 12 years reveals their true buying behavior. They've selected the lowest price bidder in every case. Once they even chose the lowest bidder despite their technical evaluation team determining that the "winning" shipyard was incapable of building the ship proposed. NAVAIR (the US Navy's buyer of airplanes), on the other hand, also claims to award on "best value." NAVAIR will pay a significant price premium for a technical solution they like better or one that is of lower risk. For example, they paid a 60 percent price premium to Northrop Grumman for the Broad Area Maritime Surveillance system. And 60 percent on a $10 billion contract is money executives like to capture. Therefore, one does not want to bid into NAVAIR like they would into the US Coast Guard, and vice versa. It's crucial to identify your customer's behavior, so that you can best architect your bid and avoid leaving "money on the table."

Even within customers, different organizations buy differently from one another. For example, NAVSEA, the contracting office responsible for buying the US Navy's ships, is very cost conscious and tends to technically level competitors, unlike NAVAIR.

The customer analysis focuses on understanding how and why the customer has made source selection decisions. This analysis looks at specific similar sales, who was selected, and why. Did they pick the lowest price, or did the winner receive a price premium?

What reasons did the customer give for picking the winner—greatest capability, lowest risk, or fastest schedule? Who were the key customer decision-makers, and what roles did they play? Did the customer rigidly adhere to their rules, or were the rules flexible? Does the customer request a best and final offer (BAFO), or multiple rounds of price concessions? As you accumulate answers to these questions, you'll uncover the patterns that the customer repeats over and over again.

—Strategy in Action—

Customer analysis provides excellent insight about how to position your company. For example, a bidder can see an interesting pattern when examining the Australian Ministry of Defense's (MOD) selection behavior. The MOD always likes to have three bidders and uses the three players as leverage against each other in lengthy negotiations before announcing a winner. They often go with someone other than the low-price bidder, such as on the Lead-In Fighter, F-18, P-3 Upgrade, and Penguin Missile programs. When the MOD intends to select a higher-priced offering, they tend to behave in a consistent way. They begin defining and interpreting the requirements to disqualify the low-cost offerings as noncompliant. Knowing this, a shrewd supplier can discern where a competition is going by watching how the MOD is evolving the requirements. However, most importantly, this knowledge helps guide the team in developing an influencing plan to shape the competition toward your offering.

One critical issue that some proposal teams neglect to fully consider is what price the customer will evaluate. Some customers evaluate development cost, some consider unit production cost, and still others look at the entire expected life-cycle cost of the program. NAVAIR, at Patuxent River, asks for development costs, low rate production costs, and life-cycle costs as part of their RFPs. However, when analyzing their behavior, you'll find that they focus almost exclusively on development costs, whereas Qantas Airways measures a total rolled-up cost per seat mile when deciding what model of aircraft to buy. Analyzing prior purchases can help the analyst answer the question "What will be priced?" Failing to answer this question can cost you the competition, as one contractor discovered on a guided-bomb bid. The contractor knew that the Air Force would pick the lowest price for this program, so the contractor set an aggressive price target for their bomb and rigorously drove their design team to meet it. Unfortunately, the RFP surprised them. They found that the customer would evaluate the cost as the bomb plus the bomb carriage (the sophisticated component of the aircraft that carries the bomb to target). The contractor had not optimized the bomb carriage for low cost, and its high cost was a key reason they lost.

Like in the commercial rocket-launch business, the price you submit isn't the number the customer evaluates. Customers add launch-insurance costs to each supplier's bid to create an evaluated price. Launch insurance covers the buyer in case of a launch failure and is based on their record, so the proven Proton rocket with its nearly perfect record has a proportionally smaller insurance premium than other launch vehicles. Customers like the US Army, Navy, Air Force, NASA, and the UK MOD all adjust one's bid for risk. We've seen these customers add dollars for risk adjustments up to 50 percent on a bidder's price to generate the evaluated price.

In projects where the supplier requires financing, price may be only a part of the evaluation. In these cases, one provides not a price per se but a business deal. With a business deal there will be revenue and risk sharing, which offset price. For example, when

General Motors decided to outsource its information technology (IT), they struck a deal with EDS. EDS agreed to take over GM's existing IT staff and assets and then sell its data processing and computer services back to GM. In this deal, there are two key prices: the price EDS was willing to pay for GM's IT department, and the service fees EDS was willing to charge GM.

The customer evaluates the overall return of a supplier's offering versus its perceived risk. In these cases, you do not conduct a price-to-win. Instead, the analyst conducts a *deal-to-win*. The deal-to-win is an analysis that determines the competitor's likely business proposition to the customer and recommends your winning deal. In this case, the analyst must understand the competitor's financing capabilities, willingness to accept risk, and return expectations, as well as their bid aggressiveness.

Figure 15.4 shows the award behavior for one customer. Of the five awards examined (we replaced program names with letters), this customer awarded to the higher-priced bid in three cases. In those four awards, the customer awarded to the company with the higher technical evaluation score. For example, in ARM2, the

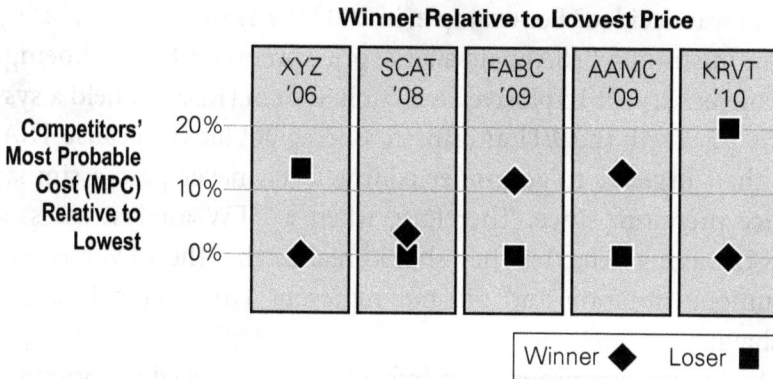

Winner Relative to Lowest Price

Figure 15.4. Tracking customer award behavior.

winner had a higher evaluation in two of the five evaluation categories. In BTA, the loser had a higher evaluation score in two areas, but was 20 percent higher in price. The conclusion one can draw from this analysis is that the customer will award to a company with a higher evaluation score (in at least two areas) as long as their price is within 12 percent of the lowest-priced offer (as it was in AMS and ATS), but not to a bidder with a 20 percent higher price.

Customer buying behavior can be commodity-specific. Customers are much more willing to pay a premium for a higher-performing solution that addresses a significant mission shortfall than for one that improves a non-mission-critical support service. For example, one construction company always chooses the lowest-cost bidder when selecting a concrete supplier. However, they believe that the quality of the architectural and engineering firm's design determines the success or failure of their projects. As a result, they are willing to pay a significant price premium for the firm they think is most technically competent.

The analyst needs to understand the context of each past procurement—how important was this competition to the organization's mission, and what were the funding constraints and other environmental pressures on the organization when this procurement was decided? For example, in 2002 the Transportation Safety Administration (TSA) paid a large price premium for the Boeing/Siemens Airport Explosive Detection System (EDS) to field a system quickly in the 9/11 aftermath. Boeing got lucky because TSA, in their urgency to get under contract, has never paid a similar price premium since. Therefore, when a PTW analyst assesses TSA's buying behavior they should realize that the EDS buy was a unique situation and did not represent TSA's typical buying behavior.

Including inappropriate purchases in the precedent program analysis is a fairly common mistake that analysts make. Buying behaviors are a function of an organization's procedures, precedents, and individuals. Therefore, when analyzing precedent programs, it's important to only examine purchases that were made by the same procurement organization you're selling to. For example, when you try to sell a ship to the US Navy, FFG(X), their next-generation frigate, would be a good precedent program. Ships like FFG(X) are purchased by the NAVSEA Command. You would not examine the Presidential Helicopter competition, which was bid into NAVAIR, which buys all the US Navy aviation assets. NAVSEA and NAVAIR have some similar procedures, but their buying behaviors are very different. If you were selling the same ship to the English Navy, it would be insightful to analyze their buying behavior on other complex development jobs such as a command center or aircraft, as well as ships, because the MOD centralizes all military purchases.

A customer's buying behavior can change. General Motors dramatically changed their buying behavior with the promotion of Jose Ignacio Lopez to the head of Worldwide Procurement. Lopez was aiming to obtain cost savings of 20 to 40 percent out of their suppliers to help GM avert a financial crisis. Lopez destroyed GM's cozy supplier relationships by reopening contracts and ruthlessly competing supplier contracts to drive down prices. Lopez changed GM's buying behavior overnight. Changing an organization's buying behavior brings a significant cultural change as well. These changes are typically well publicized both in and outside the company as leadership tries to implement its desires.

The customer analysis helps determine where the price needs to be relative to the competition, as shown in figure 15.5 for two different customers, NASA and the US Coast Guard. To win a Coast Guard procurement, one must bid a lower price than any other competitor. However, when selling to NASA, the winning price depends on how desirable your offering is relative to the

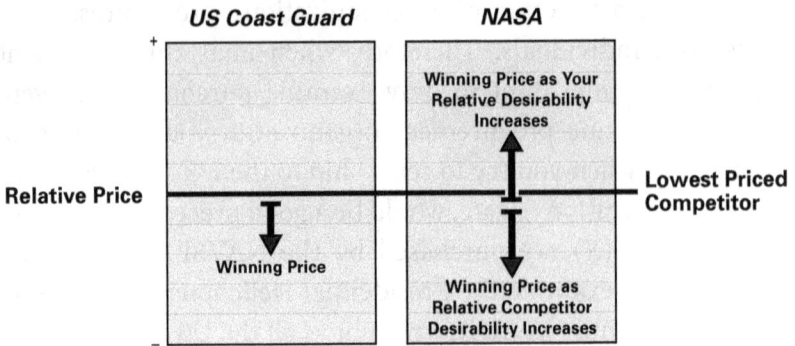

Figure 15.5. Using customer analysis for the price-to-win.

competitors'. The more desirable your offering over the competition's, the greater price premium the customer can justify. Conversely, if the competition's offering is more desirable, you must be much lower in price.

Building the should-cost model

One starting point for estimating the bid price of a competitor is their past bids. If you have a past bid, you need to do your homework to understand what the number included. You need to discover what the work scope, order size, and delivery schedule of the bid was, in addition to understanding how competitive it was. Once you determine this information, you adjust the bid for inflation, differences in quantities, bid aggressiveness, and technical differences to develop a cost baseline. In some cases the analyst may have list prices for the competitor's product or at least part of their solution. For example, when estimating the competitor's bid price for a search-and-rescue helicopter program, we were able to begin with the competitor's list pricing. After interviewing the salesforce to determine the competitor's discounting policies, we estimated their green aircraft price (a green aircraft is the base flyable aircraft with no interiors or customer equipment). Because this competitor had not bid on any search-and-rescue configurations yet, we then had to use our should-cost approach to estimate the additional costs of their aircraft modifications and avionics suite.

Another point of departure for developing an estimate for the competitor's bid is your cost baseline. Your current cost baseline incorporates a significant amount of knowledge. The cost baseline incorporates much of the company's knowledge about how much it will cost to satisfy the potential customer's requirements. The PTW analyst will use this knowledge together with competitive intelligence to calculate the differences in the two cost baselines. Unfortunately, initial program cost estimates frequently contain errors and cannot always be used. By the time a proposal goes to the customer, its pricing has gone through many reviews and management has wrung out most of the cost inefficiencies. Some competitive intelligence professionals mistakenly use this initial cost baseline for developing a competitor cost buildup. If they do, they embed these inefficiencies into their estimate of the competitor's costs. As a result, the projected competitor's cost is too high and the PTW is inaccurate.

Since the PTW analysis is always trying to predict the "end-game"—the final competitor price—analysts must develop accurate estimates early on, before this wringing-out process is complete. A key part of the PTW process is to analyze the company's current cost baseline and develop a should cost. To create this should cost, the PTW analyst builds a cost model going down to at least the third level of the work-breakdown structure and usually the fourth or fifth level. The should cost is an estimate of the company's proposal price with all of their costing and design inefficiencies eliminated. We call it a should cost, but it might be more appropriate to call it a should price, because it does include profit margin. Later in the process we use the should cost as the basis for estimating the competitor's bid price. We do that by making adjustments to the should cost for the differences in approaches between the offerings.

The first step in creating the should cost is to analyze your team's current cost baseline, or to invent one if they haven't begun yet. When a should cost is done effectively, it uncovers cost-savings ideas from across the company. The analyst evaluates all these factors against the customer's requirements to eliminate overscoping, redundancies, unnecessary features, and poor bidding practices. A good PTW analyst is experienced and knows cost-estimating relationships. This allows them to spot uncompetitive functions and support ratios that are out of line. For example, the should cost may find that management has underbudgeted some functional areas. Underbudgeted functions can result in overruns and schedule delays once the contract is awarded.

The should-cost process typically reduces the overall program budget by a double-digit percentage. Should-cost findings have included these:

- Support ratios for quality assurance, document control, reliability, and production control are double what they should be (based on similar programs).
- Logistics padded their budget by 50 percent because they were used to having their budget slashed in the review process.
- A supplier of a key component learned that the prime contractor knew little about their costs and decided to include a large nonrecurring development cost in their bid.
- Another supplier buried first-class travel in their bid to support an overseas project.
- Substantial low-skill work has been earmarked to an underutilized high-cost facility.

Using the current cost baseline, you identify the key cost drivers for your company. These cost drivers are likely to be the same for the competition, which helps focus the competitive analysis on the most important questions to address. Through interviewing your own engineers, you can determine what cost tradeoff alternatives your engineers faced in developing their estimates. Usually, these will be the same tradeoffs that the competition faced. The PTW analyst then second-guesses all the major trades and assumptions driving cost. They look for divergent opinions in the company's own staff as well as competitive intelligence about what the competitors are doing. For example, the analyst can discover that one engineer believes that a requirement interpretation might create discrepancies in the bids between teams. A single assumption can create huge cost differences between competing solutions. We've seen many situations where an engineer has made a very conservative interpretation of a requirement that results in a significant increase in a proposed solution's estimate.

—Strategy in Action—

One engineer working on a train control system concluded that to be "absolutely certain" of never losing a signal between control relay stations, the antennas must never be more than four miles apart. Another engineer found that there would be no operational impact due to lost signals if the antennas were six miles apart. Putting the antennas two miles farther apart reduced the bid cost by over 15 percent. In an analysis like this, where a requirements interpretation has a significant cost impact, it's critical that the engineers bring these issues forward to management. Management should decide how much risk they want to take on to win the business.

Competitive intelligence can also help develop the should cost.

—Strategy in Action—

In one case, a company was designing a new handheld gas detector for an upcoming pursuit. The engineering staff insisted that the design required 12 batteries. However, the company's PTW analyst was concerned about the battery count because the customer would evaluate the life-cycle cost of the solutions. In fact, battery costs dwarfed the price of the gas detectors over their life. The competitive analyst went to a trade show and visited the competitor's booth. He found the competitor's unit on display. He picked it up, turned it over, and found that it had slots for only eight batteries. When he returned to his company, he informed the executives and the engineers of his finding and of the competitor's low estimated evaluated price. Given their previous reluctance to consider a design with fewer batteries, he commented, "We are going to lose, because their engineers are better than ours." That was all the company's engineers needed to hear. The engineers took up the challenge and were able to redesign the unit with improved power management, reducing the battery requirement to eight, and achieved the PTW, thus eliminating a key competitive disadvantage. The PTW analyst's should cost pointed the engineering staff to an improved solution.

The PTW analyst needs to examine the customer's likely evaluation criteria and compare these to the solution, removing features that are costly and that have minimal impact on the evaluation criteria. We have seen features included that the customer didn't require, and that provided only an additional 2 percent of evaluation credit, but that drove up the solution's cost by more than 20 percent. The executives must remove such features from the proposal baseline but could offer them as an option. This makes the customer's job easier because they won't need to justify the high cost of these features in their source selection decision but will still have the choice to add them.

The should cost should exclude any engineering "pet rocks." Pet rocks are features or exciting technologies that your marketing or engineering departments are dying to get into production that are not desired by the customer. Since these features are not required or desired by the customer, they won't be in the competitor's solution, and they'll provide little or no evaluation credit. If pet rocks are bid, they create a competitive disadvantage.

The analyst should assess the solution's cost tradeoffs versus the customer's likely evaluation scoring. Costly technical features need to be assessed against their likely evaluation credit. For example, on an unmanned air vehicle program, the engineers were pushing to propose a radar under development instead of a commercial off-the-shelf item. The development radar would have added millions to the bid price, six months to the flight test program, and a huge amount of risk for a mere 3 percent improvement in the evaluation score. The analyst put the off-the-shelf radar's price into the should cost and not the development radar.

Estimating the competitor's bid price

The should cost is critical to modeling the competitor's bid, as shown in figure 15.2. Typically, this cost, without inefficiencies, is the starting point for developing an estimate of the competitor's bid. Once the PTW analyst deduces the competitor's technical approach, they adjust the should cost based on differences with the competitor. Developing the PTW requires a thorough understanding of the competitor's likely approach. It's our experience that it's usually better to concentrate on the strongest competitor than to analyze many. You uncover greater insights by going in depth into a single competitor's technical solution; if you spread your resources across many, you conduct a less-thorough analysis and miss critical subtleties that can drive the analysis. One accurate competitive bid number is better than two inaccurate ones. However, sometimes we do analyze more than one competitor. This might be done, for example, if the competitors have very different approaches whereby each has some unique discriminators highly valued by the customer. If the competitors have different approaches, one of which may lead to a drastically lower price that we are not able to confirm without conducting a second detailed cost analysis, then more than one competitor may be analyzed.

The analyst begins by conducting an analysis of the field of competitors to identify the top competitor. This is a critically important step. We have lost two pursuits by focusing on the wrong competitor. In both situations the customer sent mixed messages about what they wanted, which made it difficult to select the most formidable competitive solution. The best approach is to assess which competitor will have the best price and evaluation from the customer's perspective. You conduct your competitive analysis and cost analysis on the most formidable competitors and delve into more and more detail until you can deduce with confidence who is the strongest. This is a critically important step: getting it wrong can cost you the win.

The next step is to deduce the architecture of the competitor's likely solution. For most bids, differences in their architectures, not variations in labor and overhead rates, drive most of the cost differences. The analyst should focus on the messages that this competitor is communicating to the marketplace. Are they trying to be the low-risk/low-cost solution or provide the highest performance? In most procurements, a company's basic strategy is widely broadcast. They announce it in press releases and product brochures, and they communicate their strategy through actions: who they team with, who they hire, what components they buy, and what messages they send. The PTW analyst should systematically seek out these signals, piecing together data to assemble a picture of their offering.

Once you've identified the competitor's technical solution, you want to estimate its cost. While competitive intelligence alone is a powerful motivator for executives to change their assumptions and ideas, its influence is magnified if you dollarize it. For example, while competing for a maintenance services contract in the Middle East, the two companies bidding both used a mix of Americans and foreign nationals as mechanics, warehousemen, and truck drivers. When the PTW analyst told the executives that their proposed ratio of American nationals to foreign nationals was one-to-one whereas the competitor was likely to bid a one-to-three ratio, they expressed mild interest. However, when they were told that the competitor's staffing mix cut their competitor's cost by $60 million, their interest level jumped.

Using knowledge of the competitor's technical architecture, the PTW analyst works with the various internal experts (engineering, procurement, business management, etc.) to create a bill of material for all the significant cost items. *One of the biggest challenges in developing a PTW is converting qualitative competitive intelligence into a cost estimate.* A PTW analyst seeks to quantify the cost impact of all the qualitative differences in the competitor's architecture. At the lowest level, they can identify cost differences between your solution and the competition's, within the constraints of time. For each purchased component in the bill of material, they'll determine whether the competitor's component will be more or less expensive than your components based on the source or its level of complexity. For the competitor's software, they'll assess the product's functionality and consider what new functionality they must build to meet the customer's requirements. For software, assembly, engineering, installation, and other labor tasks, the PTW analyst should estimate the labor-months required for the solution and apply to that estimate the competitor's labor rates and burdens to determine their likely final bid. Labor rates can be estimated by comparing and correlating market intelligence with such factors as geographic location, structure, size, and levels of automation. For each major cost, the PTW analyst looks for adjustments to the cost baseline.

Working with your technical staff to estimate cost differences is key. While engineers frequently are precision-oriented and reluctant to make "guesses" on anything less than perfect information, it's imperative that they do. By making rough estimates at a low level in the work-breakdown structure, one finds a high level of accuracy at the system level. Underestimating some elements is compensated by overestimating on others, and rolling these costs up with the appropriate burdens and overhead rates leads to a more accurate system estimate than if the engineers did not offer their best estimate.

The following example illustrates how the PTW analyst assessed a vessel-tracking system bid to a port authority.

—Strategy in Action—

A vessel-tracking system consists of a control station connected to a series of radars that locate, identify, track, and direct all ships into a port to prevent collisions. In previous competitions, the port authority always went to the lowest price. The analyst began the process by developing a current bid baseline (the first cost column), which priced the sum of all the functional cost estimates (see figure 15.6). Next, the

PTW analyst adjusted this baseline to eliminate expensive and unnecessary software development and hardware that could have been proposed as future upgrades. In addition, the analyst added in missing bill of material items and revised some of the overhead factors to develop the "should cost" (the second cost column).

To develop the competitor's bottom-up cost, the PTW analyst studied the system's cost drivers. One of the most significant costs of a vessel-tracking system is the design and installation of the radar towers. From the competitor's marketing literature, the analyst identified the competitor's radar frequency, while a press release announced their radar supplier. Knowing the supplier and frequency allowed the PTW analyst to identify the competitor's radar from its specification in the supplier's catalog. The competitor's radar was larger, more expensive, and more capable than the capture team's radar. When the capture team's engineers overlaid the competitor's radar capabilities on the port's geography, they calculated that the competition would need only 20 radar towers to the team's 27. Each tower had to have a foundation sunk into the river and a tower erected, so each tower required a geographic survey, foundation design, foundation placement, power and communications interconnection design, and radar attachment. The competitor's per-tower erection cost would be the same as the capture team's, despite the heavier radar. Since the cost of the "Radar & Tower Hardware," "Location & Design," and "Tower Erection" were directly proportional to the number of radar towers the competitor required, with fewer towers they had a $3 million cost advantage (see the third cost column). The company's position looked bleak.

When the PTW analyst presented this information, the capture team brainstormed how to get their costs down to meet the competitor's. One engineer came up with the idea of using existing towers or buildings instead of erecting new towers. The team explored this idea and discovered that their smaller radar could be installed on 12 existing towers or buildings. This approach eliminated the erection costs for 12 towers and slashed the location and design costs, resulting in a "revised should cost" (the fourth column in figure 15.6). In addition, because they were able to remove so much cost, the company was able to incorporate some additional features in their software development and increase their profit margin while keeping their price well below the competitor's.

With competitive insight, the company was able to innovate and win. This is a simple representation of a PTW analysis. The should-cost analysis was actually conducted at a much greater level of detail, and the customer and the competitive analysis were significantly more complex than what was presented here.

	Current Bid Baseline	Should Cost	Compet- itor Bid Baseline	Revised Should Cost
Radar and tower hardware	$945	$945	$952	$945
Location and design	$5,535	$5,535	$4,100	$3,495
Tower erection	$12,150	$12,150	$9,000	$6,750
Control center equipment	$210	$120	$165	$120
Communications	$130	$130	$240	$130
Software development	$4,800	$3,900	$5,100	$4,485
Systems integration and test	$1,440	$1,170	$1,530	$1,346
Program management	$3,373	$3,238	$2,730	$2,210
General and administrative	$6,860	$6,525	$6,431	$4,675
Profit	$5,316	$4,046	$4,537	$4,831
Total	**$40,759**	**$37,759**	**$34,785**	**$28,987**
Number of new sites	27	27	20	15

Figure 15.6. Using competitive analysis to set the cost.

The following three examples show how the PTW analysis uses a variety and combination of techniques to develop the competitor's should cost and to accurately deduce their bid price.

—Strategy in Action—

An analyst needed to know the bid price of a large quantity of sophisticated multispectrum cameras for a pursuit. In this case, the analyst began with a should-cost analysis of the company's product to identify the key cost drivers for the competitor's solution. From a photograph of the competitor's unit, the analyst concluded that the competitor had one more lens, and from the size and shape of their box, the analyst could tell that the competitor had only one large circuit card versus their smaller two. As a result, the competitor would not require a flex cable like the analyst's company used to connect their two cards. The analyst estimated that as a smaller, more entrepreneurial company, the competitor's labor rates were about 9 percent lower. The system's key component was a focal plane array (FPA)—a sensor that converted an image into electronic signals. The competitor had purchased an FPA factory the year before, so the analyst believed they would have designed their product using their newly acquired FPAs. Since the analyst's company had purchased FPAs from that plant prior to the acquisition, their engineers had a good idea what prices the competitor's FPA factory charged. The analyst assessed the competitor's bidding history and found them winning new business, and no market signals indicating that the competition would bid any more aggressively than they had in the past, so the analyst concluded that the competitor would bid their standard margins. Working with the capture team's engineering and procurement personnel, the analyst estimated the costs of all these differences and was able to predict the competitor's final price within 5 percent and win the program.

—Strategy in Action—

On another pursuit, our client was bidding on a train navigation system, and the electronic enclosures to protect the equipment from heat and vibration were a significant cost driver. To determine the competitor's enclosures cost per unit, we analyzed their design versus ours and found one substantial cost difference. From our engineers we learned that the competitor wired their units differently than we had. They required more electromagnetic interference (EMI) filters and therefore more assembly time. Through interviews with our enclosure supplier, we found that the competition had similar production volumes in their plant but greater levels of automation for fabricating sheet metal. We also learned that both suppliers bought the maximum buying-unit quantities of material, so neither had an advantage in buying economies. We adjusted the competitor's costs for the automation and their plant's lower labor rates, as theirs was located in Mississippi versus our supplier's being in Michigan. Our supplier's vice president told us that he had been competing with this competitor for the last 10 years, and he believed his company had a consistent 8 to 9 percent price advantage. Our client's procurement specialists had experience buying from both companies over the years and confirmed this assessment. We did not understand why our supplier appeared to have a price advantage when the competitor had less costly processes. Which brings up a critical point: *when conducting a PTW, you need to resolve discrepancies in your findings, because an erroneous conclusion that results in a higher cost of a few percentage points can make the difference between winning and losing.* We continued our investigation and discovered that the competitor's factory carried the cost of an R&D center at their facility in their overhead. When we included an estimate of the R&D center's cost in the competitor's overhead, it explained our cost advantage despite their manufacturing's location and automation cost advantages. Having understood the competitor's cost buildup, we were then able to accurately estimate the competitor's bid and win the program.

—Strategy in Action—

This example describes how a PTW analyst developed a PTW for a field services contract to the Navy. The Navy required all the bidders to propose staffing and an hourly labor rate for a large set of job categories. Because their principle competitor had won a similar field service contract to the Army in 2017, the PTW analyst used this as a baseline for identifying cost differences between the companies. The analyst's company had lost this bid to the competitor; therefore, the analyst had his company's failed bid as a starting point for the analysis. The analyst knew the competitor's winning price, as well as his company's losing price and their cost proposal. The analyst then collected intelligence on the competitor to identify and explain differences between the competitor's bids. For example, the competitor claimed that their spares forecasting was so sophisticated that it typically reduced warehousing demands by 12 to 15 percent, so the analyst estimated how many fewer hours of warehousing and inventory control the competitor would have likely bid. To determine the hourly labor rate for each labor category, the analyst began with the competitor's overall bid and staffing levels to derive an average labor rate. Then the analyst used other labor-rate data sources for the type of job categories used in the program, such as published General Services Administration (GSA—which are blanket government buying contracts) rates and labor rates in previous contracts. The analyst adjusted these rates for such issues as inflation, changes in work rules, and different locations. To estimate the cost impacts of these changes, the analyst needed to dissect the competitor's current fringe-benefits offering and its costs. The analyst visited the competitor's website to determine their vacation, health care, and retirement policies. Then the analyst worked with his own human resources manager to estimate the costs impact of these policies and the changes for the new proposal. The analyst estimated how differences in such items as supervision ratios, rent, and utilities affected overhead. From this intelligence and analysis, the analyst was able to reconstruct the competitor's 2017 bid price. Once he understood those differences, the analyst was able to project how these differences would apply to the Navy job. Their resulting estimate was within a few percentage points and won the job.

Sometimes a competitor's product may be different enough from yours in design, production processes, or culture that extrapolating from your cost baseline is not appropriate. In these cases, you should seek out some top-down intelligence on the competitor's pricing to validate or supersede your bottom-up cost build. For example, on one bid for an arctic-based processing facility, one key component was a pumping station. The competitor's pumping system was designed for different applications and would require significant modifications to survive the arctic weather and meet the required safety standards. The company's engineers estimated that their competitor's modified system would cost $23 million. Yet we picked up intelligence from three independent sources that the competitors were quoting prices of $16 million. We believed our engineers' estimates truly reflected what it would take to build this pumping station, but because the competitor lacked prior arctic experience, we also believed that they didn't fully understand the true cost of adapting their product to operate in prolonged subzero conditions. As a result, we believed that the competitor would bid $16 million, not knowing their system would quickly break down if they won. It became critical for the capture team to educate the customer on how our solution was designed for the harsh arctic conditions, how our competitor's was not, and how this difference would affect the customer's operations.

In estimating your competitor's price, the analyst must make many judgments about the competitor's approach. They will develop a range for various cost elements and must predict what the competitor will choose to do. As we discussed earlier, the analysts use their knowledge of the competitor's culture and outlook to make these predictions. Does the competitor think this cost element is important? How will the competitor interpret the customer's requirements? For example, if you're trying to estimate how much the competitor will bid to support a customer service help desk, you can estimate approximate staffing based on the service levels the customer requires. But to estimate what the competitor will precisely bid, you need to understand how that competitor views itself and the customer's needs. If the competitor prides itself on being responsive and having excellent customer satisfaction, they will propose higher staffing levels for lower help-desk wait times and call-abandon rates. However, if the competitor always tries to be the low-cost provider, they'll staff to the bare minimum.

Amazingly, sometimes the competitors will even tell you what their pricing strategy is. On the Joint Strike Fighter pursuit, the customer had set price targets for each of the aircraft variants. Lockheed's executives believed these cost targets would be very difficult to achieve, and they were focusing on providing the maximum capability for that cost. However, Boeing broadcast their strategy in their advertisements: "The Air Force Is Committed to a Joint Strike Fighter That's *Affordable*. So Are We." Affordable is code for "low price." Most importantly, Boeing's capture team leader told the press that his team would come in well below the customer's price targets. He gave away his pricing strategy on a $200 billion pursuit! One axiom of competitive intelligence is that *big people tell big secrets*.

The PTW analyst should also analyze the competitor's past bidding behavior. On what basis do they traditionally differentiate their offerings (technical features, low price, minimal risk, support)? This information is used to help focus the analysis of how the competition is likely to behave—where and how they are likely to innovate. The PTW analyst identifies the opportunities on which the competitor has bid aggressively in the past, and those on which they have not. Analysts do not blindly use history as a predictor of the future, however. They look for patterns and discontinuities to understand the competitor's underlying behavior. Figure 15.7 describes one competitor's erratic bidding pattern.

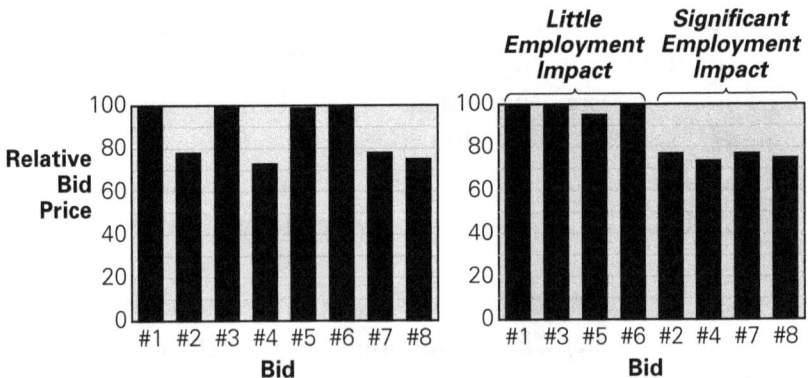

Figure 15.7. Example buying behavior.

The competitor was bidding aggressively on some projects compared with our company, but not on others. Further analysis of these bids showed that the aggressive bids coincided with those having a potentially large impact on the factory's employment. This conclusion made sense: the company had a large skilled-labor force that was difficult to ramp up or down. In addition, the company president was promoted out of human resources and was an extroverted, gregarious, feeling-oriented, "people" person. Because of this background, the company president bid to try to stabilize their staffing. This analysis helped us understand that the competitor would bid aggressively on future opportunities only if that bid would have a significant effect on the company's staffing level.

—Strategy in Action—

In another situation, we were analyzing a competitor's past bids. We'll call this competitor "TB" for the purposes of this example. TB's business strategy was to invest in cutting-edge products to dominate emerging markets. We found that in two cases TB had significantly dropped their price during campaigns. We wanted to understand this pricing behavior, so we interviewed the marketing managers on those jobs. In the first pursuit, we found that, initially, because of the customer's challenging performance requirements, TB thought they were the only viable bidder. However, when it became apparent that another company met the minimum requirements, TB's price dropped 21 percent. In the second competition, the customer was going to award a sole-source contract to TB because the customer demanded a very quick delivery schedule. When another company protested the customer's decision to give TB a sole-source award, the customer decided to initiate an accelerated procurement. In that case, TB dropped their price 15 percent. These findings were important because in the competition we were working on, TB was trying to create interest in the program and quoting prices in the press. We believed those prices reflected their belief that they had no competition. Our conclusion was that this competitor raised their prices 15 to 21 percent when they believed they had no competitors and cut their prices by that amount whenever a competitive threat loomed. When we took 20 percent off their quoted public prices, this target aligned with the bottom-up estimate we'd developed for their solution, so we set a price below this target for the client's engineering team. They designed a more affordable solution that won the competition.

A company's bid aggressiveness also depends on the competition. If a company is competing for a contract and a known low-cost company is bidding, it usually causes all other bidders to lower their prices. For example, a European telecom equipment provider was competing with their traditional rivals for a multi-million-dollar contract in Africa. When a low-cost Asian competitor entered the competition, all the competitors cut their pricing to historic new levels to compete.

Once the analyst has estimated the competitor's technical approach and understands their bidding behavior, they will add in profit and subtract out any likely competitor investment. From the competitor's past bidding history, the analyst should be able to deduce what margins the competitor targets. Do they bid lower or higher margins, and under what circumstances? To assess the competitor's business considerations and bid aggressiveness, you need to "get inside their head." To do that, look for signals including the corporate website and press announcements. You'll also want to assess the caliber of their executive and pursuit team. Do they have their "A team" on the program? If a company assigns a top executive to win an opportunity, it communicates the opportunity's importance. How much are they spending on advertising and demonstrations, and have they hired expensive consultants to help them win? If a competitor is promoting the opportunity to its shareholders, that says a lot. These are signals that indicate how important the pursuit is to the competition, which gives you an idea how much they're willing to invest or cut margins to win.

Conversely, if a company knows that their approach is significantly less costly than the competitors', they can bid with significant margins and still be confident of proposing the lowest price. Note that if a company doesn't have competitive intelligence and PTW capability, they won't know if they have a cost advantage and may fail to take advantage of cost discriminators. Our experience is that companies bid significantly lower than necessary to win about a quarter of the time. These companies' lack of competitive intelligence and PTW precludes them from leveraging cost advantages, and they squander shareholder value. One must consider how each company views an opportunity in order to project behavior.

We've seen competitions where a company thought they had an insurmountable advantage, so they proposed a monster bid—as much as they thought the market would bear. The PTW analyst should assess how strategically important this opportunity is to the competitor. On the other hand, if a company has experienced a string of losses, they usually begin to dive on price. For example, we saw one company bid thin margins and cut budgets despite having many discriminators and a customer who hated their competitor. They wanted to get their price as low as possible because, after having lost three big jobs in a row, the executive team thought that if they lost again, they'd also lose their jobs.

The more you understand about the competition's thinking, the more precise your pricing can become. For example, a company that sold a line of expensive products implemented the PTW process. Their PTW analyst studied every sale, and the executive team tried to price each sale optimally—adjusting their price up or down by millions depending on their relative competitive position. This approach significantly improved their win rate and profit margins. By studying the competition, the PTW analyst knew that the competitor was more bureaucratic and that they used a standard, but complicated, pricing model. By studying the competitor's pricing over time, the analyst was able to reverse-engineer their pricing formula. The analyst's company began beating the competitor time after time, even winning with some of their competitor's long-favored customers. The analyst's company kept waiting for the competitor to respond by changing their pricing policy. Finally, the competitor lowered their price on a small bid in an obscure market by 7 percent. The PTW analyst spotted the price change. Because the competitor lacked any PTW analysis capability, the PTW analyst could imagine the competitor's executive team struggling with loss after loss, not understanding how they were being beaten repeatedly. They probably held a long series of executive meetings to change their pricing policy. This small sale was the first sale after the likely policy change and revealed the size of their price cut. The PTW analyst got his executive team to adjust their pricing immediately to this change. His company then continued to ring up a whole new set of sales while the competitor took months to respond again.

To obtain a high level of confidence in the prediction of the competitor's bid price, you must try to triangulate your bottom-up cost analysis. Optimally, you'll have three independent approaches for estimating the competitor's prices to verify each other. One good method is to look at your competitor's past bidding behavior to understand how aggressively they tend to price. You can also use lateral analysis by asking industry experts for their estimates of competitors' costs, and create a parametric estimate based on similar types of project prices. If these three approaches line up, we have confidence in our estimates, as shown on the left in figure 15.8. However, if the bottom-up competitor estimate falls outside the other approaches, then you need to either find an explanation for the disconnect or look for errors in the analysis. The most detailed and highly weighted analysis is usually the bottom-up should cost.

How accurate can this process be? On the KC-135 Tanker Replacement Program, we used six different approaches to estimate the competitor's price. In the end, our estimate was off by $1 billion, which may seem like a lot, but it was out of an evaluated cost of $108 billion, or less than 1 percent.

Developing the evaluation

After the PTW analyst develops the competitor price estimate, they determine where to put the company's price relative to the competition. This doesn't always mean a lower price than the competition; people are willing to pay more for some attributes. The methodology must identify and justify the differences in

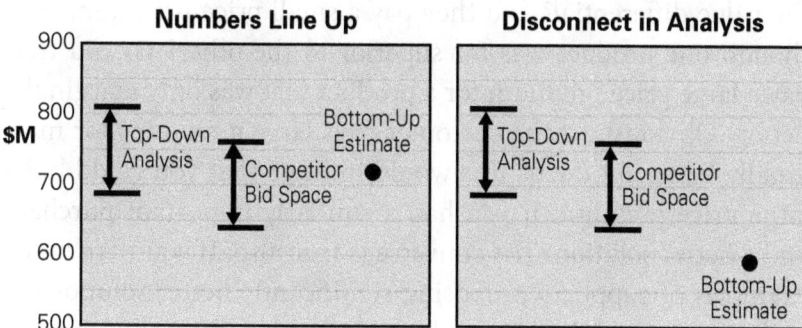

Figure 15.8. Multiple perspectives test the analysis.

value between your solution and the competition's. This value difference allows you to optimize your price and still win. Since commercial customers usually use relatively simple evaluation scoring, whereas government customers tend to use formal and very detailed evaluations, we will describe two different methodologies for estimating value—one for commercial sales and one for government sales.

For commercial sales, competing solutions differ for characteristics such as capacity, range, quality, reliability, schedule, and safety. Every product is different, but any product can be described, and measured, in terms of a list of attributes that characterize its performance from the customer's perspective. It's challenging to calculate directly the monetary value of all the performance differences among products. However, using the right methodology, you can infer the worth of your comparative advantages and disadvantages. If you know how your product stacks up attribute by attribute, you can evaluate its overall performance and determine an appropriate price premium or discount. To do this, you must assess your desirability to the customer versus the competition to know where to place your bid relative to the competitor's.

Examine the customer's past buying history to understand to what extent they pay price premiums. How much and what was the value differential? Did they pay a small price premium, even though one product was far superior to the other? Or did they pay a large price premium for a product that was only marginally better? Obviously, if the customer pays large premiums for marginally better products, this would indicate that you could bid a large price premium if you had a similarly important purchase and a better solution. The converse is true also. If you have many examples of suppliers proposing significantly better solutions at higher prices and they always lose, that says bidding anything but low price is a risky strategy.

Next, analyze the customer's business case to understand how much your advantages (or those of your competitor) are worth to their business.

—Strategy in Action—

For example, Acme Construction and Conway Brothers were competing for an industrial construction project. A PTW analyst employed by Acme identified Conway's likely bid price as $100 million and quantified their discriminators. From discussions with people who worked with the customer before, the analyst learned that the customer was a sophisticated buyer of construction services and considered such factors as schedule and construction quality in the evaluation. The most important customer value for this bid was the project's completion date. The sooner the construction was complete, the sooner the customer would be able to begin to lease out the property. Acme was promising a 21-month schedule; Conway was proposing a 24-month schedule. This earlier schedule would allow the customer to begin leasing the property three months earlier, which translates into $9 million of additional revenue for those three months. The customer had already sold the leases on the property, so if the construction was not finished on time, the customer would have to pay stiff penalties. This meant that schedule confidence was also very important to the customer's key decision-makers. The customer had more confidence in Acme's ability to make their completion commitment, based on their industry record. Since Conway's industry reputation was that they tended to miss completion dates, Acme's PTW analyst estimated that the customer would conservatively add another month to Conway's proposed schedule. As a result, improved schedule confidence was estimated to be worth $3 million. This customer highlighted the high quality of the facility's foundation, plumbing, and electrical systems to their potential tenants, so the customer was likely to value high quality. Acme had a good reputation for providing higher-quality construction. The analyst estimated that Acme's higher quality would translate into a slighter higher lease price for the space under construction, which was estimated at $5 million. All told, the PTW analyst estimates that Acme's bid was worth $17 million more to the customer than Conway's, as shown in figure 15.9. Since Conway was likely to bid $100 million, Acme could win if they bid less than $117 million.

While it is difficult to quantify value by tracking and analyzing award behavior, with time, intelligence, and experience you can begin to predict outcomes. The rewards for this investment are great—they significantly improve a company's win rate and profit margins. Most companies on large projects consider non-price attributes in their decision-making, and these non-price attributes can be translated into dollars. The trick is quantifying them. Note that if you calculated a $17 million advantage, as in the above example, that doesn't mean you have to bid as if you will receive all of that additional value. You discount the $17 million

Customer Values	Acme Construction	Value ($M)	Conway Brothers	Value ($M)
Completion date	21 months	$9	24 months	
Construction quality	High	$5	Fair	
Schedule confidence	0	—	+1 month	($3)
Total		**$14**		**($3)**
Greater value		**$17**		

Figure 15.9. Determining bid value to customer.

based on your level of confidence; this gives you room for error but still protects your profits.

In the case of government acquisitions, the PTW analyst tries to duplicate the customer's proposal evaluation criteria, and then score both their offering and the competitor's against it. This mock customer evaluation should be completed as soon in the pursuit as possible, usually before the customer has published any guidance. From the customer's past evaluations, as well as any published rules or guidelines on source selections, you should try to identify where the customer's evaluation factors come from and how are they scored. The best sources for this information are past debriefings and RFPs that your company has bid on for this customer. Finding and interviewing former customer employees involved in these source selections is invaluable to understanding how both the formal and informal processes work. The analyst should attempt to replicate the customer's likely evaluation criteria and weightings, and they should also try to duplicate the form and even the presentation of the evaluation to be as consistent with the customer's evaluation as possible. The more accurate you make the analysis, the more insight you will gain into the customer's thinking. Like the rest of the PTW analysis, this mock customer evaluation should be updated as the customer provides your team with their actual evaluation or more insight.

Once the evaluation criteria are developed, the analyst should identify strengths and weaknesses for the competitors and for themselves against each evaluation factor. When examining the strengths and weaknesses, the analyst will try to put themselves in the evaluator's place and objectively assess each competitor's offering against the evaluation criteria, creating a score. The scores are then compiled using the same method the customer will use. From this analysis, the PTW analyst is able to estimate each competitor's relative score.

—Strategy in Action—

Figure 15.10 shows an example of how NAVAIR might evaluate the offerings from Elite and Gold Wing for a new reconnaissance aircraft for the US Navy. As the figure shows, NAVAIR has four major evaluation categories: technical, past performance, similar experience, and cost.

Proposal Ratings	Weights		Merit Rating	
			Gold Wing	Elite
A. Technical	60%		**Mar**	**HS**
1. Technical approach	40%		Mar	HS
a. Effective range		7%	Mar	Out
b. Cruising altitude		7%	HS	Mar
c. Speed		7%	Mar	Out
d. Sensor capability		7%	Mar	HS
e. Logistics and readiness		6%	Sat	HS
f. Ease of maintenance		6%	HS	Mar
2. Program and schedule	20%		Mar	Sat
a. Risk analysis		5%	Sat	HS
b. Ability to achieve schedule		5%	HS	HS
c. Test and evaluation approach		5%	Mar	Sat
d. Software risk		5%	Mar	Sat
B. Past performance	10%		**Low**	**Mod**
C. Similar experience	10%		**HS**	**Out**
D. Cost	20%			
		Total score	53%	68%

Merit ratings: Out = outstanding; HS = highly satisfactory; Sat = satisfactory; Mar = marginal; Unsat = unsatisfactory
Past performance risk: VL = very low; Low = low; Mod = moderate; High = high; VH = very high; Unk = unknown

Figure 15.10. Example proposal scoring.

To estimate a quantitative category like "Effective Range," the PTW analyst would provide competitive intelligence to the company's aerodynamicists. They would assess the drag, payload, fuel capacity, and burn rate of the competitor's aircraft to estimate its effective range. In the example above, the PTW analyst found that Gold Wing's aircraft could barely meet the customer's minimum range requirements, which would result in a "Marginal" scoring. Elite's aircraft would easily exceed the customer's requirements and provide significant additional benefits to the customer, so the analyst projected that they would be scored as "Outstanding."

Technical is further decomposed into technical approach and program schedule. The analyst tries to break the evaluation down to the lowest-level evaluation factors possible. As with most competitive cost and technical analyses, the more detailed the assessment, the more accurate it becomes.

For qualitative categories, like "Ease of Maintenance," the analyst lists strengths and weaknesses for Elite and then compares them with Gold Wing to create a relative scoring. In this case, Gold Wing's simple design offered easy access to the engines and avionics compartment, while Elite's systems were more difficult to access. As a result, Gold Wing was rated "Highly Satisfactory" and Elite was rated "Marginal." It is important to use the likely evaluation criteria as a guide to collect intelligence on the competitor's capability in those areas. It is frequently difficult to get good specific competitive intelligence on elements of the evaluation, but one needs to collect enough to make good judgments. For example, it is unlikely that an analyst will know many details of a competitor's software development process, but they can get a good sense of whether their software capability is a strength or a weakness compared with their industry peers. By conducting searches of papers written, press releases, association memberships, and hiring ads, a competitive intelligence analysis can determine whether a company is leading, following, or pacing the industry's software development practices. If the company is publishing several cutting-edge papers and has industry-renowned personnel, one can assume a state-of-the-art capability. If they never claim software as a core competency and they are hiring managers requiring only basic qualifications, the competitor may be lagging behind the rest of the industry. It's critically important to remain dispassionately objective when conducting this analysis. It's just as important not to overestimate a competitor as it is not to underestimate them. A biased analysis can cost you the competition.

In the above example, Elite had a rather significant evaluation advantage over Gold Wing. If their customer's key decision-makers favored Elite's offering and the customer historically paid price premiums, Elite's PTW target could be set significantly higher than Gold Wing's estimated bid price. How much higher would be based on the size and consistency of the customer's historical price premium.

Setting the price

We've seen companies with the solution that key decision-makers want most lose because their price was too high or their evaluation score too low. And we have seen companies with the highest evaluation score and lowest price lose because the key decision-makers desired the competition more. To ensure a victory, you must have the solution the key decision-makers want most *and* your solution must balance the price and the evaluation score so that it's easy for the key decision-makers to justify selecting your solution. For example, the Kwajalein Reagan Test Site (RTS) is used to track intercontinental ballistic missiles fired from California into the South Pacific. The Army awarded Bechtel the management of the

RTS, even with a $600 million higher bid price (29 percent), which is a really big price premium. The Army justified this price premium by saying that the technical and management criteria were of much greater importance than the cost because of "the critical importance and extremely high cost of the customer programs supported by the RTS." Individual tests often cost in excess of $100 million each and were critical to national security. Despite the size of the price premium, the Army decision-makers could easily justify it.

Key decision-makers can choose whomever they want, if they are willing to take the political backlash from their board of directors, elected officials, or procurement bureaucrats to whom they must justify their actions. Choosing the lowest-priced offeror is always easy to explain. The bigger the gap between the lowest offeror's price and the winner's, the more scrutiny the decision is likely to receive. The greater the transparency of the decision and the less autonomy the procurement team has, the more pressure they are susceptible to. NASA has a great deal of transparency and oversight from the GAO and Congress, for example, whereas no one questions the decisions of Saudi Arabia's royal family. Typically, as potential political pressure increases, more-reluctant decision-makers begin to award larger price premiums. On the other hand, the more sophisticated the procurement organization, the greater their ability to justify higher prices with analysis. So NASA, despite its transparency and oversight, allows its talented organization to justify choosing significantly higher-priced bidders if they can create a persuasive rationale.

The correct balance between the evaluation score and the price comes down to how much higher an evaluation score needs to be to justify a higher price. The acceptable balance is based on the norms of behavior of the customer and key decision-makers. Some customers seem unable to justify a 3 percent price premium, while others routinely justify 20 percent. It's not just the magnitude of the price difference but also the relationship between the evaluation score difference and the price difference. The wider the gap between the two evaluation scores, the greater the customer's ability to justify a price premium.

Using your assessment of the customer's likely evaluation scoring and routine buying behavior, you can determine where your price needs to be, relative to the competitor, and how big the gap can be. If your solution will likely receive a higher score, and the customer's buying behavior shows a willingness to pay a price premium, then you can set your price higher than the competitor's. If your score is equal to or less than that of the competitor, then your team should set a PTW target comfortably lower than the competitor's.

The PTW target is the final price after all rounds of the post-proposal submittals or negotiation. You must shoot for the end game of the competition. After developing your PTW, you must develop your negotiation strategy so that you can set your proposal price. Your negotiating strategy determines what price concessions you're willing to make from the proposal price to the final negotiation, so you need to include this pad in your proposal price.

Sometimes an important customer will say "Bid the funding line; we want you to spend all of the budget." If you're bidding on a research and development contract, this may be true. Otherwise, ignore this direction. The customer program manager is naively saying this because they have worked hard to get their budget and have no incentive to give unspent money back. However, they forget that there is a competition and that if one company bids 20 percent below the funding line while your company bids the funding line... it doesn't take a rocket scientist to figure this one out. The other guy wins. The decision-makers need to justify awarding a price premium, and while the program manager is only worried about their project, the decision-makers usually have many projects to fund. If they can save some money on one project, then they can spend it elsewhere.

Packaging the price

When the PTW analyst has completed the analysis and is prepared to present their recommendations and target price, it's important that this information be presented to senior management, especially the CFO. Senior management will make the pricing decisions in the end, and they need to understand the rationale behind the PTW.

From our experience, approximately three quarters of the time, the client's current cost baseline is above the PTW target. In those cases, the PTW analyst needs to show a roadmap of low-risk cost reductions that take the current cost baseline down to the PTW target. The analyst uses ideas gleaned from the should cost and from the competitive analysis to provide a set of cost reductions. Developing this roadmap enhances the "believability" of the analysis by reconciling the PTW target with the current price estimate and should cost. This process helps the PTW analyst sell the PTW target. If it seems unachievable, the PTW target gets ignored at the company's peril. We have seen a few cases where it was impossible to get a company's should cost down to the PTW. In those cases, the company either needed to make an investment or no bid. In cases where our clients have bid significantly below our should cost, the clients won but their programs went significantly over their budget-contract execution. Bidding below the should cost is a very bad idea.

—Strategy in Action—

We worked on the PTW for a data collection system where the majority of the cost consisted of handheld data collection devices. We determined that our client needed to lower their bid cost by $60 million, or 25 percent, to undercut the competitor in price. When we studied the client's solution, we found that one of the most expensive components of the handheld devices was the transmitter. The client's operational concept was for their data collectors to transmit data to headquarters after each reading. We also learned that the data collectors meet with their supervisor each day. Therefore, since all of the handhelds had Bluetooth capability (they could electronically transmit data within a few feet), we recommended that instead of having a transmitter in every handheld, the client install one in the supervisor's unit only. When the supervisor met with the data collector, they could transfer all of their readings to the supervisor using Bluetooth, and then the supervisor could upload all the data from their data collectors to headquarters in one transaction. By requiring only the supervisor's handheld to have a transmitter, this solution eliminated the need for 90 percent of the transmitters, saving $60 million. We also estimated that by having the supervisor consolidate all the data into a single transaction, it would reduce daily data-transmission volume by more than a factor of a hundred. We believed that this reduction would significantly reduce the complexity of receiving and processing telecommunications transactions at headquarters, as well as operator training requirements, because they would not have to deal with transmission errors and resends. The client capture team believed that the customer thought of handhelds like smartphones and would think of nontransmitting handhelds as antiquated technology. However, the should-cost analysis using the nontransmitting handhelds showed the client that the PTW was achievable—they had previously thought it was impossible. The client's engineering team went to work and developed a new design that included a transmitter in every unit, a very aggressive cost challenge, which hit the PTW target and won the program. However, the program ended up being canceled because of program management failures, technical problems achieving the cost target, and data transmissions overloading the telecommunications system.

Interestingly, we find that the greatest resistance to our PTW targets is in the 25 percent of the cases where we recommend raising our client's price. The objective of the PTW is to identify the highest price a company can bid and still win. Frequently, the only advocate for this objective is usually the CFO. The capture team leaders are incentivized to win. They typically behave like typical salesmen and want the price target as low as possible to increase their probably of winning. Whether the company can perform or make a profit holds less importance to them. The analysis is also an independent view of the pursuit, and some of the recommendations may contradict the positions pushed by the capture team leader. We've seen capture team leaders hide the PTW results from their senior management because they disagreed with those results.

For example, we were working on a large pursuit with four companies competing where the customer was going to award two contracts. Our client was desperate for a win, as they had lost their last two major pursuits, and many of their executives believed they'd be fired if they lost another one. Before we were brought on to conduct our PTW analysis, the capture team had made all the right decisions—they'd selected the right strategy, chosen the right technologies, and picked the right teammates. The competitors had revealed enough information in the press about their solutions that we could accurately estimate their costs. We did extensive competitive analysis leveraging the world's most renowned designers to build our cost analysis. We found that all three of the competitors had significant risk and cost problems. In fact, we believed there was a good chance that two of the competitors would be disqualified because their technology was so immature. We told the capture team leader that the company could raise his price by $60 million and still have a 95 percent win probability. In our experience it is significantly more difficult to get executives to raise prices than to drop them, and this situation was no different. The capture team leader wanted a very low price because he wanted to make sure they won. He had no prior pursuit experience and didn't want to believe what we were telling him, despite the overwhelming evidence. He hid the PTW results from his executives. After finishing our PTW analysis, he had us update our analysis twice with new intelligence, hoping we would raise our estimates for the competitors. Each time, as we gained more intelligence and improved our understanding, all three of the competitors' relative positions grew worse. Finally, he hired another consulting firm to give him the answer he was looking for—that the competition would be close and that his team needed to bid extremely low. He bid low and won. The ironic result was that this customer published the two winning bidder's prices showing that our client had underbid their competitor by $70 million. When the CEO of the corporation called the capture team leader after the announcement, he did not congratulate him. Instead, the CEO asked, "Why did we bid so low?" It's critical to have the PTW analysts brief the senior executives so they can make informed pricing decisions and maximize shareholder value.

Deploying cost targets

The PTW process does not end with providing a price target. It should also produce a host of actionable recommendations for improving one's competitive position. A PTW is a comprehensive analysis, and the process always brings to the surface many critical competitive issues. It can provide executives an unparalleled and independent assessment of the capture team's win and pricing strategy. For example, the Joint Strike Fighter PTW identified some significant issues that triggered changes in the avionics architecture, the allocation of engineering resources, and the operations and support approach.

Once management has agreed on the PTW target, finance and the PTW analyst need to work together to set cost targets with support from the leaders of the functional organizations. Costs targets should cover all the elements of cost that the customer will evaluate as price. For example, if the customer is including operations and support (O&S) in their price assessment, then cost targets for O&S should be developed. From the PTW process, your finance manager should flow down cost targets, called "bogies," to the functional departments and be consistent with the work-breakdown structure (WBS). If business management sets cost targets at too high a level, the cost target will encompass areas outside one manager's area of responsibility and no one will have accountability for hitting the number. The cost targets need to be set at a level at which budget estimates are made and used for DTC. The targets should be broken down so that functions such as tool design, production control, and software quality control have their own cost targets. Having business management develop this baseline ensures that burdens, G&A, and fees are also included, items that the technical staff so often forgets. This avoids lots of rework later.

When deploying these cost targets, it's important to explain their rationale to cost area managers so that they understand that the numbers are not arbitrary and have logic behind them. This helps them accept the targets. Once the cost targets are set and deployed, the team's business manager must manage to those targets. They should have a spreadsheet where the cost targets are tracked against the functional estimates and are updated as revisions come in.

While we have frequently heard the comment "The functions should develop grassroots estimates without targets; otherwise, they won't make their best efforts," our experience is that functional organizations rarely estimate too low and that people almost always overscope their work. By deploying cost targets prior to the estimating process, the capture team sizes the work up front and brings up scope issues before engineers spend countless hours estimating to the wrong assumptions. Likewise, people have difficulty going down to a target after they've created and justified a higher number. Functions and subcontractors end up thinking that you're trying to squeeze them out of profit, hours, or work scope. It's better to set cost targets early on and let them drive the design. If a company has trouble meeting the target, they need to get innovative, like McDonnell Douglas did on JDAM.

The PTW must be derived early enough to allow it to drive the solution architecture. Also, the resulting cost targets become critical design parameters. Only by having the market-derived PTW drive product development can profit margins be maintained while creating a winning approach. The business manager should monitor and record in a database how each group is progressing against their cost target. In this way, the business manager can keep the technical lead and the program manager abreast of progress toward the PTW target. Continuous dialogue with the functions and subcontractors is necessary so that neither side is surprised as costs are refined. The technical lead must ensure that these cost targets are a key design parameter and are monitored across the development process.

When should a PTW be conducted?

Effective pricing is critical to winning. A company must know early on whether they have an affordable solution for their customer. If not, they should "no pursue" and find other opportunities. The company also needs to ensure that the solution they'll be proposing is cost-competitive. They must avoid making any decisions that put them in a cost bind. Even early in the pursuit, the customer may ask questions whose answers may lead to the company being burdened with a costly solution. It's imperative to develop a price target very early in the pursuit.

As figure 15.11 shows, the PTW is iterated throughout the capture process. It also shows the percentage of the PTW work during each phase. The analysis becomes more detailed and evolved as the opportunity matures. The analyst adjusts the targets as the customer changes their acquisition strategy, requirements, or available funding and as more competitor intelligence is uncovered. In addition, the capture team continually assesses their own progress in meeting the targets.

An initial PTW target is developed prior to the company's "pursue / no pursue" decision, well before the company has made significant investments. At this point, the PTW should consist of a top-level parametric estimate compared with the customer's likely budget as well as rough-order analysis of the competitors' likely bid prices. This analysis validates whether you have a solution that will fit within the customer's funding and is affordable compared with the competitors'. If there's insufficient funding or a significantly lower-priced competitor, you shouldn't bid. Initial PTWs resulting in "no pursues" keep companies from squandering millions in discretionary marketing and sales funds.

Once a capture team is committed, they should have an extensive PTW analysis conducted, which includes the should cost and competitive bottom-up cost analysis. Even though this may be well before the customer has finalized their requirements, it allows the capture team to develop and deploy cost targets early. The PTW process brings up the key cost issues and focuses the team on designing in affordability at the program outset. The PTW guides teammate selection, avoiding commitments to unaffordable work share agreements or products. The more time that the capture team has to work on cost, the more innovative they can be. Conversely, over time, capture teams become more entrenched in their existing solutions and less able to sell internally and externally innovative approaches. They are forced to fall back on traditional and potentially uncompetitive approaches. Once lost, time is impossible to make up.

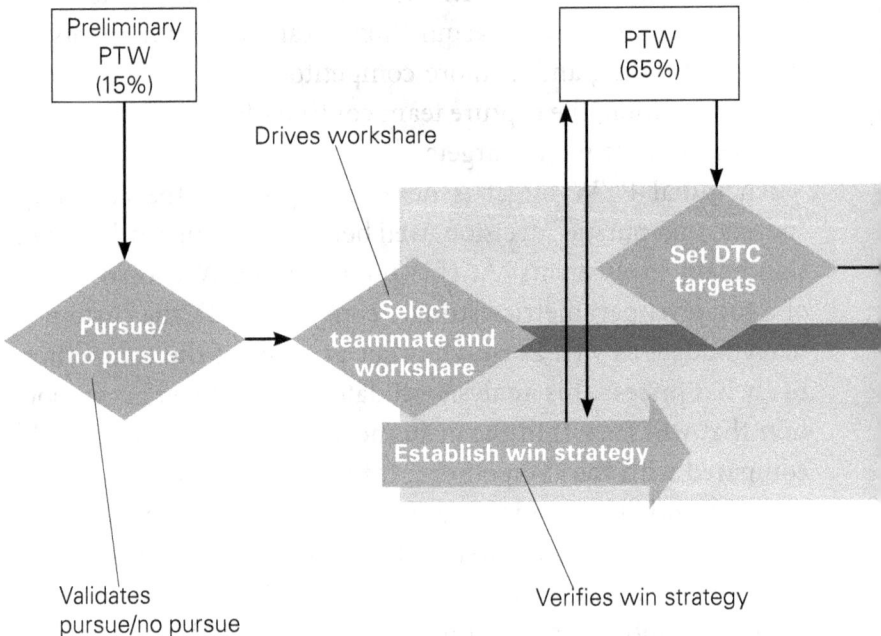

Figure 15.11. Price-to-win iterated throughout the pursuit.

The PTW analysis is updated whenever a significant customer event occurs, such as the release of the draft RFP and the BAFO. With this further definition of the customer requirements, some adjustments to the overall PTW target are typically required. The PTW may also need to be updated if significant new intelligence is uncovered that has a sizable impact on the likely price.

The PTW process continues after the award decision to understand how the customer made their decision and what the competitors proposed. This process helps companies adjust their future competitiveness by understanding what really happened on a competition. Without a competitive cost analysis, we see executives miss the opportunity to learn from experience. Frequently, they dismiss their losses by assuming that the other company

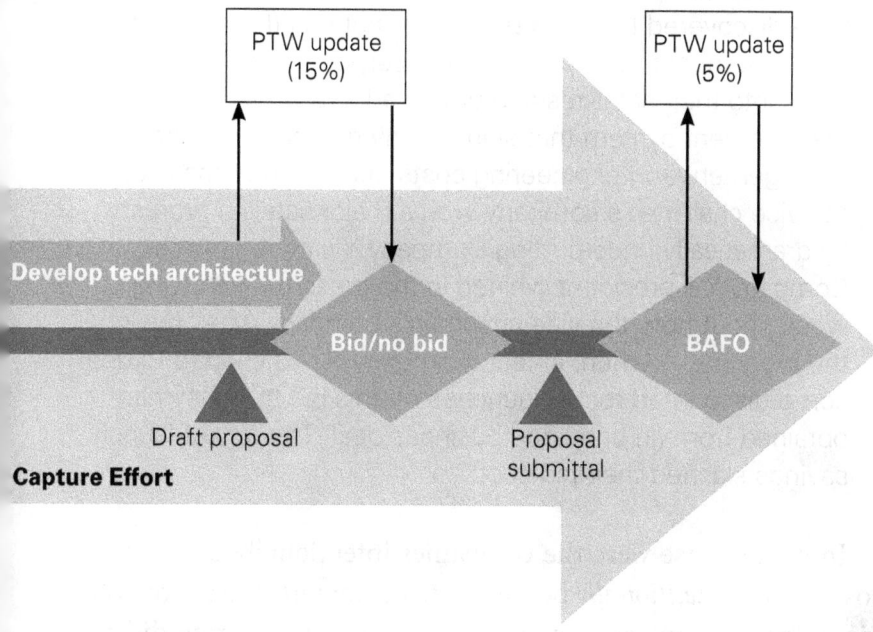

PTW update (15%)

PTW update (5%)

Develop tech architecture

Bid/no bid

BAFO

Draft proposal

Proposal submittal

Capture Effort

bid below cost just to get the business, stating, "The competition bought into the program." Despite this common sentiment, we have rarely seen American companies intentionally bid under cost (Electric Boat's bids on some large cost-plus contracts in the 1970s and Boeing's 2011 tanker bid are notable exceptions. French, Spanish, and Chinese firms are another story). This observation was ironically demonstrated in the satellite business a few years ago.

—Strategy in Action—

After losing a big satellite program, the vice chairman of Company X bitterly decried in the press that his company could not bid as low as Company Y because "my shareholders demand an adequate return." However, had the vice chairman's company conducted a competitive analysis, they would have discovered that Company Y did not win the program at a loss. In fact, Company Y had incorporated new technologies into their satellites and proposed a new information management system that significantly reduced their program management and engineering costs. Just six months later, the vice chairman's company won a major satellite program by dramatically undercutting Company Y's price. Ironically, Company Y's president whined in the press the following week about how the vice chairman's company was "buying the program"—when, in fact, Company X had elected to use some discounted rocket launches on this bid that they had obtained from an unrelated business deal. The rocket-launch savings slashed their bid cost.

In neither case were the companies intentionally bidding at a loss (we say *intentionally* because satellite manufactures are notorious for frequent cost overruns). Because these firms did not conduct a competitive analysis after the award, they remained ignorant of their competitor's successful tactics and failed to learn the correct lessons from their losses.

—Strategy in Action—

In another case, a small competitor underbid a large communication system company by 50 percent on three consecutive space-based transmitter bids. Many executives in the larger company jumped to the conclusion that the smaller company was cheaper because of lower labor rates. The PTW analyst assigned to examine these losses was skeptical of this conclusion. The analyst assessed the bids and found that the largest cost driver in the transmitter design was a set of radiation-hardened chips. These chips are required in space applications to enable the hardware to continue working properly when bombarded with interstellar radiation. These chips must go through a long and expensive manufacturing process. The large company made radiation-hardened chips, whereas the smaller competitor bought them from third parties. As a result, the large company's engineers had significant motivation to use radiation-hardened chips throughout their design. The large company's chief engineer insisted that all the hardened chips in his design were essential. However, even after accounting for their lower labor and overhead costs, the analyst found that the only way to explain the remaining cost difference was if the smaller company was not using as many radiation-hardened chips. The analyst did further research and found that there was a method of sample testing that allowed companies to certify significantly less expensive, commercial chips for some radiation-hardened use. The analyst replaced the cost of some of the radiation-hardened chips with the commercial ones in his cost model of the competitor and found that the spreadsheet hit the competitor's prices on their last three bids exactly. Initially, the chief engineer was unimpressed with the analysis. He had worked in the industry for over 30 years and had forgotten more about radiation-hardened chips than the competitive analyst would ever know. However, when the analyst told the engineer that he was going to brief the divisional president on his findings and that the engineer would need to explain why the competition could use commercial chips and his company could not, the engineer decided to rethink his position. When the president held a meeting to discuss the PTW results, the chief engineer concluded that his company could also bid sampled commercial chips. The large company changed their approach to selecting chips and won the next bid against their small competitor for the first time in five years.

In today's fiercely competitive environment, companies spend hundreds of millions of dollars on proposal development each year, but only a few top companies have an effective PTW process. Based on our experience working on over 110 pursuits, we've learned that developing an early and effective PTW, and implementing its recommendations, is the single most important factor in securing a victory.

It's very important to keep in mind that to ensure victory, a company must be certain that they are most desired by the customer's key decision-makers *and* that they have the correct balance between the price and the proposal evaluations. If a team fails to do both, the competition is a toss-up. To ensure victory, the key decision-makers must want your offering the most, and you must make it easy for them to justify selecting you. Fail to accomplish both of these activities at your own peril.

The authors

Michael O'Guin and **Kim Kelly**, partners at Knowledge Link, have helped clients win contracts worth over $386 billion. They've conducted over 100 PTW analyses and helped win the three largest awards in history, including Lockheed Martin's Joint Strike Fighter pursuit and Northrop Grumman's KC-135 Tanker Replacement Program. They authored the book *Winning the Big Ones—How Teams Capture Large Contracts*.

Since forming his company, Knowledge Link, in 1993, Michael O'Guin has worked on over 60 capture efforts, training capture teams and guiding their win strategy development. He has conducted competitive analysis for 25 years and has authored a number of articles in *Competitive Intelligence Review* on how to collect and integrate intelligence into the capture effort. When he was with Price Waterhouse, he led a two-year strategic benchmarking study of 24 aerospace and defense companies to identify best industry practices. In addition to the above book, he authored *The Complete Guide to Activity-Based Costing*. Mr. O'Guin holds a BS in Mechanical Engineering from UCSB and a MS in Systems Management from USC. He can be reached at (214) 856–3349 or at Moguin@mokrk.com.

Kim Kelly invented the PTW process in 1991 while at IBM Federal Systems, which became part of Lockheed Martin, where he worked for 20 years. He has been working full time on competitive intelligence (CI) and PTW for 29 years. He has conducted PTW analysis with a win rate of over 85 percent on over 100 pursuits. He implemented the PTW process to sell launch vehicles to commercial customers around the world. This process raised International Launch Services' market share by 30 percent and led ILS to become the market leader for the first time in just 18 months. In 1998 he founded the LMCI Working Group, the largest in-house CI association in the world. In addition to the above book, he is author of the first chapter of *Super Searchers on Competitive Intelligence: The Online and Offline Secrets of Top CI Researchers*. Mr. Kelly holds a BS in Operations Research/

Industrial Engineering from Cornell University and an MBA from George Washington University. He can be reached at (703) 378–6988 or at Kimkelly@mokrk.com.

Key Notes

Key Actions

_____

_____

_____

_____

_____

_____

_____

_____

_____

_____

_____

_____

16

Pricing Large Deals: Insights into Capabilities and Tools That Help to Win Large Deals Profitably

Andreas Hinterhuber,
Università Ca' Foscari, Venezia, Italy

I**N THIS CHAPTER,** I focus on two elements that help B2B companies increase win rates and prices on large deals: value quantification and the mapping of B2B purchase criteria. I first provide some context on pricing and on the role of large deals for B2B companies.

Offer dispersion in B2B and B2G: Highly concentrated

Offers are typically concentrated in industrial markets. An analysis of the dispersion of offer and of invoice values provides the data: in recent projects with large, global B2B companies, my colleagues and I normally find that 4 to 10 percent of offers account for approximately 80 percent of the total annual offer value. Getting pricing right on the few large deals that truly matter is thus fundamentally important to increasing overall firm performance.

Pricing: The most important, but frequently most neglected, profit driver

Pricing has a strong, but frequently underappreciated, effect on profits. A study of a sample of Fortune 500 companies suggests that the impact of pricing on profitability far exceeds the impact of other elements of the marketing mix (Hinterhuber, 2004). An increase in average selling prices of 5 percent increases earnings before interest and taxes by 22 percent on average, while other activities, such as revenue growth or cost reduction, have a much smaller impact (see figure 16.1).

Impact of price, costs, revenues on EBIT
(% improvement of EBIT)

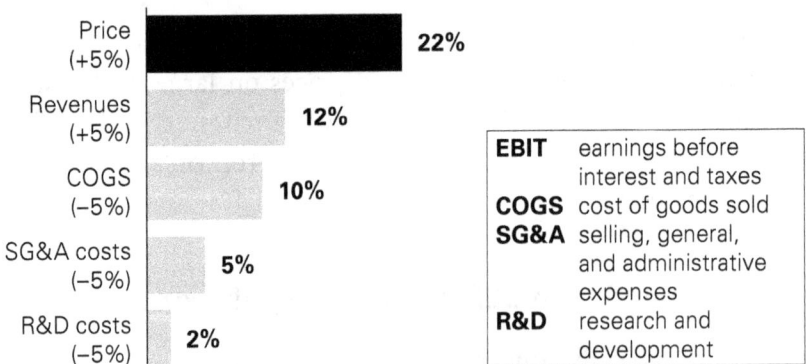

EBIT	earnings before interest and taxes
COGS	cost of goods sold
SG&A	selling, general, and administrative expenses
R&D	research and development

Price (+5%) — 22%
Revenues (+5%) — 12%
COGS (−5%) — 10%
SG&A costs (−5%) — 5%
R&D costs (−5%) — 2%

Figure 16.1. Pricing is the key profit driver. Source: Hinterhuber & Partners.

Pricing is an important contributor to company profits. It's frequently neglected, left in the hands of sales or account managers who lack the capabilities, tools, and incentives required for profitable pricing.

Value quantification and the mapping of B2B/B2G purchase criteria are activities that help sales and account managers identify price points that increase the likelihood of profitably winning large deals.

Value quantification: A key requirement for sellers in B2B and B2G

Buyer expectations of strategic account managers and sales managers are changing (Hinterhuber, 2017a, 2017b): in the past, selling was mainly about communicating product benefits and features. This is no longer enough: today, sales and account managers must document and quantify value to customers. A survey of 100 IT buyers at Fortune 1000 firms suggests that 81 percent of buyers expect vendors to quantify the financial value proposition of their solutions (Ernst & Young, 2002). Figure 16.2 provides salient insights of this survey.

A subsequent survey asked 600 IT buyers about major shortcomings in their suppliers' sales and marketing organizations (McMurchy, 2008): these buyers saw an inability to quantify the value proposition and an inability to clarify its business impact as important supplier weaknesses (see figure 16.3).

These surveys suggest the following. First, sellers in industrial markets are expected to quantify value. Second, B2B buyers do not perceive that sellers are especially proficient in value quantification. This leads to the question of whether value quantification is beneficial in industrial markets: do companies with superior value-quantification capabilities outperform their peers?

Before funding a project, how often do you expect IT vendors to quantify the financial value proposition of their solution? (% respondents)

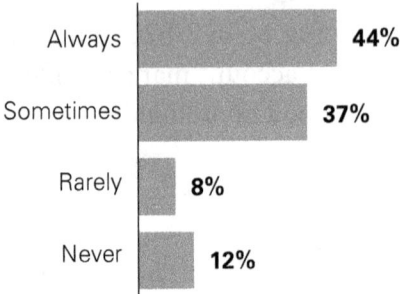

How important is a vendor's ability to quantify their financial value propositions in your vendor selection process? (% respondents)

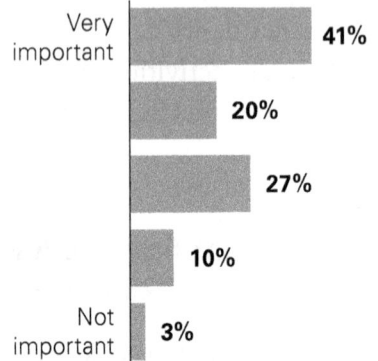

Always	44%
Sometimes	37%
Rarely	8%
Never	12%

Very important	41%
	20%
	27%
	10%
Not important	3%

Figure 16.2. Customers expect sales managers to quantify value. Source: Ernst & Young, 2002.

What are the shortcomings of IT provider sales and marketing? (% respondents)

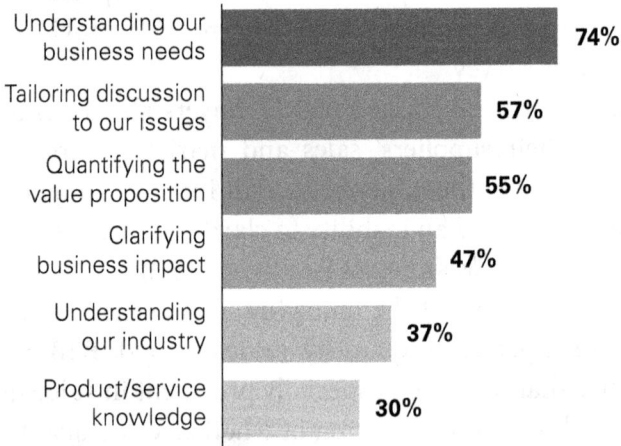

Understanding our business needs	74%
Tailoring discussion to our issues	57%
Quantifying the value proposition	55%
Clarifying business impact	47%
Understanding our industry	37%
Product/service knowledge	30%

Figure 16.3. Most sales and marketing managers lack value-quantification skills. Source: McMurchy, 2008.

A recent empirical survey provides a clear answer: the value-quantification capability, that is, the ability of sales and account managers to translate a firm's competitive advantages into quantified, monetary customer benefits, strongly improves firm performance (Hinterhuber, 2017b). Developing value-quantification capabilities is thus a key differentiator for high-performing sales organizations.

Value quantification in practice

What is value quantification? It's about the ability to translate a firm's competitive advantages into quantified, monetary customer benefits (Hinterhuber, 2017b). Doing so requires translating both quantitative customer benefits—revenue/gross margin increases, cost reductions, risk reductions, and capital savings—and qualitative customer benefits—such as ease of doing business, customer relationships, industry experience, brand value, emotional benefits or other process benefits—into one monetary value equating total customer benefits received (Hinterhuber, 2017b). White papers or quantified business cases are tools that leading B2B companies, including SKF, SAP, GE, Schneider Electric, Maersk, GE, Dell, Rockwell, 3M, and others, use to quantify the value delivered to customers. I next provide a sanitized case study of a recent consulting project of Hinterhuber & Partners.

For a client in the intelligent traffic systems industry, we quantified the financial value of intelligent, connected traffic-display systems to system integrators—companies that purchase these and other products, bundle them with complementary products, and sell a complete solution to city councils or highway operators. We interviewed procurement managers to determine purchase criteria, we collected data from third parties on the performance of competitive traffic-display systems, we conducted workshops to validate preliminary findings, and we were able, after some further research, to determine the performance implications of the competitive advantages of our client's solution for their customers' profitability. Two key factors emerged that accounted for over 80 percent of the total quantified customer value: this process thus turned an initial long list of potential competitive advantages into two factors that sales, marketing, and account managers could focus on to convey the financial benefits of their solution to B2B and B2G procurement managers.

We used our proprietary Value Quantification Tool to quantify the value of these differentiating factors. We discovered that our client's product delivered a substantial amount of value vis-à-vis competitive solutions. This allowed us to determine, in a next step, a price that would allow our client sustained profitability and the client's customers an attractive return on investment. Figure 16.4 provides the result of this analysis.

As a result of the process of value quantification, the price premium of the company's product loses its negative connotation. The price premium of 14 percent is actually small compared with the return on investment of about 380 percent for customers purchasing the connected, intelligent traffic-display systems.

Value quantification is therefore an important process that allows procurement managers to put price in perspective: it relates price differences to differences in monetary, customer-specific value. There's a catch: since value quantification determines total quantified customer benefits, it identifies just the upper boundary of selling prices; it cannot recommend a specific, profit-optimizing, selling price (Nagle, Hogan, & Zale, 2011). The process of value quantification thus leaves it to sellers to identify specific deal prices by taking into consideration other factors such as company goals (revenue vs. profit maximization), customer price sensitivity, relative power vis-à-vis purchasers, competitive intensity,

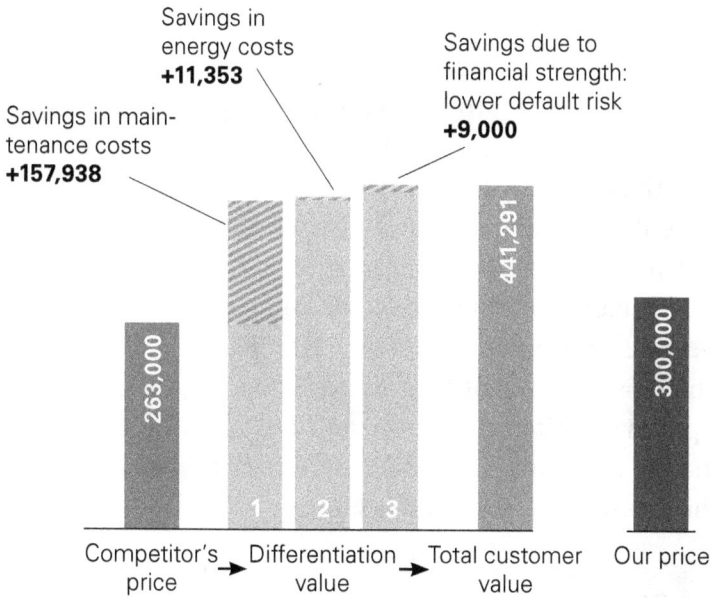

Savings in energy costs
+11,353

Savings due to financial strength: lower default risk
+9,000

Savings in maintenance costs
+157,938

263,000

441,291

300,000

1   2   3

Competitor's price → Differentiation value → Total customer value   Our price

Incremental investment: our price – competitor's price = 37,000

Incremental value: QNT + QLT – competitor's price = 178,291

ROI:
(incremental value – incremental investment) / incremental investment = 382%

The product of the client company has a price premium of about 14% vis-à-vis the customer's best available alternative: 300,000 € vs. 263,000 €. The quantification of customer benefits shows that the customer benefits exceed the price premium by a factor of 4, mainly driven by savings in maintenance.

Figure 16.4. Value quantification: Key to justifying price premiums. Source: Hinterhuber & Partners.

and customer price perceptions. The fact that value quantification provides a range of prices instead of recommending a specific, profit-maximizing price point is usually not a limitation in those instances where sellers have the opportunity to negotiate prices. Prices are adjusted in the negotiation based on new information: information on the weight of price vis-à-vis other criteria or information on competitor price levels or product features. In a negotiated setting, the process of value quantification can therefore help win the deal by providing buyers compelling arguments on the business case of one supplier vis-à-vis a variety of other suppliers with apparently lower prices.

In competitive bidding situations, there's usually no chance to renegotiate prices. There's one shot to get pricing right. The process of value quantification needs to be complemented with data on competitive offerings and data on customer purchase criteria. Two of the most prominent approaches providing these insights are B2B purchase-criteria mapping and bid-response functions. In this chapter I focus on B2B/B2G purchase-criteria mapping; on bid-response functions, see Phillips (2005).

Mapping B2B/B2G purchase criteria

Sales managers typically have an important weakness: "They do not listen," says Bernard Quancard, CEO of the Strategic Account Management Association (Hinterhuber et al., 2017, p. 44). Numerous empirical studies confirm that B2B buyers perceive their sales managers as lacking in listening skills: understanding client business needs is the most important shortcoming that IT buyers mention about sellers in the study cited above (see figure 16.3). An earlier study similarly finds that a top complaint about sales managers is that they "do not listen" (HR Chally Group, 2002).

Mapping B2B/B2G purchase criteria is a systematic process that aims to understand the importance and weight of B2B/B2G customer purchase criteria and the relative performance of alternative suppliers on these criteria in order to determine a selling price that maximizes the chances of winning the deal. Mapping B2B/B2G purchase criteria of course requires understanding them in the first place. One way to map purchase criteria is to use a matrix that B2B or government procurement organizations frequently use to evaluate alternative suppliers. Figure 16.5 provides an example.

This matrix requires two main inputs. First is an understanding of customer purchase criteria. Sales and account managers should rank and weigh these criteria: for public tenders the criteria are,

The initial proposal of senior management was to price substantially below expected price levels of competitors in order to win.

Rating on a 1–5 scale: 5 is best rating.
For price, 5 is lowest price.

Criterion	Weight	Performance Hinterhuber & Partners client	Performance competitor A	Performance competitor B
Facilities: space, decor, layout	30%	4	3	4
Price	25%	⑤	4	3
Accessibility	20%	2	4	4
Ease of doing buisness: speed, proposal quality	15%	5	3	3
Track record, credibility	10%	3	3	3
Total	**100%**	**3.9**	**3.5**	**3.5**

H&P client: lowest price

Figure 16.5. Mapping of B2B/B2G purchase criteria: Pricing low to increase win rates. Source: Hinterhuber & Partners.

this is clear, published. Second are insights into one's own performance and the performance of key competitors on these purchase criteria. Sales managers should measure the performance of their own company and the performance of two or three key competitors on the purchase criteria. They should of course take the perspective of the specific procurement organization that is evaluating the bid. Data sources are customer interviews, customer surveys, or third-party data on performance in actual field conditions.

The example, also from a recent consulting project of Hinterhuber & Partners, illustrates how our client initially attempted to win the bid. Client management at first suggested bidding below key competitors to achieve the highest score on the supplier evaluation matrix.

Our research helped the client win the deal at a price premium vis-à-vis the main competitor. The research uncovered purchase criteria first. We then measured customer-perceived performance and objective performance against these criteria. We also identified ways to further differentiate the client's offering from those of key competitors along the most important purchase criteria (see figure 16.6 for details). The research provided insights into unmet customer needs that helped differentiate the product and create a truly distinctive offer. Mapping of purchase criteria on the matrix led to the conclusion that the client had a reasonably high chance of winning the bid at a premium price vis-à-vis the main competitor. This turned out to be the case.

Putting the idea into practice
in pricing decisions for public tenders

Pricing has an immediate, substantial impact on profitability. Pricing isn't easy. Pricing that is too low leads to low profits;

As a result of the research by Hinterhuber & Partners on purchase criteria, the client company improved the product, increased the price and won the bid—despite a substantial price premium vis-à-vis the main competitor.

Rating on a 1–5 scale: 5 is best rating.
For price, 5 is lowest price.

Criterion	Weight	Performance Hinterhuber & Partners client	Performance competitor A	Performance competitor B
Facilities: space, decor, layout	30%	5	3	4
Price	25%	③	4	3
Accessibility	20%	2	4	4
Ease of doing buisness: speed, proposal quality	15%	5	3	3
Track record, credibility	10%	3	3	3
Total	**100%**	**3.9**	**3.5**	**3.5**

H&P client: premium price vis-à-vis main competitor

Figure 16.6. Mapping of key purchase criteria: Improving differentiation to win bids at premium prices. Source: Hinterhuber & Partners.

pricing that is too high leads to low revenues. The pricing sweet spot is thus low enough to win the deal and high enough to do so profitably.

In simple terms, this article highlights the importance of one key factor in winning large deals profitably: preparation. Preparation wins deals, as opposed to an escalation involving ever-more-senior management levels depending on deal size. Value quantification translates competitive advantages into customer-specific economic benefits and thus identifies the upper boundary of selling prices. B2B/B2G purchase-criteria mapping plugs a specific, profit-optimizing selling price into a matrix comparing the overall attractiveness of alternative offers in order to understand the likelihood of winning the deal at any given price.

Purchase-criteria mapping is particularly effective if sales and account managers can influence procurement criteria in the first place. White papers on value quantification can thus also be seen as an important tool helping to influence procurement criteria.

Winning the next big deal profitably is the ambition of every sales manager, every account manager, and every CEO. Big deals are few: value quantification and B2B/B2G purchase-criteria mapping can help identify the sweet spot of pricing that identifies profitable price points that win the next big deal.

Acknowledgments

This article is reprinted with permission from Andreas Hinterhuber, "Pricing Large Deals," *Velocity, 21*(1), 2019, the magazine of the Strategic Account Management Association.

References

Ernst & Young. (2002). *Fortune 1000 IT buyer survey: What could shorten sales cycles and further increase win rates for technology vendors?* Economics & Business Analytics white paper.

Hinterhuber, A. (2004). Towards value-based pricing—An integrative framework for decision making. *Industrial Marketing Management, 33*(8), 765–778.

Hinterhuber, A. (2017a). Value quantification—Processes and best practices to document and quantify value in B2B. In A. Hinterhuber & T. Snelgrove (Eds.), *Value first, then price: Quantifying value in business markets from the perspective of both buyers and sellers* (pp. 61–74). Milton Park, UK: Routledge.

Hinterhuber, A. (2017b). Value quantification capabilities in industrial markets. *Journal of Business Research, 76,* 163–178.

Hinterhuber, A., Snelgrove, T., & Quancard, B. (2017). Interview: Nurturing value quantification capabilities in strategic account managers. In A. Hinterhuber & T. Snelgrove (Eds.), *Value first, then price: Quantifying value in business markets from the perspective of both buyers and sellers* (pp. 39–48). Milton Park, UK: Routledge.

HR Chally Group. (2002). *Ten year research report.* Dayton, OH.

McMurchy, N. (2008). *Tough times in IT: How do you exploit the opportunities?* Gartner presentation.

Nagle, T., Hogan, J., & Zale, J. (2011). *The strategy and tactics of pricing: A guide to growing more profitably.* Upper Saddle River, NJ: Prentice Hall.

Phillips, R. (2005). *Pricing and revenue optimization.* Stanford, CA: Stanford University Press.

The author

Andreas Hinterhuber is an Associate Professor in the Department of Management at Università Ca' Foscari, Venezia, Italy, and has been a Partner of Hinterhuber & Partners, a consulting company specializing in pricing, based in Innsbruck, Austria. He has published articles in leading journals including *Journal of Business Research* and *MIT Sloan Management Review* and has edited many books on pricing, including *Innovation in Pricing* (2012), *The ROI of Pricing* (2014), *Pricing and the Sales Force* (2016), *Value First then Price* (2017), and *Pricing Strategy Implementation* (2020).

Key Notes

Key Actions

Interview with an Expert

17

Larry Newman,
Vice President and Partner,
Shipley Associates

Stephan   Thanks again for giving me some of your precious time. Can you introduce yourself and your role at Shipley Associates?

Larry   I've been with Shipley for more than 30 years; I'm now a vice president and partner. I hold a bachelor's and a master's in engineering, so I had a technical background when I joined Shipley in 1986, when Shipley was primarily a business communications training company. The original version of Shipley Associates was focused on effective business, technical, and scientific writing. A technical writing client asked if we could teach their engineers to write better proposals. In response, we developed proposal writing and then proposal management workshops. Shortly thereafter, I joined the Shipley Associates, as they had asked about costing issues relevant to bids and proposals. Because of my prior employment with an industrial equipment manufacturer, my first project was explaining typical costing approaches.

After several years of teaching Shipley proposal workshops, consulting with clients, and writing proposals, I was asked to develop a costing workshop. Our client's primary concern was to improve cost rationale to support cost volumes. Inadequate cost rationale led to major price concessions when negotiating government contracts.

When developing the original Shipley costing workshop, I interviewed multiple experts, focusing on government cost volume evaluators and senior individuals who both managed and trained cost proposal evaluators and negotiated contracts. They emphasized several key points:

- Solid cost substantiation equals lower price concessions and less time to finalize the contract.
- Easily evaluated cost volumes receive higher "scores," much like the technical and management volumes. While not technically "scored," price concessions are reduced during negotiations.
- One senior US Air Force evaluator emphasized *traceability and trackability,* saying that he should be able to open a cost volume anywhere and rapidly determine where that item was

summarized at a higher level and supported at a lower level.

- Decision-makers and influencers, such as the Source Selection Authority and their trusted advisors, are usually forced to rely on the cost volume evaluator(s) because most cost volumes are dense and poorly organized.

My take-away from this last point was to prepare a succinct, clear, persuasive cost volume summary that could be understood by non-costing-experts. Ideally, a good cost volume summary is read by the source selection authority and senior evaluation team or is used by the cost volume evaluator to support his selection recommendations.

Subsequently, some of our key, highly competitive clients were focusing on something called capture planning. Multiple clients asked us to develop a workshop to train their capture managers. Much as with our initial cost volume preparation workshop, I researched sales and sales management methodologies, identified common elements and best practices, and adapted them to capture management.

Essentially, sales training focuses on strategic and tactical elements. The strategic elements focus on planning how to approach the customer. Often, the strategic focus in on multiple sales to a major account. The tactical elements are actions that implement the strategy, the face-to-face practices between the sales professional and customer.

Our capture planning approach contrasts *simple* and *complex* sales. A simple sale involves a single seller and one or few buyers. A complex sale involves selling and buying communities. In our view, a capture manager orchestrates a team to position the buying team to prefer their organization as the source of the preferred solution. Our Capture Planning workshop and the Shipley *Capture Guide* both teach and document this Shipley capture process.

As the US federal government expertise of Shipley's consulting cadre increased, I increasingly focused on non-US government clients—B2B and international B2G clients, often in concert with Shipley's network of international affiliates. The fundamental principles are equally applicable, within the different purchasing processes.

Stephan   You have a wealth of experience in the capture process in the B2G sector. What trends do you see emerging that might influence the way the federal government procures?

Larry   Historically, US government procurement professionals understood that increased competition reduced acquisition costs. The impetus for the 1984 Federal Acquisition Regulations (FAR) was to increase competition by standardizing the US government purchasing process. But as a seller you seek to eliminate as many competitors as possible. While this conflict is not new, most trends arise from this conflict.

- The speed of contracting is often faster, with shorter bid-response times, page-limited proposals, task orders issued under blanket or master contracts, and oral proposals.

- Governments adapting procurement best practices from the commercial or private sector. For example, performance-based contracting and service-level agreements originated in the private sector.
- Contractor consolidation often reduces competition to the point that procurement officials are concerned that they might be left with a single source. So, selection decisions might be influenced by the desire to maintain viable competition.
- Sole-source procurement. While sensitive, agencies do develop favorite or preferred sources but need to preserve the appearance of a fair, full, and open competition. Protested awards reflect negatively on purchasing officials and delay awards.
- Consideration of life-cycle cost elements in addition to the initial acquisition cost. Depending upon how a program is funded, life-cycle considerations can be a negative or positive influence.

Stephan Do you see among these trends much greater professionalization, a moving away from what would be more cooperative and partnership-based procurement to more like very professional procurement teams, as in B2B?

Larry It varies. I would not necessarily concede that most B2B procurement teams are highly professional. Such trends depend more on individual purchasing professionals that move from one job or position to another. For example, a major company might hire a procurement professional from government and you'll see more government-like processes incorporated. Similarly, a B2B purchasing professional that moves into government often incorporates B2B-like practices within government guidelines.

Other trends are driven by politics. For example, in 2008, Recovery Act funds were approved for *shovel-ready* projects. Local politicians wanted local businesses to win these contracts, but many of these businesses were ill equipped to compete because they were unfamiliar with government procurement processes.

Stephan   I come from the B2B world, where I would say that 40 percent of the decisions are made on cost, probably 40 percent on following the competition, and the remaining 20 percent are customer-value based. But when I started in the B2G world working in the capture and the bidding management process, it's very much cost oriented, which kind of surprised me. There are few value discussions. There's a lot of cost building and then the cost plus. How do you explain that?

Larry   I think there are a couple of explanations initially driven by FAR. Governments, especially at a national level, are often the only buyers for many products and services, so FAR regulations require bidders to disclose their costs. Thus, the RFP requirement to disclose cost and pricing data leads to a cost orientation in the bidding and selection process.

But the focus on cost does not necessarily eliminate value as a consideration. As in the B2B world, as the perception of the product/service shifts from *commodity* to *unique,* value becomes a greater potential consideration.

Another consideration might be the *color of the money,* meaning the type of funds: maintenance funds, operating funds, and timing, or when the funds are available. Different funds cannot be comingled, and unobligated funds often cannot slide into the next budget cycle. One key question is "When must/can the customer pay?" And, "*What are their options, if any, to get more funds?*" If you can't fit within their budget, and they have to go back and ask for more money, you're probably in trouble.

Stephan   Can you really do value-based pricing when you deal with the federal government?

Larry   Yes, provided you can persuade the customer that your solution isn't a commodity. Essentially, value-based pricing grows increasingly valid as the solution moves along a continuum from commodity to unique.

The US government has two primary purchasing processes under FAR Part 14 and FAR Part 15.

- Part 14 is a two-phase procurement. In *phase 1,* the technical bid is evaluated to determine whether the proposal meets minimum qualifications. In *phase 2,* the cost portions of bids meeting minimum qualifications are opened, and low price wins. The implicit assumption is that exceeding the specification offers no additional value. One procurement official said he uses a two-phase procurement to keep the buy within the budget, to limit technical users with *stars in their eyes,* meaning those enamored with a more elaborate and costly solution.

- Part 15 governs competitive source selection procurements, designed to select the best *source* to deliver the products/services, where the buying authorities' perception of value matters.

In general, as the purchasing process advances, sellers' access to the customer is increasingly limited. Here, capture planning becomes relevant, as the goal of capture planning is to influence the customer to value your solution over competitors' solutions. Throughout the capture process, sellers identify the customer's issues, perceptions of the value of addressing those issues, and then collaboratively develop a solution the customer prefers or values over competitors' solutions.

Another procurement trend is customers' increasing use of systems and software to support proposal evaluation. Computer systems are used to eliminate some of the drudgery: they can cut and paste from the proposal to justify higher or lower factor scores.

Sellers often overlook how proposals are scored. If the bid meets the requirement, it's easy to score. Regulations require evaluators to justify, usually in writing, scores above the minimum requirement. Ideally, evaluators find that justification in your proposal, then *copy and paste* it into their evaluation. If your value proposition is easy to identify and extract to support a higher score, they have the support to justify paying more for a superior solution.

Stephan In essence, you must make it easy for the evaluators to do their job!

Larry If I'm an evaluator and I'm having a hard time finding your value proposition, then I have to make it up. Given time pressures, I'm more likely to give the vendor an average score. Making an evaluator's life easy will lead to a higher evaluation. A former evaluator said: *"We would go to the charts, graphs, and tables first. If we could find the answer, then we didn't have to read the text."* Evaluation is much like a take-home exam. You read a question, look for the answer, score it, and then you go to the next question. If you can't find the answer, mark *zero,* note a *deficiency,* and perhaps ask a clarification question. If evaluators have to read your entire proposal, you've probably lost. Evaluation is a search for the answers. If you make it easy to find the answer and easy to justify a higher score, you'll get a higher score, get a higher total evaluation score, and be better positioned to more rapidly negotiate the order at a higher price.

Stephan So the proposal evaluators play a key role in the procurement selection process.

Larry There are many key roles influencing a customer's buying decision. A key aspect of the Shipley capture process is to identify, understand, and influence those individuals. Some are obvious, and some might be hidden. When we discuss hot-button issues, note that different people have different issues. Financial buyers, users, and owners have different sets of issues and different views of the costs of those issues.

The pre-proposal focus should be on determining your approach to addressing the customer's diverse issues. What tactical action(s) will you take to reduce or eliminate an issue? If you don't meet the requirement, might you persuade the buyer to change that requirement? Can your organization improve your performance? Can you find a teaming partner to address that issue?

Stephan How was price-to-win (PTW) included in the Shipley *Guides* and the capture process?

Larry As you begin to understand the customer's issues, performance requirements, and evaluation criteria, you can evaluate your capabilities versus your likely competitors. What value does this customer place on these issues? Only the customer determines the value, not the seller.

A key consideration in the Shipley approach distinguishes *differentiators* from *discriminators*. If you read the sales literature, a differentiator is a feature of your solution, your product, your service or an additional condition that the customer cares about. If they do not care about the difference, it does not matter.

Imagine you're purchasing a car and have the choice of *red* versus *black*. If you don't care about the color, then color is not a discriminator. So what does this customer value and how much is that worth to them? The fact that a car has far greater horsepower might be desirable to a person who really wants racing performance. For someone else, it might imply poor gas mileage and higher operating and maintenance costs. So value depends on what they care about, what they value.

The only way to determine value is to collaborate with your customer—what's your value to them? You can't determine value in isolation. PTW also involves your customer and your competitors: what are they likely to do?

Stephan   PTW is very cost oriented, and I see a little bit of a disconnect between discriminators, hot buttons, and willingness-to-pay. Potentially, PTW begins as a bottom-up exercise.

Larry   PTW usually begins as a bottom-up cost development exercise for yourself and competitors. Then asking "What can I do to influence my costs?" And if my costs are higher, then asking *"What can I do differently?"*

Stephan   You see my point when I talk about PTW. We spent a lot of time on hot buttons and doing black hat sessions and doing the blue sheet and all that stuff. But then when it comes to PTW, it seems that it derails the logic of value and we go straight back into cost, and I have a tough time.

Larry   Yes. Think of it as having two areas. One is a competitive assessment: how will we price it, how do we think the others will price it, and what is our competitive position? Second, what's it going to take to win? Because once you've got the cost basis, then it's *How much money do they have?* Can we put together a solution that will fit within their budget and the timing of their funds, the color of the money? That gets more into PTW as opposed to competitive assessment. What's everybody's best estimate of cost? Then, *How much risk are the corporate guys going to tack at the end?* Management typically adds a percentage in the end to get the corporate approval of the price.

Stephan   In the pricing area, we talk about proposal managers, bid managers, capture planners, capture managers. I often found that in an organization entering the B2G world, there's not a very strong pricing team per se. Pricing belongs to either finance or costing or, you know, bid—versus the B2B, where you have dedicated pricing teams and they call them pricing. Have you seen this in the field?

Larry   It varies. The traditional approach with systems contractors was to ask the technical people, the engineers and scientists, for their time and material estimates. Their estimates are passed to a pricing or finance group to enter these estimates into their pricing model, add overheads by applying *wrap rates,* and arrive at the total cost and price. Senior management will review the bid, potential profit margin, and risks, and further change the bid price. Then the arguments commence. Technical people want to make sure their estimate is safe, so they often add a risk factor. When risk factors are added at multiple levels, the price might double. The capture manager, understanding the customer's budget, declares the price *uncompetitive.* This extends to subcontractors' and vendors' bids. Everyone gets input; senior management decides.

Stephan   Thanks. Let's switch gears. What are your top recommendations for a successful capture management process?

Larry   First, engage the customer in collaboratively determining the value of your solution. You need to cultivate and support one or more individuals in the purchasing organization to advocate for your organization and solution when the buying decision is being made. So that gets back to your customer discussions and what you include in your proposal. Is your pricing premium justifiable as offering the best value? Working intimately with the customer allows you to receive signals about how pricing is positioned versus competition.

Second, determine individuals' roles in the buying-decision process and what process they follow. Don't assume prior bid behaviors will repeat.

Third, team sell every time. There's a buying team, and you need to have a selling team. Determine who needs to convey what messages and to whom. That's a vital role of the capture manager, whether or not they have much contact with the customer. Who do they want to talk to in that customer organization? Who's best equipped to do it, and can we make that happen in some manner?

Fourth, determine what the customer values. What you value is irrelevant. I can't tell you how many times I've worked with people, particularly in the tech industry, that will tell you that corporate marketing has rebranded something. They'll rave about a new feature, yet few can explain how it might benefit this customer. Features with no perceived benefit deemed more expensive, complex, and unnecessary. If somebody tells me about how much they spend on R&D, I might think you need a higher margin to pay for that R&D. So, focus on customer-perceived value.

Finally, understand the color of the client's money and their budget over time. What kind of funds do they have? When do they have them? Are the budgeted funds sufficient? Can you price your solution compatibly?

Stephan   Glad you have many recommendations for our readers!

Larry   To be successful in B2G pricing and the capture process in general, focus on *alignment* and *discipline*. Pricing and capture management are multifunctional activities. For these, you need a strong team working closely together with a strong alignment on the strategy. That's not enough. The discipline to maintain an aligned capture process bid after bid is essential. Some companies refer to this as a bid factory, but that description ignores the front end of the capture process. Industry-leading contractors increasingly emphasize *phase zero* in the bid process. They engage the customer very early to gain a strong, trusted position in their mind.

Post-win is also essential. Quality delivery facilitates pricing and winning the next bid. Some vendors focus on the very large pursuit, and then they disappear after contract award. So consider the program management process pre-sales, during implementation, and post implementation. Align team members with the customer and opportunity.

Stephan   Thanks for all the sharing. I encourage our readers to connect with Larry Newman and Shipley Associates. See Larry's bio for more information. Thanks again Larry.

The author

Larry Newman is vice president and a founding partner of Shipley Associates. He has 30 years of commercial, international, and government business development experience as a consultant, author, trainer, and coach. He has developed and taught many of Shipley's proposal writing, proposal management, capture planning, and costing workshops. He authored Shipley's *Proposal Guide, Capture Guide,* and *Business Development Lifecycle Guide.*

As a long-time member of the Association of Proposal Management Professionals (APMP), he was selected as a Fellow, honoring his contributions to the profession. He was asked to kick off APMP's 2009 conference and has presented at more than 20 professional association conferences.

Key Notes

_____

_____

_____

_____

_____

_____

Key Actions

_____

_____

_____

_____

_____

_____

Section 4

INNOVATION IN PRICING

18

Using the Pricing Model Innovation Canvas for B2G Pricing

INNOVATORS, CAPTURE LEADERS, AND marketers use a business model canvas when they need to think strategically about a new opportunity, gauge the attractiveness of an existing offer, or pivot an existing opportunity to a new business model. With the emergence of business model innovation as part of strategic innovation, it isn't surprising to see an increased adoption of canvases, as discussed in chapter 8. They're great tools for mapping ideas, discussing high-level concepts, and creating alignment around a new idea. Business model canvases are also used by digital incubators, design thinking teams, and creative marketing minds. They can assist in the construction and delivery of a strategic bid, a complex offer, or a new-to-the-world technology.

Traditional business model canvases propose a series of blocks that are aggregated and integrated into a business model. Both include a "revenue streams" block. Block 5 of the Lean Canvas includes elements such as revenue model, lifetime value, revenues, and gross margins (when combined with the other side of block 5, focused on cost structure). The Strategyzer canvas also proposes a "revenue streams" block (block 9) focusing on types of revenue streams, fixed pricing, and dynamic pricing. They also discuss willingness-to-pay. Having revenue management included in both canvases is good news. But neither methodology provides the types of analysis that need to be conducted, the detailed sources of information that need to be collected, or the integration of all information needed to make intelligent and informed pricing decisions. They barely cover some of the very critical components of value-based pricing, price-to-win, price-to-compete, and, potentially, digital pricing. So there's room for improvement.

The four C's of pricing

For the past five years, I've worked at developing and testing the Pricing Model Innovation Canvas (PMIC) in both the B2B and the B2G worlds. The purpose of this canvas is to offer a framework to innovators, marketers, capture experts, and pricers to conduct deep dives into the revenue model block. It can also be used without the development of a business model canvas. It's generally preferred to tie the PMIC to the customer-value proposition. The PMIC focuses on the three C's of pricing (cost, competition, and customer value) and one C related to change management to support the design and execution of new or revised pricing models. The PMIC describes the various methods, analyses, and outcomes of the four C's. Working with it leads to the selection of the proper pricing model(s), to the relevant pricing test plan, and to a better-informed pricing decision (see figure 18.1).

PRICING MODEL

INNOVATION CANVAS (v1.2)

Designed for:

Owner:

Date:

The 4C's of Pricing

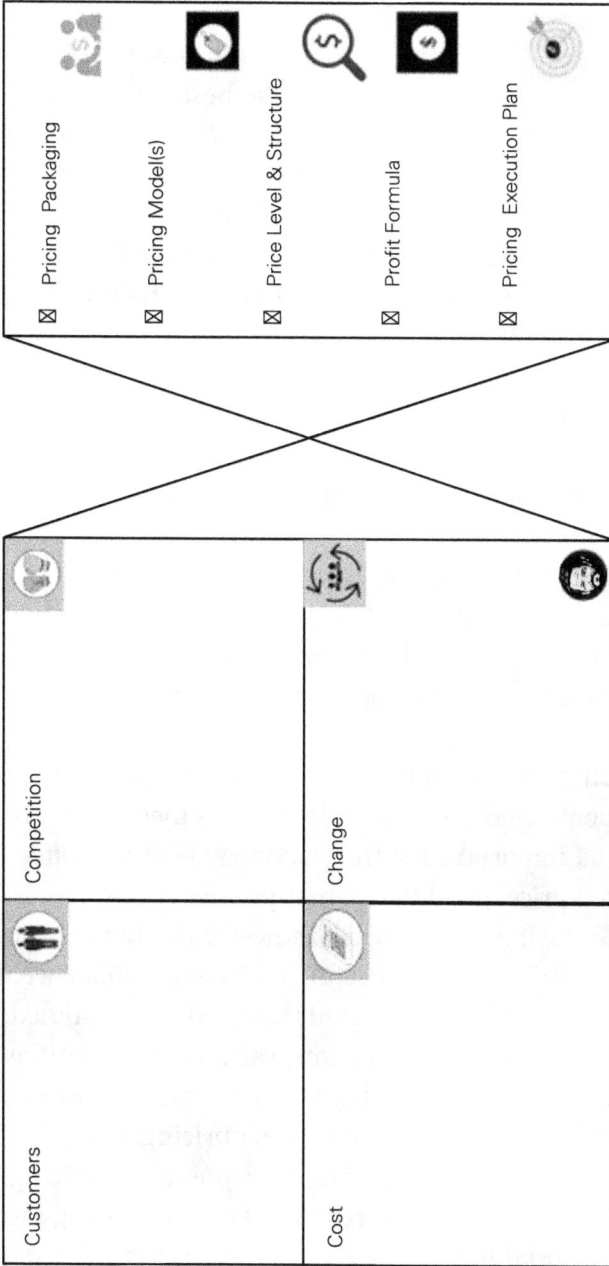

Framing Decisions

Customers

Competition

Cost

Change

☒ Pricing Packaging

☒ Pricing Model(s)

☒ Price Level & Structure

☒ Profit Formula

☒ Pricing Execution Plan

Figure 18.1. The Pricing Model Innovation Canvas.

The information contained in the PMIC isn't new. In fact, pricing based on the three C's of pricing has been used for a while under the leadership of some of the best pricing scholars. Kent Monroe's 1990 book *Pricing: Making Profitable Decisions* highlights concepts of the final price discretion by integrating the three C's (customer, competition, and cost).

The PMIC uses these three C's and adds a fourth C (change). For each of the C's, five methods, tools, or analyses are proposed, for a total of 20. Of course, it's not always necessary to use the 20 methodologies for every opportunity. Frankly, it's also not required to use the PMIC for every deal and offer. But I highly recommend using the canvas for strategic bids, disruptive commercial offers, and new business models. Innovators, marketers, and pricers select the most relevant methodologies to use and assemble the information using the canvas. The end game is to generate the outcomes and outputs necessary to better frame an opportunity and to make better pricing decisions. I recommend five of these framing decisions as shown in the PMIC:

1 **Pricing packaging.** The packaging of your price will be connected to your customer segmentation process and what's important for the customer. Will you offer one integrated price, good-better-best pricing options, a pricing offer à la carte (open or closed bundles)? Most of the time, the customer RFP will give useful information about what type of pricing proposal is expected (bundled or unbundled, separate pricing for some components, variations of solutions, etc.).

2 **Pricing model(s).** What's the right pricing model or models for this opportunity? Is it product pricing, subscription-based pricing, usage-based pricing, outcome-based pricing, or a mix of these? Of course, there are a variety of pricing models, and it's essential to pay attention to the customer's requirements.

Does the customer prefer a pay-as-you-go pricing model, or do they want a fixed up-front price?

3 **Pricing levels and structure.** What's the right price level for the new opportunity? What's the right pricing structure and discount level? What rebates might you offer in addition to discounts? This section of the model shows the actual price decision for your offer. You might have several price levels based on your structure and your model. For complex offers, the pricing structure might also cover financing and payment components.

4 **Profit formula.** With the pricing model(s) and price point selected, what does the P&L look like? What happens to earnings before interest and taxes and cash flow? What are the impacts of switching from an ownership model to a consumption model? Are there specific P&L scenarios that top management might want to consider and choose from?

5 **Pricing execution plan.** Last but not least, who does what in pricing? Who's accountable to implement the guidelines and scaling plan? How is pricing governed for this innovation when it moves back into the core business? How do we train the salesforce, especially if there's a new pricing model? How are the price and the customer proposal delivered? Remember that execution is half the battle to reach the ROI of your pricing strategy. So it must be prepared seriously.

The PMIC focuses on key questions

Much of the information needed to fill out the PMIC should be already available from the analyses conducted in the rest of the business model blocks and/or in preparation of your bid costing models. Data may come from other processes as well. The key is to assemble a multifunctional team of experts to have a dedicated and intelligent discussion on pricing as part of the framing process of the offer using the canvas. That team might be an MVP team, a capture team, or a bid team, for example. That discussion will lead to the uncovering of information gaps and neglected areas. Some of the questions we need to answer for each of the four C's are listed below.

Customer
- What are your customer's key stakeholders in the buying center?
- What are your customer's hot buttons?
- What is your customer's buying style and buying behavior?
- Who makes the final acquisition decision?
- What drivers impact the customer's P&L?
- What are the customer's addressable and maximum budgets?
- What are the measures of willingness-to-pay and ability to pay?

Competitors
- Which competitors might be finalists on the offer or bid?
- Which competitors are in the best position to win?
- What are your discriminators versus theirs?
- What are your WOW differentiators?
- What are marketing and technical switching costs?
- What are your main competitors' bidding styles?
- What are your competitors' price levels and pricing strategies?

Costs
- What are your main cost drivers?
- What are your top-down margin targets?
- What's your breakeven point?
- What are your cost advantages versus competitors'?

- How do costs evolve during scaling?
- What is your customer's price sensitivity?

Change
- Who's in charge of pricing pre/post launch of your innovation?
- Are your sellers trained on value/pricing models?
- What are the expected pricing objections?
- How are price special conditions approved, and by whom?
- How do you quickly scale commercially?
- How is a hybrid pricing model operationalized in your ERP?

Benefits of using the PMIC for B2G offers

There are many benefits of using some sort of canvas to manage pricing. The PMIC is a good option. There might be others available. The PMIC

- Harmonizes the review of the four C's across the organization.
- Reinforces the voice of the customer in the capture process and the bid development phase.
- Identifies the information gaps and the need to pursue additional knowledge.
- Focuses on essential information needed to make an intelligent pricing decision.
- Allows capture teams to track progress on pricing by updating the canvas during the capture process.
- Shows top management that pricing was paid attention to and was not a second thought.
- Allows one key person in the capture team to keep track of pricing input and output.
- Allows teams to be trained on the 20 techniques and methodologies related to pricing while performing practical work.

- Serves as a condensed summary to answer a simple question during the bid-gate review: "How did you come up with this pricing level?"
- Helps better frame value for new-to-the-world innovations.

When do you use the PMIC?

There's no ideal time and place to use the canvas. Like any canvas, it's part of developing a mindset of using tools to frame opportunities. In my experience, there are five situations that are well positioned for PMIC use:

1 **For complex offers.** These are multicomponent and multidimensional. They might integrate products, services, software, and data. There is also an intangible part of the system that needs to be accounted for. So, pricing will be more complex and might require a framework.

2 **For innovative offers.** The same thinking applies to innovative disruptive offers that may be new to the world. A focus on the four C's is required and information synthesis is needed to make the right pricing decisions.

3 **For new revenue and business models.** When a bid or offer is based on a new business and revenue model (CapEx to OpEx model, for example), the PMIC is ideal for preparing the change and for focusing on the change management dimension of the new models.

4 **During the early capture process.** When a capture team is assembled very early in the bid-preparation process, it's essential to begin working on the components of the PMIC early before and at Gate 0. PMIC offers a great centralized point of information collection for discussion and convergence.

5 **To track pricing strategy during a long pursuit.**
Finally, for long capture and pursuit cycles, using the PMIC
might allow teams to track progress and justify changes in the
pricing strategies as new information becomes available and
the bid requirements change over time.

Additional remarks

A full version of the Pricing Model Innovation Canvas is available
on Slideshare, and videos are available on YouTube. You'll find
the basic version of the canvas, a version with questions, and a
detailed version with all 10 methods and analyses with relevant
outputs/outcomes. This is a work in progress, and it can certainly
be improved. I'd also like to promote the use of the PMIC in digital incubators, in startups, and in marketing circles. It's the right
time for the pricing function to push for wider adoption of key
concepts. A dedicated pricing model canvas does just that. To
help with adoption, this canvas was designed and released with
the Creative Commons (CC) attribution. A CC license is one of
several public copyright licenses that enable the free distribution
of an otherwise copyrighted work. It's used when a creator wants
to give people the right to share, use, and build on a work they've
created. So be bold, share widely, and make use of it. Updates and
revisions will be made on a regular basis.

Key Notes

_____

_____

_____

_____

_____

_____

Key Actions

_____

_____

_____

_____

_____

_____

19

Get What You Pay For in B2G Deals

Kate Vitasek, University of Tennessee, and Michele Flynn, SIREAS, LLC

WHY DO SO MANY companies and B2G commercial managers find themselves back at the negotiation table after they've negotiated a "deal?" It's the nature of the pricing process itself that causes consternation.

There are three significant reasons for pricing discord. First, dissatisfaction is often directly related to the pricing approach used, or, more appropriately, the lack of a well-thought-out and aligned approach. In their rush to "get to yes," parties negotiate and lock-in early on a "price"—only to find that business conditions change, unknowns become discovered, and the price is now no longer "fair." By definition, B2G services, for example in facilities management, vary substantially based on uncontrollable issues such as weather, changing business needs, and corporate growth strategies. We advocate for companies to understand and know when to use a "price" versus a "pricing model."

A second reason for pricing discord stems from companies adopting a muscular, lowest-price-possible mindset in which buyers aim to squeeze short-term price concessions from their suppliers. Procurement philosophies introduced in the 1980s, such as the Kraljic model, encouraged businesses to assert their buying power to condition their supply chains and force a change in the demand curve to minimize dependency on suppliers. This has led to the commoditization of services in many industries as companies seek to "bid and transition" to pit supplier against supplier. The more companies apply these dominating "I-win-you-lose" methods, the more suppliers hunker down to protect margins and use short-term tactics to win the business, knowing they'll be back at the table with tactics to increase their price once work is transitioned.

Finally—and all too often—companies rely on a conventional transaction-based business model rather than using a more appropriate outcome or investment-based sourcing business model that will best meet their business needs. Research conducted by the International Association for Contract and Commercial Management validates that most companies operate in a conventional transaction-based model constrained by formal, legally oriented corporate policies ("Contract Negotiations Continue to Undermine Value," 2010). There is growing awareness that this approach is ineffective given the dynamic nature of today's business environment and does not always achieve each party's intended long-term results. Rather, it creates perverse incentives and missed opportunities to drive investments and innovation.

Bottom line: companies that want to prevent these common traps should begin by first understanding—and using—the right tools. This article provides insights and recommendations that B2G professionals can use to align the right pricing mechanisms with the right sourcing business model that best fits their sourcing situation.

Aligning pricing mechanisms with the business model

As an organization's need becomes more complex, riskier, and/or requires higher levels of continuous improvement or innovation, sourcing business model theory suggests that the organization should shift to a performance-based or Vested® model as the foundation for their outsourcing relationship. One of the biggest mistakes a company can make when trying to establish fair pricing is to use the wrong sourcing business model. The problem worsens when a company does not align the right pricing mechanisms (compensation method, price vs. pricing model) with their chosen sourcing business model (Keith, Vitasek, Manrodt, & Kling, 2016).

This chapter provides a deep dive into why and how to construct the most appropriate pricing approach for each sourcing business model, beginning with transaction-based models. We share typical pricing mechanisms and discuss inherent incentives and pros/cons for each model.

Transaction-based models

Transaction-based business models have been the cornerstone of business endeavors for centuries and remain the most common of sourcing business models in use today. There are three transaction-based sourcing business models: basic, approved provider, and preferred provider. As the commitment between a buyer and supplier increases, buyers will often shift their suppliers to an "approved provider" or a "preferred provider" status.

Typical pricing mechanics used

Transaction-based models typically use *prices* instead of a *pricing model,* and payment is triggered when transactions are completed. The supplier gets paid by the transaction; therefore, the greater the number of transactions, the more revenue for the supplier. The transaction price can be based on labor, product, or unit of service. Some common examples are as follows:

- An HVAC contractor supplies labor to manage PMs on a blanket PO, supplier bills for staff on a fully loaded cost per hour.
- An interior designer provides design development documents for a flat price per usable square foot designed.
- A move labor contractor provides services inclusive of trucks, labor, boxes, and supplies at a set price per person moved.
- A local broker provides transaction support for a set price per rentable square foot.

There are two common pricing approaches for transaction-based agreements: staff augmentation and price per transaction. The main difference is that staff augmentation typically is tied to labor (number of hours/days worked), whereas price per transaction is tied to completing a product unit / unit of service. Figure 19.1 summarizes the typical characteristics of staff-augmentation and price-per-transaction approaches.

While transaction-based agreements can be open- or closed-book, it's very common to use a closed-book, fixed-price compensation method where the buyer and seller establish a unit price per transaction for a particular task with limited visibility for the buyer into the composition of the unit price.

Characteristic	Two Most Common Transaction-Based Pricing Approaches	
	Staff Augmentation	Price per Transaction
Typical business drivers	Overhead reduction and variable staffing	Variable costs (people and infrastruture)
Work definition	Focus on *who* and *how*	Focus on *how*; use statement of work to define work
Desired outcomes	Hours of work completed	Transactions completed at desirable quality specifications
Economics/ compensation method	Price vs. pricing model: hourly/daily rate per FTE Can be *cost reimbursement* or *fixed price*, with more tendency to be *fixed price with profit and OH as a markup on people cost*	Price vs. pricing model: per unit/activity (cost per call, cost per unit, cost per shipment) Can be *cost reimbursement* or *fixed price* with more tendency to be fixed price
Governance structure	Direct oversight/supervision where "boss" signs off on work	Oversight through quality metrics, volume tracking, service level agreements. Larger "preferred" suppliers may be managed under a supplier relationship management program
Typical mindset	Zero sum/win–lose	Zero sum/win–lose

Figure 19.1. Summarized characteristics of common transaction-based approaches. Source: University of Tennessee.

Inherent incentives: Pros and cons

By far the biggest advantage of a transactional pricing model is simplicity and flexibility. Agree on a price and pay for what you use. The strength of transactional pricing is also the Achilles' heel because the supplier revenue is directly tied to the volume of transactions: the greater the number of transactions, the greater the revenue; the greater the revenue, the greater the profit. Transactional pricing creates an inherent perverse incentive for the supplier to focus on performing activities versus driving efficiencies. It makes sense when you think about it. If you're paying your supplier a price per hour or per person for a custodial worker, the supplier is most profitable when they use a lot of hours and have many people.

Recommendation

A transaction-based pricing model is effective for simple transactions with an abundant supply, low complexity, and little asset specificity (unique or custom requirements). If the level of dependency and the shared value is low, transaction-based models are the way to go. They also work well when there's high variability in volume—that is, when you don't need full-time ongoing services but need them occasionally.

Transaction-based pricing doesn't work well if there's a high degree of customization, significant training, or the service requires tight integration with the buyer or other supplier organizations. Each variable requires investment and consistency of supply base, which means higher fixed costs unique to one particular customer.

Output- and outcome-based models

There has been a trend in B2G to shift to output- and outcome-based models for more complex environments. Output- and outcomes-based models link the compensation of a supplier to their ability to perform against prenegotiated goals or commitments.

Rolls-Royce PLC was the first known organization to explore outcome-based approaches in the 1960s while making engines for aircraft clients. In this approach, the buyer often increases the scope of work and reduces the level of detail in the statement of work—focusing on "outcomes." Rolls-Royce's outcome-based model is called the "Power-by-the-Hour" program.[2] Under the model, Rolls-Royce assumes the risk for operational uptime and receives a fixed fee per hour of operational uptime. This flexibility allows Rolls-Royce to use its expertise efficiently and cost-ffectively to deliver the desired outcome—a well-maintained engine that decreases aircraft downtime for its clients. Rolls-Royce benefits by having a steady revenue stream that it can use to level load resources and budget for optimized maintenance during the life of the engine. The airline benefits because regularly scheduled, expertly provided maintenance results in fewer planes that require unexpected repairs, increasing the number of hours the planes are operational.

Output- and outcome-based business models have increased in popularity in the last few years. There are two broad classifications: performance-based agreements (which focus on supplier-controlled outputs) and Vested agreements (which focus on boundary-spanning business outcomes). Figure 19.2 summarizes the typical characteristics of performance-based and Vested business approaches.

We explore both models in more detail below with an emphasis on the pricing models for each.

---

2   Power-by-the-Hour is a registered trademark of Rolls-Royce. For details about the Rolls-Royce Power-by-the-Hour initiative, see http://www.rolls-royce.com /media/press-releases/yr-2012/121030-the-hour.aspx

Business Model	Performance-Based Managed Services	Vested
Economic model	Output-based	Outcome-based
Relationship model	Relational contract—collaborative	Relational contract—collaborative
Vision and intent	Performance to SLA—process efficiencies	Shared vision, desired outcomes and value creation
Scope of Work		
Statement of work and objectives	"What" (narrowly defined as the supplier's responsibilities, as defined by the client)	"What" (broadly defined as the areas to be addressed as collaboratively agreed)
Performance Management		
Performance focus	Output-based service-level agreements	Strategic desired outcomes
Performance measures	Operational + relational (values and behaviors)	Operational + transformational + relational (system-wide KPIs)
Pricing		
Pricing model and incentives	Price or pricing model with incentives and/or penalties	Pricing model with value-based incentives
Governance		
Relationship management	Oversight emphasis: supplier relationship management	Insight emphasis: strategic relationship management
Improve, transform, and innovate	Supplier driven to meet SLAs/price	Joint and proactive transformation management
Exit management	Performance-based termination for cause, with safeguards	Joint exit management plan
Compliance and special concerns	Corporate-based audit requirements	Outcome-based joint requirements

Figure 19.2. Summarized Characteristics of Common Outcome-Based Approaches. Adapted from B. Keith, K. Vitasek, K. Manrodt, and J. Kling, *Strategic Sourcing in the New Economy: Harnessing the Potential of Sourcing Business Models for Modern Procurement.* New York: Palgrave Macmillan. Copyright © the authors 2016.

Performance-based agreements

A performance-based agreement (sometimes also referred to as a managed services agreement) seeks to create a formal, longer-term relationship with the intent that the supplier's compensation is linked directly to performance and/or to the ability to deliver cost savings or other service improvements. Buyers typically define the level of performance required and competitively bid the work to determine which suppliers can meet the buyers' needs at the best value. Performance-based pricing agreements are sometimes called "pay for performance" because they often have positive and/or negative incentives tied to outcomes (often called gainshare/painshare).

Typical pricing mechanics used

Performance-based agreements can be structured as fixed price, fixed price per unit, or cost reimbursement. One approach is referred to as a "guaranteed maximum price" (GMP). GMP deals have grown in popularity for facilities management because they enable budget predictability. As outsourcing has matured, organizations have shifted to more of a hybrid approach using a mix of fixed price (management fee), transactional, and cost reimbursement components in their pricing models to better align with the breadth and complexity of services within the scope.

At its core, a well-designed performance-based agreement provides behavioral incentives for the supplier to keep costs low and performance high. A hallmark design principle of a performance-based agreement is the use of incentives and at-risk fees to help align the parties' interests by creating a band of performance tied to the supplier's price. The incentives and at-risk fees help align the economics of the relationship based on the level of service received. For this reason, performance-based agreements typically require high levels of interaction between a supplier and a buyer to review performance against service-level agreements

(SLAs) and assess the incentive or at-risk fees typically embedded in the contract. These reviews are periodically scheduled and include representatives from the supplier and the buyer company.

Inherent incentives: Pros and cons

A powerful advantage of a performance-based agreement is that it ensures that a supplier keeps its eye on performance and costs. Well-structured pricing models tightly align the economics of the deal to the supplier's performance and inherently incentivize the supplier to meet contractual SLAs at committed prices. GMP deals, in particular, allow buying organizations to have a predictable budget because the supplier commits to keeping costs at or below the price they quote.

A good performance-based pricing model also creates a self-executing contract with clearly defined metrics and measurement methodologies; determining the actual incentive payment simply becomes a reporting requirement. While the self-correcting nature of the agreement is a core strength, it can also be a downfall because often there is a tendency toward oversimplification, which can create inherent perverse incentives.

One inherent perverse incentive is that the supplier optimizes service/costs only for themselves and just for the duration of the contract. For example, a city utility district that operates a large water treatment plant hired a supplier to manage maintenance of the plant. If in the performance-based agreement, the supplier is incentivized to achieve operational SLAs only, focusing on operational SLAs will allow the supplier to get a green scorecard every month. While this is great for them, it would be far more beneficial for both parties if the supplier did more proactive maintenance to maximize the performance of the plant's lifetime. Unfortunately, more preventive maintenance would increase the supplier's costs (potentially decreasing its margin). Suppliers easily justify forgoing maintenance in the short term if there's no risk to operational performance (achieving their green scorecard). After all, why invest now when the buyer is likely to bid out the work at the end of the contract? And if the supplier made the investments and lost the bid, they truly would face a lose-lose scenario. Correctly structuring metrics to focus on the total life cycle and not just operational SLAs can mitigate this risk.

Many companies, like the city utility district above, struggle with how to properly apply incentives. A great example of a bonus system gone awry is the idea that if a supplier outperforms a service level, it should automatically get a bonus. This only works if there's a corresponding business benefit. If a customer needs a supplier to complete employee moves before 5 a.m. on Monday morning, the value of the service will likely be degraded if the supplier is still moving people into the workweek; however, it's unlikely that getting the moves completed on Saturday instead of Sunday will provide any additional value, so an offset or bonus isn't appropriate. Contrast this with a development project where beating a deadline may mean going to market earlier with a product. The key decision point should be whether incremental value is gained from incremental performance improvements against SLAs.

GMP deals have several perverse incentives built in. By definition, GMP means that the supplier cannot go back to the buyer and request more funds unless there's been a change in scope. This means that the supplier must factor all potential risks into the pricing structure. As an example, because the supplier cannot predict snowfall, it will likely assess what is the "average" snowfall for a given site and then include a contingency factor to cover their risks in case there's extraordinary snowfall. As a result, the buyer will pay for that risk. If the snowfall's average or below average, the buyer will receive no rebate. Another perverse incentive is that GMP deals are by design rigid. A supplier will be far less flexible in assuming more work under a GMP because they have bid a fixed price for a fixed set of services. Each new service or activity will need to be scoped and bid separately, and the contract will need to be amended to accommodate the negotiated incremental costs.

Another potential drawback of inappropriate application of a performance-based contract is what University of Tennessee researchers call a "watermelon scorecard." This happens when suppliers are meeting SLAs but the buyer perceives that the supplier is still failing to meet the company's business objectives. Simply put, performance is green on the outside, red on the inside—like a watermelon. If you're experiencing a watermelon scorecard, it may be a signal that your business is better suited for a Vested business model or that you're not measuring the things important to the buying organization. Ongoing governance and review of the performance measures throughout the life of the contract and relationship can help mitigate this risk.

Other potential drawbacks occur when clients bury the cost of governance into the supplier's transaction price or management fee without ensuring that there are sufficient funds to cover this responsibility. Suppliers also suffer when their clients don't invest in proper governance. Suppliers often will bring ideas to buyers to help drive efficiencies, only to find that the buyer does not have appropriate mechanisms to drive sound decision-making and support the implementation of these ideas. Or worse, they make investments right for the relationship, only to find that a "new sheriff" rides into town and does not honor previous decisions, which places their investments at risk.

Finally, when suppliers are held accountable to meet guaranteed glidepath price reductions, they may feel margin pressure. When this happens, buyers can quickly see the "A team" on their account move off and be switched with the "C team."

Recommendation

Performance-based approaches can succeed wildly or be hugely disappointing. Failure occurs most often when companies use a performance-based sourcing business model when another approach would fit better. A performance-based approach works best when the supplier is placed in a static "black box" and asked to optimize productivity and costs in the "box." It is simply unfair to ask a service provider to sign up for putting its compensation at risk if the nature of the business itself is risky. We recommend using a performance-based agreement only *if the level of dependency and the shared value is medium.*

Before adopting a performance-based pricing approach, ask these questions:

- Do you have a sound baseline where the supplier feels comfortable signing up for "guaranteed" performance or cost reductions?
- Is the scope of work very stable and predictable? If it's variable, can you ensure that the supplier won't be taking on inappropriate risk? Under a performance-based model, the supplier will place a "bet" on the risk and the buyer must live with the predictable consequences. (If the risk turns out well for the supplier, they will earn high margins. If the risk is too much for the supplier to bear, the supplier will have an inherent incentive to marginalize performance or come back and ask for a price increase.)
- Can a discrete scope of work be carved off into a "black box" for the supplier to optimize? Work that requires significant input from the buyer or external sources probably isn't a good fit, because it imposes risks that are likely not appropriate.
- Are the cost components controllable? A general rule of thumb is that a supplier shouldn't be held accountable for

"guaranteeing" a price decrease if there's a substantial potential risk (e.g., foreign currency exchange, commodity fluctuations, service demand fluctuations).

- Are you prepared to devote proper governance levels to the
relationship? This is especially true for the supplier, as governance is typically absorbed into the transaction-based price
versus part of a more comprehensive *pricing model.*

If the answer is "yes" to each of these, a performance-based
agreement is potentially a good fit. If the answer is "no," the parties will likely create friction in their relationship because the
supplier will be signing up for risk outside of its control. Here,
the parties should consider either a transaction-based or a Vested
approach.

Vested agreements

A Vested agreement—like a performance-based agreement—purposefully seeks to create a formal, longer-term relationship with
the intent that the supplier's compensation be linked directly to
performance. However, the mindset and design principles are
different. The Vested approach consciously shifts toward viewing the supplier as a business partner—not simply as a supplier.
Vested takes buyer–supplier alignment to a new level, structuring a true "win-win" pricing model by establishing an economic
engine that generates value for all parties at a high level. Procter
& Gamble (P&G) uses the analogy of having buyers and suppliers
"tug on the same side of the rope" when referring to its Vested
agreements because a Vested supplier sits on the same side of the
table. The better P&G does, the better the supplier does...and the
worse P&G does, the worse the supplier does (Vitasek, Manrodt,
& Kling, 2012).

Typical pricing mechanisms used

There are five characteristics of a Vested pricing model:[3]

- Foundation based on transparency, TCO/value, and appropriate risk allocation.
- Flexible framework based on the logic of Maslow's hierarchy.
- Incentives (not penalties) drive behaviors.
- True value sharing with high incentives for innovation/transformation (ROI).
- Margin matching to ensure continual alignment.

Each is discussed below.

Foundation based on transparency, TCO/value, and appropriate risk allocation

A Vested pricing model is based on three foundational principles: flexibility, transparency, and a shift to TCO/value versus price/budget. Most Vested agreements use a *cost-pass-through model* where "the costs are the costs are the costs," and there's no markup by the supplier. The profit of the supplier is "broken" from the cost and linked to their value/performance. Decoupling costs and profit eliminates the perverse incentive for a supplier to have more costs. It also prevents "markup on markup" when using subcontractors—which is common in highly complex deals.

---

3   The term *Vested outsourcing* was originally coined by University of Tennessee researchers to describe the highly successful outcome-based outsourcing agreements they studied as part of a large research project funded by the US Air Force. Their research revealed that Vested agreements combined an outcome-based model with the Nobel Prize concepts of behavioral economics and the principles of shared value. Using these concepts, companies enter into highly collaborative arrangements designed to create value for all parties involved above and beyond the conventional buy–sell economics of transaction-based or performance-based agreements (see Vitasek, Ledyard, & Manrodt, 2013).

The cost-pass-through model promotes transparency, enabling the buying organization and supplier to take "price" and turn it into visible cost drivers where they can collaborate on how to best reduce the overall total cost—not just the supplier prices or the buying organizations budget. While the pricing model should be transparent, the parties may decide to use mechanisms that are easy to administer and as such may have some components that are translated into fees for billing purposes. For example, the supplier's profit and overhead could be charged as a monthly "fixed management fee."

The underlying nature of the pricing model also shifts from a "price" and "budget" focus to one of TCO/value. In addition, the parties view risk from a very objective perspective. Risks are not something to shift to the other party but are instead a fact of the business. The parties complete a thorough risk analysis and determine which party is the most appropriate to bear the risk. If a supplier bears the risk, they're paid a risk premium.

Once the cost drivers and risks are understood, the buyer and supplier organizations develop the most flexible and fair way to pay for the various goods and services under scope, using Maslow's hierarchy as the logic.

Flexible framework based on the logic of Maslow's hierarchy

Vested pricing models mirror Abraham Maslow's hierarchy of needs. Maslow's theory states that it is vital to meet certain lower needs before higher needs can be addressed (McLeod, 2018).

The base of Maslow's hierarchy is "physiological needs and safety." The equivalent of Maslow's base in a B2G outsourcing deal is the "base services" consisting of the repetitive and stable costs associated with the basic service requirement (e.g., keep the lights on, keep the facilities clean, have compliant processes). For the buying organization, basics tend to be around feeling safe in that the service provider can deliver on basic service and prove they can get the job done. For the service provider, the basics come in creating fair pricing that ensures they won't lose money—especially on uncontrollable risks. Simply put, a supplier can't possibly help their client solve complex business problems if they're not at least covering basic costs.

A general rule is that a supplier earns a "small" margin for base services when there's little risk and where the actual activities/work are more of a commodity. This typically translates into below-market margins if the work is competitively bid—often as low as 50 percent of "market" margin. For example, if the work was put to bid and the "market" margin was 10 percent, a Vested deal might have a 5 percent margin for the base services.

The pricing in the base services is somewhat similar to a performance-based agreement in that the economics are tied to performance. However, the mindset and approach in the pricing model is different. Rather than have a fee-at-risk for nonperformance, Vested pricing strategically guarantees a minimum profit for the supplier for the base book of work. The supplier will never lose money on the deal. This gives everyone peace of mind, knowing that the work will be done effectively and efficiently, while also guaranteeing that the supplier's lights will stay on, payroll will be covered, and the equipment or facilities will be properly maintained. The supplier can then earn incentives (see more under "Incentives").

The middle of Maslow's hierarchy is "esteem and love/belonging." Here the Vested pricing model addresses the more complex aspects of a commercial real estate (CRE) deal and includes two design principles. The first is how the parties will address how they'll manage "other services" that are more variable and riskier, and the second is governance.

In a Vested agreement, there is a commitment to the partnership. Thus, when new work is added to the supplier's scope, it should go to the partner by default, provided the partner is capable and cost-effective. Other services typically include either ongoing costs with significant variability, one-off needs, or new services. In essence, other services enable the parties to have a fair and predefined way to pay for "scope creep," which significantly reduces tension in the relationship. The general rule is that the margin for other services is higher than the base—but less than the market margin. The rationale is that the buying organization commits to providing "other services" to the supplier under a no-bid situation as their strategic partner, and that the supplier agrees not to hold the buying organization hostage because of lock-in. Having an agreed-upon way to manage "other services" designs in flexibility and reduces friction associated with lock-in and scope creep.

A Vested pricing model also incorporates the fact that the relationship is long-term and future-focused. Thus, governance is essential, even more so than in a performance-based agreement. Vested pricing models always design how the organizations will fund and pay for governance—on both sides. The general rule is that the supplier should earn above market margin for governance, as they have an inherent incentive to hire the "A team." Governance costs should not be embedded in the "base services" because buyers by nature want to reduce their costs. If governance costs are part of the base services, the supplier will have a perverse incentive to reduce the cost of governance and replace the "A team" with the "C team."

The top of Maslow's hierarchy is "self-actualization." Most businesses—like people—have desires. A desire is something that a business wants but doesn't have. A Vested agreement is anchored on the buyer and supplier working jointly to create desired outcomes. But it's almost always imperative to make investments and innovation and/or transformation initiatives to achieve the desired outcomes. For this reason, desired outcomes reside at the top of a company's needs pyramid. And also for this reason, the pricing model needs to highly compensate the supplier with high margins for their risk and investments. Using 10 percent as the "market margin," a Vested pricing model would allow the supplier to earn two to three times the market margin—or up to 20 to 30 percent profit margins—if the supplier successfully incorporates transformation and innovation to achieve desired outcomes. Most often, compensation for achieving transformation and innovation is paid as an incentive.

Incentives (not penalties) drive behavior

A Vested pricing model uses incentives (not penalties). The supplier earns incentives when it performs well. Do a good job? Make more profit. In addition, in cost-pass-through deals, the supplier is not motivated to drive up costs because their profit is tied to performance—not costs.

Incentives are typically linked to each of the pricing model components. For example, incentives can be linked to the base services (e.g., achieving SLA targets), other services (e.g., reducing time to market on a project), governance (e.g., improving a corporate objective such as increased Tier 2 supplier diversity spend), or transformation (e.g., developing an innovation that achieves a desired outcome to improve the buying company's employee productivity).

True value sharing

Performance-based agreements often use a concept known as *gainsharing*. A Vested pricing model goes beyond gainsharing and expands the thinking to value sharing.

Harvard Business School's Michael Porter and Mark Kramer (2011) focused on the "big idea" of shared value in their excellent *Harvard Business Review* article "The Big Idea: Creating Shared Value." While the article relates primarily to how companies can work with society to create shared value, the concept of shared value is crucial to the Vested approach. The pricing model must share any value gained from achieving the desired outcomes.

Value sharing seeks to improve the overall value for the organization—not just to reduce cost, as in gainsharing. Incentives can be a powerful motivator when designed appropriately. A good example is the environmental services contract between the Department of Energy Superfund site known as the Rocky Flats Closure Project and Kaiser-Hill. The supplier—Kaiser-Hill—earned a base management fee of 3.7 percent (market margin was 4.1%) with incentives enabling it to earn up to an 11.7 percent profit margin when predefined outcomes were met (e.g., beating budget, raising safety levels, developing innovations that sped up closure). Kaiser-Hill developed over 200 innovations and ultimately earned incentive payments of $560 million; this may seem excessive until the full story is known: Kaiser-Hill saved US taxpayers $30 billion in costs and closed the site safely 65 years ahead of schedule—something almost all thought was impossible (Vitasek et al., 2012).

Of course, it's important to realize that value cannot always be expressed monetarily. For example, in one Vested agreement, a desired outcome was to increase the J. D. Power ranking for customer satisfaction in bank branches. The CRE supplier could influence the desired outcome but not control it. In this case, the parties used nonmonetary incentives. Nonmonetary incentives include things such as automatic contract-extension incentives, expanded scope of services, and even the customer's willingness to provide references.

Margin matching to ensure continual alignment

Vested agreements use margin matching to keep the economics of the deal in continual alignment. Typically, this means that the pricing model itself is monitored to ensure fairness for both the buyer and supplier organizations. This is crucial because complex outsourcing agreements will probably evolve. When the pricing model generates a payout to the supplier below their minimum profit guardrail or above what can be deemed a reasonable ROI on the total book of business, the margin-matching trigger flags the parties to review the model and assumptions and, if needed, make necessary changes.

Inherent incentives: Pros and cons

Organizations that make the shift to Vested find that they have a significant increase in trust because the parties are speaking the same financial language.

One might think that moving to a Vested pricing model is risky for a company and its supplier(s). Obviously, anything new and different involving investment in time, effort, and resources implies some risk. But the rewards can significantly outweigh the evaluated risk. One of the biggest advantages to using a Vested sourcing business model is the tight alignment of interests between buyer and supplier. Alignment on transparent win-win economics creates an inherent incentive for the parties to work together to shift from "pay for doing work" to "pay for delivering on value."

While a Vested model can deliver on the promise of transformation, the biggest challenge is that it's both different and hard. To succeed, it's imperative that buying organizations understand that a "bigger payoff" must be shared. This requires a mindset change for most organizations. Companies that choose a Vested sourcing business model must resist the urge, and corporate pressures, to demand the lowest possible price from suppliers. Suppliers must get comfortable with an open and transparent approach with financials. And both companies must make the shift toward a collaborative approach to developing a pricing model as the parties truly co-create the pricing model versus "negotiate" prices.

Organizations must also go beyond merely saying and using the term *partnership* to actually creating a commercial pricing model that equitably allocates risks and rewards to create shared value during the agreement. If they can't do this, they shouldn't enter into a Vested approach.

The biggest complaint about a Vested approach is the amount of time it takes. While it's possible to create a Vested agreement in less than three months, most take four to seven months once the provider has been selected, as the Vested methodology is often thought of as a paradigm shift.

Recommendation

A Vested pricing model works best when both parties are prepared to sit on the same side of the table conducting transparent, fact-based discussions about the business. Each party must clearly understand the goals and financial drivers of the relationship. A Vested approach is effective when

- a company has transformation or innovation objectives it cannot achieve itself and needs to create a "win-win" pricing model to incentivize the supplier to make investments needed to achieve the transformation/innovation objectives (desired outcomes).
- there is a need or desire to share risks and rewards. Vested deals are ideal when the business is complex and risky. They are also ideal when the buyer has decided that CRE is not a core competency and wants/needs a strategic business partner to make investments on its behalf.

- there is a high level of dependency (e.g., integration, high switching costs).

It's important to remember that a Vested pricing model will only work when a buyer and supplier agree to adopt the Vested business model in totality; a Vested pricing model is one of the five rules of the Vested approach, as profiled in *Vested Outsourcing: Five Rules That Will Transform Outsourcing* (Vitasek, Ledyard, & Manrodt, 2013).[4]

Market vision

Some will read this chapter and think "The authors put forth a good theory, but my situation is unique."

The simple answer to that is "Yes—you're right." But does that mean that the concepts outlined in this chapter won't work for you?

The lion's share of B2G contracts today are transactional. Regardless of whether you're buying facilities management services as shown in this chapter, the same logic can be applied to almost any type of procurement—especially when purchasing services. For example, in logistics contracts the transaction costs are cost per shipment or unit stored rather than cost per hour. Likewise, in IT support, they're cost per call or cost per minute. This, of course, imposes a perverse incentive on the supplier to perform more transactions regardless of the type of transaction being procured.

---

4   Rule 1: Focus on Outcomes, Not Transactions; Rule 2: Focus on the What, Not the How; Rule 3: Agree on Clearly Defined and Measurable Outcomes; Rule 4: Optimize Pricing Model Incentives; Rule 5: Governance Structure Should Provide Insight, Not Merely Oversight (see www.vestedway.com/category/5-rules/).

The second challenge is that far too many companies are still emphasizing simple "cost reduction" and "guaranteed savings" instead of value for money and total cost of ownership associated with the maintaining the business, compared with the quality of the service delivery and employee satisfaction with the workplace service delivery. This is exacerbated by suppliers who are willing to "buy" the business and commit to guaranteed savings commitments, sometimes funded by the profits from the transaction business.

At this point many would say that the supplier and client goals diverge. But we argue that they really don't. We argue that at the heart of B2G deals, clients and providers share a common vision—to deliver effective business results. The supplier wants to make money / a profit. The client wants their supplier to earn enough profit while delivering efficient and effective services. The supplier also wants to continue to help the client achieve the vision. We believe well-designed longer-term partnerships purposefully seek to align the buyer's and supplier's interests. A well-designed performance-based agreement is a good first step for those willing to drive to deeper integration and tighter alignment of pricing to service. Alternatively, a Vested model has proved very effective for organizations willing to truly shift to a transparent approach geared toward optimizing value for money against mutually defined buyer–supplier desired outcomes.

The bottom line? Our vision for the future is that buyers and providers work together to achieve common goals that will ultimately generate a true win-win for them. Don't assume the current market norms around pricing or old-fashioned perspectives that clients and suppliers have different objectives preclude building an effective relationship that can achieve your goals.

Conclusion: Implications for B2G pricing

Collectively the authors have been involved in hundreds of buyer–supplier agreements. One thing is certain. The saying "you get what you pay for" is as true today as when it was coined.

There are no magic potions or easy answers for pricing. And there's no generic template or spreadsheet that provides the "answer." Rather, you should view developing a pricing model as a process that parties go through to reach—and maintain—equilibrium. Doing so will ensure that they don't find themselves returning to the negotiations table after they have reached "yes."

If we had a magic wand? We'd challenge companies to resist the urge to simply get to "yes" on a price and challenge themselves to explore more advanced sourcing business models such as performance-based or Vested agreements. We'd also ensure that more business people consciously choose to use the sourcing business model that best fits the characteristics of their business and actively seek to use pricing mechanisms that prevent perverse incentives.

If you do make the shift to a performance-based or a Vested model, take the time to develop a fair and flexible pricing model to ensure that the economics of the commercial agreement stay in equilibrium over the life of the agreement.

Remember that no one approach fits all circumstances but that they all—when chosen correctly—can lead to sustainable and successful relationships.

The bottom line? It's time to adapt and adjust procurement and negotiation processes to address the rise of today's more dynamic and complex environments to create much-needed innovation.

References

Contract negotiations continue to undermine value. (2010). *International Association of Contracting and Commercial Management 9th Annual Top Ten Terms Report.*

Keith, B., Vitasek, K., Manrodt, K., & Kling, J. (2016). *Strategic sourcing in the new economy: Harnessing the potential of sourcing business models for modern procurement.* New York: Palgrave Macmillan.

McLeod, S. (2018). Maslow's hierarchy of needs. *Simply psychology.* Retrieved from www.simplypsychology.org/maslow .html

Porter, M. E., & Kramer, M. R. (2011). The big idea: Creating shared value. *Harvard Business Review,* January–February, 62–77. Retrieved from http://hbr.org/2011/01 /the-big-idea-creating-shared-value/ar/1

Vitasek, K., Ledyard, M., & Manrodt, K. (2013) *Vested outsourcing: Five rules that will transform outsourcing* (2nd ed.). New York: Palgrave Macmillan

Vitasek. K., Manrodt, K., & Kling, J. (2012). *Vested: How P&G, McDonald's, and Microsoft are redefining winning in business relationships.* New York: Palgrave Macmillan.

The authors

Kate Vitasek is an international authority for her award-winning research and Vested® business model for highly collaborative relationships. Vitasek, a faculty member at the University of Tennessee, has been lauded by *World Trade Magazine* as one of the "Fabulous 50+1" most influential people impacting global commerce.

Her pioneering work has led to six books, including: *Vested Outsourcing: Five Rules That Will Transform Outsourcing, Vested:*

How P&G, McDonald's and Microsoft Are Redefining Winning in Business Relationships, and *Getting to We: Negotiating Agreements for Highly Collaborative Relationships.* Vitasek's work also won the Supply Chain Council's Academic Advancement award for its impact in advancing business.

Vitasek is internationally recognized for her practical and research-based advice for driving transformation and innovation through highly collaborative and strategic partnerships. She has appeared on CNN International, Bloomberg, NPR, and Fox Business News. Her work has been featured in over 300 articles in publications like *Forbes, Chief Executive Magazine, CIO Magazine,* the *Wall Street Journal, Journal of Commerce, World Trade Magazine,* and *Outsource Magazine.*

Prior to her joining the University of Tennessee, Vitasek's storied career includes positions with P&G, Microsoft, Accenture, Stream International, and the founding of Supply Chain Visions—a boutique consulting firm recognized by ARC Advisory Group as one of the "10 Coolest" Boutique Consulting firms.

Michele Flynn is a visionary and expert in the fields of outsourcing, facilities management, real estate, and governance. She serves as executive chairman for SIREAS, LLC (a Vested Center of Excellence), working directly with clients to provide vision, strategy, and guidance in their pursuit of excellence in corporate real estate. As the founder and CEO of Expense Management Solutions, her leadership and expertise were integral to the development of performance-based contracting for global outsourcing relationships in corporate real estate and administrative services. She has authored many articles on facilities, real estate, and governance best practices, and is a sought-after speaker. She can be contacted at flynn@sireas.com.

Key Notes

_____

_____

_____

_____

_____

_____

Key Actions

_____

_____

_____

_____

_____

_____

20

Best Practices in Pricing B2G Software and Software-Enabled Systems

Scott D. Miller, Miller Advisors

THERE CAN BE A high degree of complexity around pricing, monetization, and offer design in the world of B2G software and software-enabled systems. These range from managing large multiyear deal opportunities, to selling into government procurement arms, to developing a multifaceted product portfolio that addresses a high volume of varying B2G requirements and challenges, to supporting clients on a variety of differing software versions, differing delivery architectures, and differing revenue models. It's no wonder that B2G pricing and offer design can be a confusing undertaking with so many considerations. *Enter the need for best practices in B2G software pricing.*

Achieving best practices in B2G software pricing is both a journey and a process for one's organization. From a journey perspective, this chapter highlights short- and long-term approaches to improving your organization's pricing capabilities. From a process perspective, this chapter introduces the Software Pricing Framework, a series of processes and tools with a specific focus on the *offer design* phase to not only help simplify the complexity of B2G pricing but to also create a best-practice approach for developing value-based pricing (VBP) and offer structures that improve your company's overall growth and profitability performance.

Pricing is a process

Frameworks and processes are not uncommon in the world of software. Consider the likes of Agile, Waterfall, Scrum, and V-Model (Eriksson, 2016). Even the product management discipline itself is governed by frameworks such as the Software Product Management Framework (ISPMA, 2019). Such processes and methodologies are the cornerstone of software project success and positive outcomes. B2G software pricing processes are no exception.

The Software Pricing Framework

Pricing processes help establish best practices, consistency, and improved end-to-end delivery across an organization that surpasses, from a growth and financial perspective, outcomes that would otherwise be achieved under more ad hoc pricing approaches. Successfully developing a VBP approach for software involves using the right design inputs, the right company-wide price-value training, and the right approaches to executing pricing within B2G tenders. The Software Pricing Framework®

(figure 20.1) addresses this end-to-end process cycle using three key activities: *offer design, enablement,* and *execution.*

Offer design. From strategy, to value analysis, to price structure development (packaging, metrics, tiers), to financial stress testing—the offer-design phase ensures that product and pricing teams bring in the right inputs and analysis to drive the most favorable value-based segmented pricing and offer structures.

Enablement. Whether it's internal sales teams or with channel partners, sales enablement is a critical activity for successfully

Figure 20.1. The Software Pricing Framework.

selling the pricing strategy and linking this to the software "value story." Change management must be considered to create an "all on board" organizational alignment, especially where there are major transformational changes to product and pricing strategies. Finally, effective communications, both internally and externally to clients, are key to helping avoid confusion when implementing new strategies.

Execution. Applying an effective bid-evaluation process, assigning pricing negotiation policies, and applying pricing approval matrices avoids a "race to the bottom" price approach when submitting a best and final offer (BAFO) for bids. As well, consistently monitoring results with key performance indicators (KPIs) and insights from post-bid-award feedback reports is critical for acting as an early warning system for ongoing adjustments to pricing and offer structures.

The pricing ecosystem (PECO). At the center of the framework is what is termed PECO; this includes all other people, processes, and systems within an organization that are impacted by changes to pricing strategies, structures, and policies. Cross-functional teams including accounting, legal, sales operations, contracting, reporting, IT, and customer service (to name several) are all impacted by pricing and must be informed and consulted during the pricing review process to identify implementation implications, risks, and compliance requirements across the organization.

The importance of viewing pricing "as a process" cannot be understated. And not only is it a process, it's also an approach that requires a continuous cycle of improvement: client and segment value perceptions change over time, new strategies emerge, and market innovation will continue to change—especially in the fast-paced era of digital transformation.

B2G Software 101: The fundamentals

Understanding the fundamentals for B2G software pricing helps create a foundation for pricing best practices and set the stage for the offer-design phase within the Software Pricing Framework. In this section, we discuss B2G revenue models as well as an overview of industry practices around contractualizing B2G pricing.

Software revenue models

Revenue models serve as the basis for how clients pay for, and use, one's software solution. The most commonly used B2G software revenue models include the following.

Perpetual license. This is a type of software license that authorizes a government entity to use a particular version of a software package indefinitely. Most often, a perpetual license is applied toward on-premise deployments (whereas subscriptions are applied to cloud environments). From a pricing perspective, clients will pay a one-time software fee that, in many cases, also includes a recurring annual maintenance and support (M&S) fee (see "Maintenance and support").

Term-based license. This is somewhat similar to a perpetual license, although instead of a one-time up-front fee, there is a lump-sum fee alongside a recurring annual M&S fee; this lump-sum fee is payable at each time of renewal. Clients are entitled to use the software only during the term of the contract. Term-based license pricing can be quite lucrative from the software vendor standpoint compared with perpetual licenses, benefiting from the lump-sum payments at each time of renewal; however, this license approach is known to create client "sticker shock" during the renewal process, increasing the risk of a client issuing a new tender.

Tip

Consider using a subscription revenue model rather than a term-based license model. Not only are payments spread over the course of the term, but it helps to avoid renewal "sticker shock" and, for those clients with an on-premise solution, can simplify future migrations to SaaS.

Subscription. This is a recurring monthly or annual license fee that entitles a government entity to use the software only during the subscription term (unlike a perpetual license that allows them to use it indefinitely). Subscription fees also inherently bundle the M&S fee. Although subscriptions are more commonly used for SaaS (whereby the subscription fee also includes hosting and application management), this is now becoming widespread for on-premise solutions as well. The total annual subscriptions fees for B2G are often calculated as a roll-up of underlying metric fees (see "Metrics").

Per-usage fee. This revenue model works well for services that are more transactional, such as the number of requests processed or number of reports accessed. However, this model can also create too much variability in pricing for a government entity that operates more within fixed budget funding. In these cases, a *per-usage* metric fee can be used a baseline calculation to derive a larger ongoing subscription fee (e.g., $0.25 per transaction × 300,000 average transactions per year = $75,000 annual subscription). An *overage fee* can be included to account for any outlier usages beyond an agreed-upon +/- transaction threshold amount.

Maintenance and support (M&S). M&S involves modifying the software product to address faults via bug fixes and patches or to improve performance to ensure a software solution operates seamlessly 24/7 without any failures that can cause workflow disruptions and potential economic loss for one's client (ISO, 2006).

Traditionally, M&S is calculated as a percentage (%) relative to the one-time perpetual or lump-sum term-based license. Example: a 25% M&S fee of $1M one-time perpetual license = $250,000 M&S per annum.

Tip

If M&S is a sizable revenue stream for your organization, take the time to conduct deep-dive internal workshops to better understand the underlying activities, pricing opportunities, and potential risks. Untapped opportunities, such as creating good-better-best M&S offerings, can drive significant monetization upside (Miller, 2019).

Pricing schedules in B2G contracts

B2G software pricing schedules within B2G contracts are an excellent means to highlight exactly what has been purchased (pricing, packages, volume) and what could be purchased (future upsell), and to clearly articulate the go-forward pricing arrangement (renewal options, overages, upgrades/enhancements).

Tip

"Giving software away for free"? Buyers use price as a simple proxy for quality (Blum & Mansour, 2018), and excluding details of your software pricing in contracts (common for many software-enabled systems) can lead to an interpretation that the software provides little to no value. Including details around software pricing helps articulate its value.

Software pricing schedules typically include the following components: *one-time fees, ongoing fees, renewal options,* and *overage fee.*

One-time fees. Implementation is typically the largest of such fees and is usually calculated based on time and materials (T&M) that should, in theory, be similar in amount for similar-size clients, purchasing similar solutions, with similar deployments. Costs beyond this can vary based on factors such as integration costs with other systems, customizations, and process changes. Localized implementations and regional differences in labor rates and regulations can also impact variation in implementation fees.

Other ancillary one-time fees such as training and training materials may seem insignificant, but they can be used to drive incremental monetization opportunities, increasing total contract value by as much as 2 to 5 percent. Avoid bundling these components for free, as they provide value, especially where a considerable amount of change management is required on the client side with use of a new software system.

Ongoing fees (pricing schedule). B2G is now seeing a shift to subscription models from what was once dominated by perpetual licenses. Benefits to highlighting an annual fee schedule over the course of the contract term create an awareness with a client around receiving ongoing value from the software as well as setting the stage for redetermined price increases and renewal options.

One myth in applying subscription pricing in B2G is that "customers can cancel after the first year"—an undesirable pricing model in circumstances that involve highly complex and costly implementations. However, B2G software vendors can successfully apply subscription pricing models without this fear of initial year cancellation by including a non-cancellation clause across a fixed-term commitment. B2G subscription term commitments for complex implementations now run an average of three years to five years; compare this with legacy B2G license contracts that were traditionally 10, 15, and sometimes 20 years long (note that subscription contracts are indirectly extended to around 10 years via *renewal options*; see figure 20.2).

Other key points to highlight for B2G subscription pricing: (a) annual subscription fees are held constant each year during the term commitment, (b) fees are increased at time of renewal, (c) subscription totals can be linked to underlying metrics—identify these within the pricing agreement, and (d) overages are included should the client scale and exceed a baseline threshold (defined based on metrics/volume purchased).

Renewal options. Contracts, in particular those with subscription offers, should include renewal option(s) within the agreement—a clause that outlines the terms of renewing or extending the original agreement and, from a pricing perspective, predetermines a renewal price increase that is calculated in two additive parts: (a) a standard percentage increase, plus (b) a cost-of-living adjustment. Renewal options help indirectly extend the contract length, simplify the renewal negotiation process, and lessen the likelihood of cancellation or reissuance of a new RFP.

Overage fee. Governments can grow in size (volumes, usage, and users) over the course of a contract, and this scalability can be further monetized through an *overage* fee. Overages typically reflect the underlying *metric(s)* that are used to calculate the total annual subscription fee.

Offer design: The road to value-based structures

With an understanding of the foundation and examples of contractualization of B2G software pricing, an organization is now ready to ask the key question: "How do we go about pricing our software solution?" Enter the offer-design process within the Software Pricing Framework. This process focuses heavily on applying VBP concepts and tools to develop optimal and segmented pricing and offer structures. This stage consists of four subprocesses:

Total Contract Value (5 years)	
Total contract value (TCV)	$7,365,000

Contract Fee Summary	
One-Time Fees	
Implementation fees	$2,790,000
System support and maintenance	See hosted
Hardware	managed
Software	subscription
Training (onsite)	305,000
Training (remote, online)	65,000
Training documentation	30,000
Other	
Total One-Time Fees	**$3,190,000**

Ongoing Fees	
SaaS subscription	$800,000
Customer success premium	35,000
Total Ongoing Fees	**$835,000**

Figure 20.2. Example of a B2G software pricing schedule.

(a) strategy; (b) price-value analysis; (c) packaging, metrics, and tiers; and (d) financial analysis.

In many ways, offer design can be analogous to skydiving: the *strategy* phase begins with gathering key inputs and strategic analyses that determine pricing guiding principles, product, and customer segmentation strategies (the 10,000-foot view); the *price-value analysis* phase seeks to determine approximate price positioning based on price-value perceptions across key segments (the 5,000-foot view); the *packaging, metrics, and tiers* phase seeks to create the underlying commercial price structures (the 500-foot

Pricing Schedule			
Five-Year Term Commitment			
Year	**Annual Subscription**	**Metrics**	**Notes**
Year 1	$800,000	6,400 FTE	
Year 2	$800,000	6,400 FTE	5-year commitment,
Year 3	$800,000	6,400 FTE	non-cancelable
Year 4	$800,000	6,400 FTE	FTE: full-time equivalent
Year 5	$800,000	6,400 FTE	
Renewal Options			
Year 6	$832,000	6,400 FTE	Renewal option +4%
Year 7	$832,000	6,400 FTE	3 years
Year 8	$832,000	6,400 FTE	
Year 9	$865,280	6,400 FTE	Renewal option +4%
Year 10	$865,280	6,400 FTE	2 years
Overages			
$125 per additional FTE above 6,400 baseline			

view); and, finally, the *financial views* phase conducts profitability analysis and price stress testing to determine breaking points and rework requirements in the pricing (ground level).

Strategy (10,000-foot view)

Strategy is a first step in gathering the right strategic inputs that determine the go-forward short- and long-term pricing and offer-design approach. Not only does a strategic assessment help guide offer design, it also helps drive product strategy decisions, including product positioning, new product introductions, product marketing, value selling, as well as value innovation and portfolio investments (Gale & Swire, 2012). The software strategy review process involves integrating and interpreting the implications of a variety of inputs from the software-related categories shown in figure 20.3.

Tip

For competitive analysis, B2G pricing can be much more transparent than B2B pricing. For example, some competitors may publish government price lists (e.g., GSA Price List). Governments also commonly provide competitive details in post-contract-award summaries as well as within bid protests (US GAO, 2019).

Product management teams will need to spend adequate time to gather, discuss, and interpret strategic insights and determine how these impact the short-, medium-, and long-term go-to-market pricing, customer, and product strategies. From a pricing

- Objective measures
- Customer perceptions
- Value proposition and differentiation
- Market and industry analysis
- Competitive analysis
- Segmentation analysis
- Roadmap strategy
- Innovation strategy
- Channel and channel partner strategy
- Third-party partnerships strategy

Figure 20.3. Software strategic analysis categories.

and offer-design perspective, this strategic analysis should be documented into a set of *guiding principles* that acts as a vision when designing and selecting optimal offer structures.

Price-value analysis (5,000-foot view)

VBP is defined as setting prices primarily based on the customer's perceived or estimated value of a product or service rather than on the cost of the product or historical prices. Linking price with value can be achieved using two useful software pricing tools: (a) *economic value analysis* and (b) *price-value tradeoff analysis*. These tools will help establish the higher-level price positioning views that will serve as the price targets for the underlying roll-up of the price structure (packaging, metrics, and tiers).

Economic value analysis. This analysis articulates value in terms of client financial improvements as a result of using the software solution—this can include revenue growth, cost savings, cash-flow improvement, and/or mitigation of financial risk. Software is then priced in the context of those financial benefits: "Similar-size clients with similar challenges have achieved savings of over $1 million per year using our software. At our price of $150,000 per year, you're still getting an 85 percent discount off the worth of the product."

Tip

A useful starting point for assessing economic value is to understand all the relevant client (and user) KPIs, assess how the software impacts those KPIs, and link those KPI changes with a financial impact. Applying the client's KPIs also "talks their language" and helps to better link your solution with their direct challenges and performance measures.

A general rule of thumb is to price in the context of 15 to 25 percent of the economic value. The more confidence a client has in being able to achieve these results (i.e., backed by case studies and client references), the more likely they will have confidence in your pricing strategy. Note that competition isn't factored into this type of analysis, which is more applicable within *price-value tradeoff analysis*. In this regard, *economic value analysis* is useful in those cases for establishing ceiling prices, opening offers, or determining pricing for new innovation.

Price-value tradeoff analysis. This tool is particularly useful not only for linking the price and value relationship but also for exploring the client buying-decision drivers and how your software offering compares with the next best alternative; next best alternatives can include competition, other products within your portfolio (cannibalization), or even a client's deciding to develop an in-house solution. This analysis seeks to quantify both price and value using a weighted scoring approach, factoring in the tradeoff that a segment makes between price and value.

One major advantage to using this tool for B2G software is that it also mirrors the scoring approach commonly used by government procurement arms as part of their RFP assessment to determine a contract award (figure 20.4).

In figure 20.4, a scoring approach is applied to quantify price, value, and an overall total. The chart highlights how differences in scores and tradeoff between price and value (i.e., price sensitivity) drive different client buying decisions.

Tip

Myth: "Lowest price wins the bid." Such is not the case for best-value tradeoff tenders (versus "low-priced, technically acceptable" [LPTA] tenders). In such cases, governments are

| | Price | Value | Price Score | Value Score | Price Sensitivity (Price:Value Weighting) | | | |
					Low 20:80 Total Score[2]	Moderate 30:70 Total Score	High 40:60 Total Score	LPTA[1] 100:0 Total Score
Software company A	$1,530,000	Good	6.2	6.4	6.4	6.3	6.3	6.2
Software company B	$1,210,000	Acceptable	6.7	5.0	5.3	5.6	5.7	6.7
Software company C	$943,000	Marginal	7.5	4.8	5.3	5.6	5.9	7.5
Software company D	$2,450,000	Outstanding	5.2	6.9	6.6	6.4	6.2	5.2

▇ = most likely selected vendor (highest total score)

1 Low-priced, technically acceptable (LPTA) bid contract. So long as vendors meet a minimum technical requirement, a decision is based solely on price.

2 Total score calculated as price score × price weighting + value score × value weighting (for example, 7.5 × 0.20 + 8.0 × 0.80 = 7.9 total score).

Figure 20.4. Price-value tradeoff analysis.

more concerned with obtaining superior technical capability than with making an award to the lowest-priced offer (Watson, 2015). Understand what type of government bid has been issued and, where possible, the underlying price and value scoring evaluation criteria (figure 20.5).

As a best practice, product management teams need to integrate the price-value analysis tool as (a) part of their bid-pricing evaluation process, and (b) part of their strategic planning cycle—whereby product teams *conduct price-value analysis for each market segment* (different segments have different value perceptions, price sensitivities, and product requirements). Analysis outcomes from the tool can be used to assess short-term tactics ("How can we compete with what we have today?") as well as longer-term product development investments and pricing improvements ("Which attributes require our highest investment and priority to capture future monetization upside and RFP wins?").

Understanding your price positioning using both *economic value analysis* and the *price-value tradeoff analysis* helps to create a target range for the next pricing phase: *packaging, metrics, and tiers.*

Packaging, metrics, and tiers (500-foot view)

This process focuses on creating well-defined pricing and offer structures that target key segments while also linking to the price positioning defined in the earlier exercises. It's an opportunity for product teams to build new, or to realign current, price lists whereby some components may be published externally (e.g., GSA Price Lists) or used entirely for internal price reference purposes only.

		Scoring			
Technical Merit	Weighting	Software Company A	Software Company B	Software Company C	Software Company D
1 Technical and functional					
Software solution	25%	4.3	4.0	3.6	5.8
Implementation	10%	8.1	7.0	6.0	8.1
Hosting	10%	8.1	6.0	5.0	8.1
2 Experience and past performance					
Organization experience	10%	7.5	3.0	4.0	7.5
Past performance	10%	5.6	4.0	5.0	7.5
3 Management approach					
Approach	5%	6.7	5.0	6.0	6.7
Personnel	5%	9.0	6.0	5.0	4.5
Oral Presentation and Solutions Demonstration					
1 Oral presentation	5%	8.0	7.0	4.0	8.0
2 Solution demonstration					
Business scenarios	5%	6.0	5.0	6.0	8.0
Ability to satisfy goals	5%	6.0	6.0	4.0	6.0
Navigation and ease of use	5%	6.0	6.0	8.0	8.0
Effectiveness of team	5%	6.0	4.0	4.0	6.0
Total value score (100%)	**100%**	**6.4**	**5.0**	**4.8**	**6.9**

Figure 20.5. Price-value tradeoff analysis: Procurement team "value scores."

Tip

Myth: "B2G low-volume, high-revenue deals don't need a price list." Even an internal price list in these circumstances helps to avoid guesswork on willingness-to-pay and builds confidence that a well-researched pricing strategy is strongly linked to bid-winning outcomes that are optimized based on the software "value story." Price lists can also help standardize architecture deployments and monetize those cases outside a typical deployment (e.g., 20 integrations to other systems vs. 250 integrations).

Packaging. Similar to restaurant menus, software can be sold via an à-la-carte approach or more as a bundling approach—these bundles can be used to target different segments with differing needs (value) and differing price sensitivities.

It will be important to assess which package best aligns with the original guiding principles as defined with the strategy phase. Functional packages (see figure 20.6), for example, may be more preferred in those cases where governments integrate a mixture of different vendors into a larger system—a common occurrence with large ERPs with differing functions including finance, payroll, HR, and cash management. In this case, applying a modular approach where a client must first purchase a baseline core system before purchasing the ERP module could put a software firm at a disadvantage over a firm that sells a software component as a functional standalone offer. Alternatively, modular packages may prove more beneficial during a mature life-cycle phase that enables monetizing a legacy client base with new innovations and feature sets.

Key questions to ask when evaluating software packaging structures:

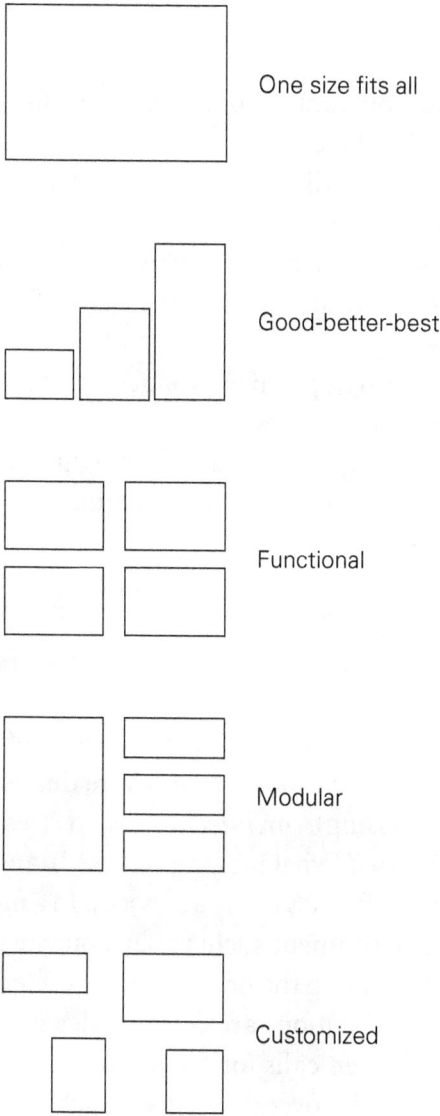

One size fits all

Good-better-best

Functional

Modular

Customized

Figure 20.6. Software packaging types. Note that packaging can also be a hybrid mixture of the above (e.g., good-better-best can be applied within functional and modular package offers).

- Does the packaging target desired segments as defined within the strategy phase?
- How does your competition package their offer? What is the advantage/disadvantage?
- Will your packaging differ between government (B2G) and commercial (B2B) offers?
- Can your packaging benefit from using a hybrid approach for those described in figure 20.6 (e.g., functional with good-better-best)?
- Does your packaging optimize product mix and new monetization (upsell) opportunities?
- Does your packaging allow you to highlight your key market differentiation? (Or do you need to unbundle this component and price/package separately?)
- To what extent will you allow for customization (vs. configuration) in your packages?

Metrics. A software metric is a standard unit of measure that links a fee structure to four possible software dimensions: *access-based* (who is accessing), *architecture-based* (resources being accessed), *content-based* (what is being accessed), and *usage-based* (how much and how often it's being accessed). In a more simplistic software pricing environment such as B2C, one metric can serve as the basis for determining the pricing strategy (e.g., *per-user* fee). However, where B2G solutions are concerned, a greater degree of solution complexity often calls for the use of multiple underlying metrics to determine the overall license or subscription fee. The metric dimensions outlined in figure 20.7 include the most commonly used metrics in B2G.

Access-Based	Architecture-Based	Content-Based	Usage-Based
Platform fees • Platform access fee • Platform (non-production/test) • Regional fees • Localization fee **User fees** • Named user • Named user (by profile) • Named user (limited) • Concurrent user • Mobile user	**Architecture fees** • Number of interfaces/ interface type • Server license • Console license • Appliance license • Per instance fee • Per connection/node • Storage (ECM)	**Workflow** • Workflow type 1 • Workflow type 2 • Workflow type 3 … **Advanced features** • Advanced reports • Analytic modules • AI features • Enhanced data/ content **Customization** • Custom reports • Custom dashboards • Custom pages	**Per usage** • Per transaction • Per reports accessed • Per message (APIs) • Per batch job vs. on-demand **Usage ranges** (such as between X and Y volumes) • Transaction ranges • Reports accessed ranges **Proxy for usage** • Company size (revenue) • Number of FTEs • Budget size • Number of customers • Number of accounts • Number of branches

Figure 20.7. Software metric types and examples.

Tip

Architecture-based metrics can be useful in a price list where clients desire an environment outside your standard deployment configuration (similar in concept to overage fees). For example, your base pricing may include up to 20 integrations; additional integrations could be charged a fee of +$X to the overall annual subscription fee.

"Which metrics are the best metrics for my software?" There's no silver-bullet answer—but there is a process for evaluating the options. Every B2G software is unique and requires an assessment to evaluate potential options while weighing the respective pros and con. During this metric evaluation phase, product teams can ask the following questions to help select the most ideal option for their software:

- Does the metric represent value delivered?
- Does it provide incremental monetization opportunities?
- Is it overly complex (black box)? Alternatively, is it overly simple (1 metric = suboptimal)
- Is it sellable and well understood by your client?
- Can it be measured and billed? (Or does it require enhancements to your billing system?)
- Does it mitigate any unforeseen risks (in particular, recover underlying third-party license costs)?
- Is it scalable? (Does your pricing model grow as your client grows?)
- How will these metrics change based on delivery model type? (on-premise vs. SaaS)

Tiering. Tiering is a methodology that creates variation in pricing and/or packaging value that targets a defined client segment. These clients can vary in size (small, medium, large), usage volumes (low to high), requirement needs (low to high features), or price sensitivity. For example, tiering can include *price-volume discounts* where a discounted *per-fee* metric is applied for larger overall volumes. Or, alternatively, a good-better-best packaging format that increases a package's content and features alongside respective increases in pricing.

- **Volume discounts.** In any B2B or B2G sales environment, it's common practice to discount per-unit prices with increasing volumes. Volume discounts can provide significant guidance during the sales negotiation process, but they can also be a major source of margin leakage when applied suboptimally. A starting point for determining volume discounts is to understand where you want to price your smallest client tier, and where you want to price your largest client tier; this helps establish your overall discount slope across tiers.

Tip

Be mindful of excessive "discounting on top of discounting," meaning, providing a volume discount price structure that is even further discounted via aggressive sales negotiation. A best-practice approach involves establishing a well-structured volume discount structure in alignment with designing the allowable sales discount range for each tier.

- **Tiering packaging value (good-better-best, or G-B-B).** A G-B-B tiering approach serves as both a packaging type and a tiering methodology. G-B-B can address several strategies, including offensive plays aimed at generating new growth and revenue, defensive plays meant to counter or forestall moves by competitors, and behavioral plays that draw on principles of consumer psychology, whatever the competitive landscape (Mohammed, 2018). Examples include applying a low-priced "good" offer to make a product accessible to more customers; applying a premium-priced "best" offer (a decoy) to drive buyer psychology that shifts an incremental mix volume from low-end buyers ("good") to a middle offering ("better"); or applying a "low-hanging fruit" tier to encourage upsell with current clients to a more value-enriched offering.

- **Price levels.** Price levels are defined categories of client segments that receive differences in pricing. For example, a software firm selling to municipal governments might create six price levels, each consisting of ranges of number of inhabitants (Level A = 1 to 25,000; Level B = 25,001 to 50,000; etc). Price levels should contain a relevant mix of clients—having too many price levels can lead to margin leakage and irrelevant discounts from one band to the next. In many cases, price levels act as a proxy for usage—consider instead applying a direct measure of usage that is a better reflection of value delivered (see "Metrics").

Throughout tiering design, it will be important to evaluate this from two views: the volume-discounted list price for each tier (opening position) and the allowable net price floor for each tier (maximum allowable sales discounted price). Especially for software firms selling to both B2G and B2B, it's critical to manage any most-favored customer (MFC) government contract clauses; these clauses seek to ensure that the contracting authority receives pricing at least as favorable as customers making similar purchases

(Ettinger & Altman, 2014)—violating this results in significant consequences.

Financial analysis (ground level)

The last process within the offer-design phase involves conducting profitability analysis and price stress testing to determine breaking points and to rework requirements in pricing structures. This can involve a few analytic approaches including *mock deal profitability analysis* and *business case* development.

Mock deal profitability analysis. Mock deal analysis should be conducted across small, medium, large, and super-sized client-type profiles. Finance teams can help link these models with direct and indirect cost allocation assumptions. Be sure to test extremes for possible metric outcomes that can "break" a pricing structure. In other cases, mock deals can also show low or negative profitability to smaller client sizes, which identifies a need to rework an offer, the respective volume curve, or to reevaluate a more cost-effective product strategy (e.g., target multitenant SaaS to small client sizes, and single-tenant enterprise SaaS to the largest client sizes).

Business case. Once a pricing strategy is determined, this can then be linked with annual volume assumptions (e.g., pipeline) and annual costs to develop a year-over-year business case view. In particular for those organizations undergoing major transformations (e.g., on-premise to SaaS), it may be important to highlight and get executive alignment in those cases where there are short-term losses in exchange for future profitability. Ultimately, the business case becomes the company's best financial estimate that links the overall strategy with the proposed software pricing and offer structures.

Implications of B2G pricing

- **Pricing is a journey...and pricing is a process.** By applying the Software Pricing Framework, teams can follow a series of end-to-end processes for designing value-based segmented offer structures, endowing sales teams with the ability to sell the software "value story" (and link this to pricing) and driving best-in-class execution across the organization. Viewing pricing as a process ultimately ensures that an adequate time and rigor are devoted to developing offer structures that optimize outcomes and drive to company objectives.

- **SaaS and subscription revenue models have changed the game for B2G.** More government entities are becoming open to SaaS over traditional on-premise solutions; this provides an opportunity for software firms to pursue more modernized revenue models while creating new product roadmaps. Ensure that your pricing evaluation occurs before SaaS product development, and link pricing initiatives to any larger company-wide transformation initiatives.

- **Focus on developing the right packages, for the right clients, at the right price.** Developing the right value-based packaging, metrics, and tiers is key to achieving your stated objectives. Ample time should be spent evaluating various options as well as their pros and cons. Tie-in with financial analysis views, and vet offers internally to determine a need for rework.

- **Apply best practices in B2G software contracting.** Clearly articulate the software's one-time fees, recurring (subscription) fees, pricing schedules, overages, and renewal options. Using best practices in software contracting sets the stage for continued revenue growth (grow as your clients grow), predetermines price increases, and simplifies the renewal process.

- **Know thy bid-tender type.** B2G software clients are often less certain about requirements and, as such, typically issue *best-value tradeoff* bids rather than *low-priced, technically acceptable* (LPTAs) bids—meaning, governments are more concerned with obtaining superior technical capability (value) than making an award to the lowest-priced offer.

- **Become masters of replicating the procurement vendor-selection scoring process.** Pricing tools not only can help you understand price positioning and respective links between price and value; they can also be used to mimic a procurement team's vendor-selection scoring process. Know when to apply premium pricing…and when to be more competitive.

- **Have an up-to-date and frequently assessed price list…even if for internal purposes only.** A price list becomes your company's official document that signals to sales teams and executives that due diligence has been performed to ensure that the pricing strategy and structures are value-based, competitive, and optimized. Price lists also considerably decrease the time that product and sales teams spend evaluating bid-pricing scenarios.

- **Highlight your differentiation in your pricing and packaging.** Avoid muting your differentiation within a larger software package—in some cases this could involve unbundling and creating a premium-priced package specific to your differentiation.

Conclusion

Pricing is a journey, and pricing is a process. With a solid foundational understanding of B2G industry pricing practices, and by adopting processes and tools defined within the Software Pricing Framework, your organization can embark on their journey toward developing and implementing optimal value-based and segmented offer structures that not only compete in the market place but also grow your client base while delivering material improvements to your organization's revenue and profitability performance.

References

Blum, A., & Mansour, Y. (2018). On price versus quality. In Anna R. Karlin (Ed.), *9th Innovations in Theoretical Computer Science conference (ITCS 2018)* (pp. 1–12). Dagstuhl, Germany: Schloss Dagstuhl—Leibniz-Zentrum fuer Informatik.

Eriksson, U. (2016, May 19). *The A to Z guide to software testing processes.* Retrieved from https://reqtest.com/testing-blog/the-a-to-z-guide-to-the-software-testing-process/

Ettinger, M. S., & Altman, J. C. (2014). Compliance with Most Favored Nation clauses: Giving meaning to ambiguous terms while avoiding False Claim Act allegations. *Notre Dame Law Review Online, 90*(1), Article 1.

Gale, B., & Swire, D. (2012). Implementing strategic B2B pricing: Constructing value benchmarks. *Journal of Revenue and Pricing Management, 11,* 40–53.

Hogan, J., & Nagle, T. (2005). *What is strategic pricing?* Monitor Group.

International Organization for Standardization. (2006). *Software engineering—Software life cycle processes—Maintenance* (2nd ed.). Retrieved from https://www.iso.org/standard/39064.html

ISPMA. (2019). *Software product management framework.* Retrieved from https://ispma.org/body-of-knowledge/

Miller, S. (2019). The do's and don'ts of pricing maintenance and support. *Miller Advisors,* October 30. Retrieved from https://www.miller-advisors.com/post/the-dos-and-donts-of-pricing-maintenance-and-support

Mohammed, R. (2018). The good-better-best approach to pricing. *Harvard Business Review,* September–October. Retrieved from https://hbr.org/2018/09/the-good-better-best-approach-to-pricing

US Government Accountability Office. (2019). *Bid protests, appropriations law, & other legal work.* Retrieved from https://www.gao.gov/legal/

US Department of Justice, Office of Public Affairs. (2015, June 30). VMWare and Carahsoft agree to pay $75.5 million to settle claims that they concealed commercial pricing and overcharged the government. Retrieved from https://www.justice.gov/opa/pr/vmware-and-carahsoft-agree-pay-755-million-settle-claims-they-concealed-commercial-pricing

US Department of Justice, Office of Public Affairs (2019, May 13). Informatica agrees to pay $21.57 million for alleged false claims caused by its commercial pricing disclosures. Retrieved from https://www.justice.gov/opa/pr/informatica-agrees-pay-2157-million-alleged-false-claims-caused-its-commercial-pricing

Watson, K. (2015). *LPTA versus tradeoff: How procurement methods can impact contract performance.* Monterey, CA: Naval Postgraduate School.

The author

Scott Miller is the founder of Miller Advisors (www.miller -advisors.com), a pricing, monetization, and offer-design consulting firm with a specialty in B2B and B2G software. He is also a speaker and instructor on best pricing practices with the Professional Pricing Society (PPS) and the International Software Product Management Association (ISPMA), bringing over 15 years of experience from a variety of consulting and global corporate pricing roles. Scott is also a Chartered Professional Accountant (CPA) and a Certified Management Accountant (CMA).

Key Notes

Key Actions

_____

_____

_____

_____

_____

_____

_____

_____

_____

_____

_____

_____

_____

Interview with an Expert **21**

Emmanuel Poidevin, CEO of e-Attestations.com

Stephan   Emmanuel, thanks for speaking with me today. Before we get started with the discussion, it will be interesting for our readers to understand your background and your experience in working with government agencies.

Emmanuel Well, I'm an entrepreneur. I'm the owner and founder of a software company called e-Attestations.com. We work in the compliance management field across Europe. Mainly my job is to ensure that the suppliers or the economic operators fulfill their requirements in terms of public procurement or business profit that goes through the supply chain. I'm also an expert for the European Commission. I've been working for the European Commission since 2010, on several programs. The first was how to enable and cut the red tape and the administrative burden regarding public procurement. And this work was finished with the 2014 regulation that spread across Europe, which has changed the rules in European procurement. We've been implementing a lot of interoperability and a common framework for all the companies and all the public authorities across Europe, enabling all of them to exchange data. And the purpose was to give a broader access, especially for the SMEs (small and medium enterprises), to the public procurement markets.

Stephan   That's interesting. You've been very involved with the simplification of procurement processes right across the EU.

Emmanuel   Exactly. Yes.

Stephan   Is that a general trend that you see in Europe?

Emmanuel   It is. Especially in Europe.

Stephan   It will make it easy for companies to have access to opportunities, contracts?

Emmanuel   Yes. The public procurement market in Europe is huge. It's a goal at both the European level and for every country within the EU. For instance, I work in France, and it's very important to reinforce the role and the access for the SMEs to public procurement. It's a way to make sure that all economic products, enterprises, are getting some proper opportunity and access to business, and especially within the European internal market.

Stephan   Good, good. When you mentioned SMEs, does that include all the startups and all these companies that are radical business models?

Emmanuel Actually, yes. I should have begun with the proper definition of the SMEs. What we call small and middle-sized enterprises depends on four different aspects. The annual turnover, the number of employees, the fact that there are subsidiaries or that they belong to subsidiaries of a larger company, and also some key figures.

Stephan When you mentioned Europe as a federal agency for these countries, trying to simplify and make it accessible for SMEs in general, given the equitable access to opportunities, do they have any specific rules or specific guidelines on how to price for them, or is that included in there—or is pricing not in there?

Emmanuel Actually pricing was not specifically included. It's a business consideration that was not taken as part of what we have to deliver. The first one was a unified framework that enabled any company in Europe to access any governance or public authority across Europe. Meaning that, for instance, I'm a French company; it's easy for me to fulfill the requirements and to get access to the German market, for instance. The main framework offers interoperability and standards so that all the governments and public authorities can use the same framework.

Stephan Yes. But it's important to understand that it didn't force a pricing methodology or a way of pricing.

Emmanuel Not at all.

Stephan Low-price compliant or best price wins.

Emmanuel Well, it's an aspect of the public procurement itself. It means that in public procurement, you have to avoid what's called unfair or predatory pricing when prices that are abnormally too low are excluded from the public procurement process.

Stephan   Okay. But I know in Europe typically we have, versus other regions in the world, we have more of a fairness, equitable position on price to make sure there's even distribution and it's fairer. Would you agree with these statements?

Emmanuel   Yes. True. While I'm not very used to bidding in India or in East Asia, Eastern Asia, it's true that here all the people have the same structure to answer to. You really can compare one pricing with another because they try to get as much of the total cost approach so that you can really compare pricing from one proposal to the next.

Stephan   That's interesting. There's a myth that when dealing with the government or a government agency, in general, they're not open to a new business model or a new pricing model. I'm referring here maybe to subscription pricing, to SaaS, to outcome-based pricing. Do you see that? What's your view on that? Do you see that as a real myth, or is it just fiction?

Emmanuel   No. First, in talking about agencies, the public sector is not just one entity. They're very different actors. For instance, if you're thinking about the town you live in or a public hospital or a large public transportation company or the government itself, they're not made the same. Some are very keen on innovation. They like innovation and they want to support local startups that can bring innovation to citizens or to public services. They're trying to do their best to encourage innovation, meaning startups, for instance. Thus, they've established some new frameworks dedicated to making innovation easier and faster. For instance, you can have a specific process dedicated to innovation that enables the startups to get a first contract when you are below 100,000 euros. It gives faster and easier access to public procurement through an innovation framework.

Stephan When they consider these innovative business models, are they able to compare apples to apples? Let's say they buy software with a perpetual license versus software with a subscription pricing model. Do they ask for help and support to understand the apples to apples?

Emmanuel Well, it's still a tough job for them because in contracting with the public sector they're not able to fully participate in the subscription economy. You must transform your pricing subscription into a yearly or a three-year contract. The forever contract doesn't exist in public procurement. You cannot get forever. There's a beginning and there's an end, so basically what we do is transform all subscription models into a yearly contract or a three-year contract. It cannot be the same framework. For them it's also tough to compare, let's say, the old licensing and service economy with a subscription offer. Today what they're trying more and more is to consider the total cost of ownership for a set period between a traditional offer and a recurring offer. But they need help, and we're here to provide that.

Stephan That's interesting. How did that come about? Is it because they read about TCO or is it because the suppliers are training them?

Emmanuel There are two different trends. The first is that public procurement is a different process than buying. They're not buyers. Public procurement is much more legal. It used to be run by lawyers focusing on the regulations, and now they're hiring people that come from professional and private procurement. They changed the way they design their contracting process to include more procurement-like dimensions using professional agents who come with their methodology and their skills. You have many people from the private sector in procurement that have been hired by the public sector.

Stephan They bring that experience—

Emmanuel That's how they change.

Stephan And then they transform internally.

Emmanuel Exactly.

Stephan Do you think these procurement methods will eventually accept the subscription model?

Emmanuel There is much work on this, and we were exchanging with them quite often. They're willing to change, but everything in the public sector relies on budgeting. In budgeting, it depends very much on a yearly contract. They're not used to buying for a month or per use or stuff like that. Right now in Europe, you must transform your pricing model into a yearly contract, which could look like a bit like a yearly subscription at the end of the day. That's what we do. The problem is that you must be able to give a price for several years. They aren't that flexible in adjustment.

Stephan It sounds you're saying that there's a willingness to do this from both sides: from the supplier and the procurement side, there's a willingness to adapt and meet in the middle.

Emmanuel True. Also, many public entities are buying centrally, relying on central purchasing bodies that are more and more efficient to run. I would say the average contract—for instance, if you want to contract with Microsoft—in the old days every contracting authority had to get this specific contract. Right now you have a central purchasing body that's able to have one contract framework for software and that other contracting authorities can reuse for their own needs.

Stephan Okay. Then it reduces the complexity and the access, right?

Emmanuel Exactly.

Stephan Maybe this is another myth that we're less aware of because we look at the public sector and we all think it's very complex and it's all red tape and so bureaucratic. And maybe for a startup it seems an impossible task, right? Do you think that's changing?

Emmanuel It is. It is. It is. And that's what I went through when I started my business: I didn't even think about the public sector because I had no idea. It was a totally different world. And then through an innovation meeting, I met some people from the public sector that were very interested in what we had to offer as a service, and then they helped us build the proposition that would fit the legal requirements. My advice is always to consider them as a prospect. I mean, if your service can be useful to them, then you can consider them a prospect and then be able to contract with them. First, I would advise you to go as a subcontractor, as part of another bigger project or opportunity. Doing this with a public entity as a subcontractor means that you don't have to do all the legal stuff because you're just a part of the main contract. And then you get used to it and then you can start thinking about contracting directly if you want. That's how I started.

Stephan   Talk to me about the scaling process. Is it a different scaling process? Usually we read about startups, about explosive growth in the commercial world, in B2B and B2C. Should entrepreneurs expect different scaling processes in the public sector?

Emmanuel I know this will sound weird, but it's easier to scale in the public than in the private sector. Let me explain why. If you manage to get a first contract with, let's say, a middle-sized city and the contract is running well, then you can go to all the other middle-sized cities that are not willing to take risk. If you manage to do well for one, they'll feel comfortable working with you. If you've got one, then you can have a hundred, because you'll have shown that you can do that—that the client is satisfied—and then the others will come.

Stephan   Wow. There's no need, maybe, for every B2B account to do a pilot, a short pilot. Are you saying that?

Emmanuel Exactly. Because you just have to show that you're already working for such a contract or for such a public body. And then you can use them as referrals. These entities will call each other because they trust each other, and they have the same characteristics and requirements. You don't have to do the same process all the time. If you've got one, you can get more.

Stephan It's interesting for the millennials reading this book, reading this chapter; most of these new generations, they want to be entrepreneurs. They may have a perception that all public agents or public actors are middle-aged, wearing gray suits and sitting in an office typing and stamping documents. This is a traditional view that they are "bureaucrats."

Emmanuel Old-fashioned.

Stephan Yes. And now you're telling me that these public procurement agents are sitting in innovation sessions and that they want to hear from startups, and they want to embrace new value propositions. That's a different world. What do you tell these new entrepreneurs? How do you connect in this public community?

Emmanuel You have to connect with people. When you meet people, they're not from the public sector or the private sector. They're just people. And people, even in the public sector, are very used to using software in their everyday lives. They also have smartphones. They're not that much older than those in the private sector and the entrepreneurs. They could be of the same generation and are very used in their everyday lives to having access to services online or SaaS or whatever. Connecting with people and showing the value of your offer and services is easy when you just meet someone. And the second step is, once you're sure that your service is relevant for or of interest to the people in front of you, you build a way to work together.

Many services that are available fit very well with the public sector. I used to say to people that the private sector doesn't exist, the public sector doesn't exist. You and I, when we meet each other, we're not in the private sector club, right? If I were working for a public company, we would have the same exchange as people. People in the public sector are seeing us, the private sector, as a different world, which is not the case. We have the same everyday lives, and in our everyday lives we use many innovative services that have been delivered by startups. Let me give you an example of a very successful service company. When you want to get an appointment with a doctor, you use your cellphone with an application like Doctolib. It began with the private sector. Then, hospitals from the public sector began using the system, and now the same application is used by a public hospital or for a private doctor. It's the same. The product is the same. You don't have to change your product because you're in the public sector. Maybe you'll have to adapt a little bit, but most of the time we're going to sell to the public sector, and you don't need to change your product or service that much.

Stephan   That's very interesting on the technical side, on the application side, on the user design side. But when you sell, when you design or go to market for your startup, did you have to have a public strategy versus a private strategy, with different pricing models and different go-to-markets?

Emmanuel Yes. And the contracting time is longer in the public sector. That's still true. But you'll keep the customer longer as you experience less churn. You'll have less churn because the contracting process is longer and because they want to make sure that your solution matches their requirements. But then, as you get more accustomed to, more involved with them, you keep them longer. The current contracting time is a bit longer, and your strategy should include a one-year time frame to get everything in place. One year after the first meeting we can sell because they have to put that in their internal budget. In the private sector, you don't have that. We sell usually between three months and six months. Then the pricing structure is just a mapping between what you would sell for a year or three-year contract. It's just transforming the subscription into a yearly or three-year contract.

Stephan   What you said before about the willingness of some public sectors is to accept the TCO, right? To understand the total cost of ownership. Are you able to capture good value for the differentiation of your software solution because of that? There's also sometimes a myth that you really must reduce your price for the private sector: we are not going to accept the value. But I interpret what you said to mean that they do accept the value in a way.

Emmanuel True. It's difficult to generalize, but I would say that most of the time we get better value in the public sector. That's because they're studying your process and your solutions, and they make sure that they match their requirements. In our case, we face public agents that want to study the total cost of ownership, and they're interested in value for money in the whole package. So our customers are more diligent and very interested in innovations that produce savings and efficiency. I can't say that this is the case for all public procurement. In the private sector, it's try, learn, and then grow. People like to have a trial period, a pilot, or a proof of concept. After that you might grow over time. The public sector, because of their structure in procurement, already begins with a bigger view of your services. It's a bit different. The strategy is different. For us, I have two business plans.

Stephan That's great insight. What are your top three recommendations for startups to succeed in the public space?

Emmanuel First, meet them. Meet them. I mean, physically go to them, knock on that door, and go to them before thinking about a contract: instead, think about interest and services. Second, listen to them. It's a bit different in terms of sales and marketing. In the private world, we used to say that we have the best solution and the best price for value. We talked about competition and our advantages. In the public sector, you go, you present your services, and then they will rephrase it to their world. They will give you the key to the treasure and will explain the value for them. It's true that this was unexpected. Sometimes the value you create for them is not the same value you might communicate in the private sector. They don't have the same keys as in the private sector.

In the private sector, you might have better pricing, a better process, better savings with fewer people involved, better quality, and so forth. In the public sector, most of the time they will come back to you with different keys to value and you must listen to their words. How do they see you? The wording is different. The marketing is different. First, meet the people and then listen to what they say. Try to understand the value they create for the public sector. Third, don't think big. Don't think big. Start and learn.

Stephan   It's a little bit of the land and expand. Land first, listen, and then adapt and expand.

Emmanuel   Exactly. But once you've got your first proof of concept with one entity, then think big and go for all the same entities in the same segment.

Stephan   Great. On the other hand, what were the rookie mistakes that you wouldn't make in front of public sector employees?

Emmanuel   Some I've done myself. First—you'll find it silly. First is to present a value proposition that focuses on time savings for public employees or head-count reduction. In the public sector, they're not hiring and firing. If you present your solution to people and you say, "Well, you will need fewer people to do the same thing," you might be kicked out. People are there and you've got to employ them. That's the first rookie mistake. Second is to begin with a lower price and try to get it higher, because it will never happen. You've got to start high and then lower your price, but start with the best value and then negotiate. It's the opposite way around. You can't change the price during the contract. So you're stuck with your initial pricing. Another mistake is to propose a proof of concept right off the bat. It's better to pursue a specific contract or opportunity and to demonstrate the real value you deliver in production. So don't run for proof of concept, because there are people in the public sector that can spend their whole time doing proof of concepts that will never become businesses. You must approach the public sector in full business mode. You are here to sell what you deliver, not to switch to a project mode.

Stephan So it's a different speed of doing business. We all understand that. The first time you'd present your solution, would you use your proof of concepts and your success stories from the private world, and show them case studies?

Emmanuel Exactly. They're very pragmatic. They want to know what you deliver, and they aren't keen on risk. The public sector doesn't want to take risks. If you go with a proof of concept, it's going to be a tough one. But if you show that you already deliver a reliable service in the private sector with a private entity, then they will just consider it and say: "Okay, can we use it for our own needs?" The buyers in the public sector want to take no risks. The most important thing for them is not to have problems during a contract.

Stephan Your own company has been doing well, right? What are the grand plans for your business in the public sector? Expand? What's your strategy for the future?

Emmanuel It's to continue to spread. We're very strong in our local market, but we've focused on 30 percent growth in the internal European market. The plan is to go for the whole European market. That's the next big thing for us. We also want to focus on three public verticals: public transportation systems, energy, and housing authorities. All three have many requirements for compliance.

Stephan Thank you for sharing your wealth of insights and your experience. I encourage all readers to visit www.e-attestations.com and to find out more about their value proposition.

The author

Emmanuel Poidevin is the founder and CEO of e-Attestations. com, located in Paris, France, and serving the interests of customers across Europe. Emmanuel is a serial entrepreneur and an expert in working with the European procurement process. He has served for almost six years as an expert to the European Commission on the topic of electronics procurement. He has participated in the design and implementation of specific procurement norms and regulations and has published numerous papers on the topic. He holds a management degree from University of Paris Panthéon-Sorbonne and several certificates in the areas of data compliance, data privacy, and economics. He can be reached through LinkedIn or at www.e-attestations.com/nous-contacter2.

Key Notes

_____

_____

_____

_____

_____

_____

Key Actions

_____

_____

_____

_____

_____

_____

22

12 Reasons Why Subscription Business Models Will Penetrate the B2G World

Michael Mansard, Zuora

T HE SUBSCRIPTION ECONOMY IS taking the business
world by storm. Gartner's Digital Commerce State of the
Union survey reports that 70 percent of companies have deployed,
or are considering deploying, a subscription business model, and
Zuora's Subscription Economy Index (SEI) finds that subscription
businesses are growing revenues approximately five times faster
than S&P 500 Index company revenues. There are thousands of
B2C companies and startups fully operating according to a subscription model and selling to millions of customers. Some consumer markets (news media, video streaming, music, for example)

have adopted this business model as a new normal. For many traditional B2C firms, it has offered new life to their declining product sales. In the B2B and industrial world, there are more and more signs that the same phenomenon is happening. Large organizations (Siemens, Honeywell, Saint-Gobain, Thales, ABB, and more) have launched subscription-based offers to complement and monetize their hardware or product offers or have launched independent startups focused on providing innovative, new connected products and services. Given the pure scope of the subscription economy, a natural question follows: Will subscription business and pricing models enter the B2G sector? If yes, when will they be more prevalent? It's just a question of time before the public sector embraces consumption-based models. Below are 12 reasons why the subscription economy tsunami will eventually consume the public space on a global scale.

1 **Public sector employees are consumers first and foremost, and they are well educated on how subscriptions work.** Most consumers have several subscriptions and use them in their daily lives. Zuora's End of Ownership survey, fielded among more than 13,000 adults across 12 countries, found that roughly 71 percent have subscription services, up from roughly half (53%) five years ago. Thus, the concept of a subscription and how it works is not foreign to them. Given the familiarity of subscription-based offers, the process of selecting and deploying a subscription-based product or service throughout a government institution would not present a significant disruption to its employees.

2 **Public entities, such as the European Union, are usually very keen on supporting equal access for small and medium businesses**, including technology startups, making it easier for these startups to bid for public contracts,

and they've worked closely with procurement agencies to help startups adjust their pricing. Monthly subscriptions can be annualized to increase predictability for public agencies and to respect budgeting requirements. Subscription recurring payments with higher frequency can also enable SMBs to better cope with working-capital and cash-flow impacts versus "in arrears" payment terms that could only be handled by larger companies with ampler treasury.

3 **Right now, in a context of geopolitical tensions and rising nationalism, budgets for military and border protection agencies are skyrocketing.** We're seeing a level of public debt reach unprecedented levels. This is not sustainable for the long term. Eventually, budget reduction and optimization will kick in. Faced with budget constraints and pressures, public agencies will be forced to reduce acquisition costs and to move from a pure CapEx model to a hybrid CapEx/OpEx or a pure OpEx model. They'll embrace much more flexible consumption models, such as pay-as-you-go or usage-based business models, to optimize OpEx budgets and minimize CapEx. This trend is beginning to hold true in emerging countries.

4 **Subscriptions are inherently flexible.** The experience from the B2C and B2B worlds is that agility, flexibility, and creativity are key to subscription success. There are, on average, four changes for a subscription each year. These include upgrades, add-ons, downgrades, and other changes throughout a subscription's life cycle. That number can be even higher depending on the business model. For example, Zoom Video Communications' CEO, Eric Yuan, recently stated that Zoom processes five changes to a subscription per month across their entire customer base. The implication is that subscription pricing levels and structures can be added to government

contracts. Monthly can be turned into annual. Usage-based pricing can be turned into prepaid packages. Pricing and marketing teams need to keep this in mind when responding to public RFPs.

5 **Many government entities have already been introduced to outsourcing models and outcome-based contracts.** In a way, they've been able to make drastic changes in their operational and procurement models. When outsourcing became a hot topic, many defense agencies outsourced supply-chain processes to third-party vendors and insisted on being paid on performance. Others have substituted the purchases of supporting assets by a usage business model. An example of this is the pay-by-the-hour business model that Thales UK offered the UN for surveillance drones. Technological enablers such as the Internet of Things, the cloud, or blockchain, for instance, also act as catalysts in such contracts. They promote transparent and fair performance measurement while expanding the fields of possibility in terms of use case or applications for outcome-based contracts.

6 **Diversified industrial groups with stakes in both the B2B and the B2G sectors have begun their transformation on the commercial side.** It's only a matter of time before this bleeds into the B2G world. Companies like Siemens, ABB, BEA, and others are well positioned to serve the energy, utilities, infrastructure, and transportation spaces. They have lasting relationships with cities, states, and national agencies. Looking at the enormous investments in smart cities, for example, it's essential to support the technological solutions with flexible and agile business models. The same can be said about 5G connectivity and smart airports!

7 **Competition among industrial players in the B2D world is intense.** For example, Lockheed Martin, General

Dynamics, Northrop Grumman, BAE, Raytheon, Thales. With more investments in digital transformation, new business models will emerge with a larger emphasis on service, software, and data monetization. These industrial actors want and need to educate defense agencies on the imperative to move away from legacy transactional models. One way to differentiate themselves is by offering disruptive business and pricing models that save these agencies millions. These industrial players also must take the risk of switching their business models in order to stop competing on price alone. To avoid the race to the bottom on price, they are changing the game with collaboration from the most progressive government agencies. The subscription model might not include the equipment—it may be focused on services, software, and support of the hardware, a good first step toward transitioning from hardware acquisition to hybrid consumption models. Zuora's SEI found that industrial organizations are exceeding S&P 500 industrial revenue growth rates by more than five times with a shift to digital services (26.0% vs. 5.0%).

8 **Government agencies can no longer use the excuses of confidentiality, cybersecurity, and sovereignty to avoid the adoption of cloud technology and SaaS cloud solutions.** For the past five years, technology, AI, and consulting firms have designed sovereign defense clouds that are secured and highly protected. The National Security Agency has moved most of the mission data that it collects, analyzes, and stores into a classified cloud computing environment known as the Intelligence Community GovCloud. The CIA has also moved to a private cloud. That opens the doors for subscriptions to SaaS solutions and apps. Secured and sovereign platforms are being launched allowing users to connect, transact, and learn.

9   **Large software companies have launched innovative subscription or usage-based pricing models
tailored to the unique requirements of the public
sector.** Take Microsoft, for example. The company designed
a specific solution called Microsoft 365 Government. They've
also adjusted their offers to meet country-specific requirements, such as Microsoft 365 Germany to match EU and
European Free Trade Agreement rules. Additionally, Microsoft offers unique solutions for education systems with Microsoft 365 Education. All are subscription-based offers. Adobe
has also made inroads into the public space. The Adobe Enterprise Term License Agreement (ETLA) is "a flexible buying
program designed to meet the needs of large agencies and
organizations." It enables agencies to "get budget predictability over a three-year term—with one annual payment due
on the same date each year" as well as "an Admin Console
and use of the Adobe Licensing Website for easy deployment,
compliance and management" so that "everyone at your government agency can gain access to the latest Adobe tools, apps
and services." The Adobe ETLA can be customized to fit the
specific needs of each department—with or without services
and storage. Bottom line: it might have taken years of preparation and certification, but it's possible to expand your SaaS
solution into the public space.

10 **Amazon Business, Alibaba, and the like are offering procurement platforms to government, state,
and municipal agencies, establishing strong relationships.** Procurement agents can subscribe to services and
deliver off-the-shelf products. For example, Amazon Business
offers category management, strategic sourcing initiatives,
automated reporting, and fast, free shipping on eligible items
with Business Prime. Amazon Business Plans start at just $179

per year for up to three users; they also offer a special dis-counted Enterprise price for public sector entities through the Amazon Public Sector Division. This enables companies like Amazon to progressively build relationships with the pub-lic sector's procurement departments. They could use those solutions as future platforms for growth by increasing their footprint through the cross-selling of other solutions—and address more and more of the public sector's core.

11 **FAAMG (Facebook, Amazon, Apple, Microsoft, and Google) are working with several governments around the world in the technology, cloud, and software areas.** PaaS (platform-as-a-service) and SaaS (software-as-a-service) models are part of their DNA. Because of their current organizational design and go-to-market struc-ture, these companies might not be able to offer on-premise solutions, legacy licensing, or pure hardware-based solu-tions. These firms are inevitable, and public agencies may have to adjust more quickly to be able to cooperate and invest with them. Recent large programs won by Microsoft (JEDI, HoloLens for Army) or Amazon (CIA) are proving that the FAAMG penetration will accelerate in the coming years, and might move progressively into more and more value-added contracts. Their innovative solutions and pricing/packaging strategies will also gradually influence buying/procurement behavior.

12 **Last but not least, governments around the world are digitizing their processes** and could begin mone-tizing those new services by leveraging monthly subscription and/or usage-based models (e.g., API monetization, recur-ring services fees). As a result, they will expect to consume their own services in a similar fashion. For example, the TSA Global Entry program allows frequent international flyers to

bypass some of the long checkpoints at immigration and customs through a subscription. The subscription is a five-year period at a low price of $100. You could call this a membership fee, but it's also a subscription price. Governments selling subscriptions…the circle is now complete!

Implications for B2G pricing

Subscription-based pricing, usage-based pricing, and outcome-based pricing will eventually be the new normal for public procurement. We're seeing the first evidence of that. Some public RFPs for software already require both perpetual and subscription pricing. The changes are being made slowly but surely to public procurement processes. Skeptics tend to say that public agencies will never embrace the subscription business model. My view is that there is nothing stopping technological evolutions, especially when paired with an even deeper business model revolution! With that, nothing will stop the subscription economy, which has grown more than 350 percent in the last 7.5 years according to Zuora's SEI. I recommend that marketers in the public world get ready to join the push to change the government mindset. The sooner the better!

The author

Michael Mansard is Principal of Business Transformation at Zuora. Michael is a seasoned subscription economy business strategist. During his five-year tenure at Zuora, he has accompanied more than 200 companies globally and across industries, from startups to large enterprises.

Leveraging his 11-year experience at Deloitte Consulting, SAP, or as a startup mentor, Mansard has developed an original multidisciplinary profile. His skills range across enterprise business processes (order-to-cash, close-to-disclose, procure-to-pay), strategic sales, financial controlling, and digital/IT architecture.

Mansard holds a dual master's degree from ESIEE Paris in Business Management and Information Technologies. He currently serves as Principal, Business Transformation and Innovation, within Zuora's Strategy and Operations field group.

He recently authored several thought leadership pieces—such as "Industry 4.0: An Executive Playbook for Business Model Transformation" and "Subscription Economy Maturity Model."

Key Notes

_____

_____

_____

_____

_____

_____

Key Actions

_____

_____

_____

_____

_____

_____

Conclusions

This book was designed and published to be a focused repository of knowledge on the topic of B2G pricing, especially when vendors can respond to best-value contracts and demonstrate the value of their offerings. Because there was a gap of knowledge that I identified in 2017, I decided to bring some of the best experts in the world and to make this contribution to the pricing field. I sincerely hope that more people publish additional work to complete this first body of work. My focus in writing this book was the following:

1 **Demonstrate that pricing is different from modeling, estimating, and contracting, and that it's science that can be applied to the B2G space.** There are certainly differences between B2C, B2B, and B2G pricing. But some of the principles still apply, especially in the context of best-value contracts.
2 **Show that value-based pricing and price-to-win analyses have key similarities and major differences.** I propose that progressive pricing professionals in the

space will embrace various methodologies and make them their own. Customer needs can also be called hot buttons. Differentiators can also be called discriminators. I recommend not falling in love with the names of the methodologies but instead being mindful and focusing on the outcome: make better pricing decisions and extract more value from markets when possible.

3 **Provide a reminder that price-to-win analysis is serious business! It requires skills, data, and a strong analytical backbone.** If you are in B2G and responding to complex RFPs, you ought to investigate conducting this type of analysis internally or allocate budgets to hire experts. Vendors can spend millions on bid costs and not be willing to spend more on customer research, competitive analysis, and PTW analysis. This must change.

4 **Reinforce the fact that value-based pricing can be applied completely or partially to the B2G world.** Some companies do this by applying TCO or by pricing services and spare parts at a premium. This isn't new. Maybe the name of the method is new, but there's a need to conduct segmentation, to focus on competitive positioning, and to quantify the value of the differentiation. Call it what you want! Proposal evaluators will conduct RFP analysis based on a set of criteria that might include technical performance, service performance, and pricing. You must be able to conduct the same analysis internally to see how you might be positioned versus competition.

5 **Project how some of the B2G trends might influence pricing.** The world is changing, and the change is reaching the public sector more and more under the leadership of progressive vendors but also because of the increased attention paid by digital players. I wanted to show that the B2G pricing

world cannot stay static and solely focused on costs. There's a need to focus on the three C's of pricing as well as innovative pricing techniques impacting contract types and pricing models.

6 **Anticipate the rise of software procurement from government agencies.** More and more government RFPs contain a software and/or data component. It's therefore essential not only to position software and data in the response to RFPs but also to educate procurement agencies on the value of software and data. Therefore, Scott Miller made two contributions to this book. He is the world expert in software pricing and has worked for many years in the B2G world.

The book does not offer a complete review of all the possible pricing topics. I didn't cover commodity pricing or commercial pricing for government business. That topic would make for an interesting next book, as more and products and services are being commoditized. It would also have been beneficial to show a few case studies for the best practices I listed in sections 1 and 2. It's challenging to get companies to agree on any pricing success stories, especially when dealing with government business. This is often considered a secret and sensitive subject. Finally, I was reminded by Marsha Lindquist that every procurement agency can have separate and specific pricing practices. This might be the main reason why there was a large knowledge gap in the space. How can a book be written for such a diversity of practices?

I hope you enjoyed reading and consulting this book. Again, I thank all the contributors for being so open to collaborating with me on this project. It's been a very enriching experience. If you're in the B2G world and involved in pricing, I wish you the best of success in your work. I encourage you to keep learning and to connect with me on LinkedIn to engage in exchange and discussions. I've been in pricing for over 10 years now, and I'm learning every day. Most of my self-learning comes from my interactions with experts and practitioners I'm grateful for now. Be bold and price well!

The Author

Stephan M. Liozu (www.stephanliozu.com) is Chief Value Officer of the Thales Group (www.thalesgroup.com) and the Founder of Value Innoruption Advisors (www.valueinnoruption.com), a consulting boutique specializing in industrial, digital, and value-based pricing. He is also an Adjunct Professor and Research Fellow at the Case Western Reserve University Weatherhead School of Management. Stephan holds a PhD in Management from Case Western Reserve University (2013), an MS in Innovation Management from Toulouse School of Management (2005), and an MBA in Marketing from Cleveland State University (1991).

Stephan holds the following certifications:

Certified Platform Design Toolkit Facilitator (PDT, 2020)

Certified IoT Professional (IoT-Inc., 2019)

Certified Black Hat Coach (Thales, 2018)

Certified Pricing-to-Win Shipley Instructor (2017)

Business Model Innovation Coach (Strategyzer, 2016)

Certified Innovation Leader—GIMI/IXL (2014)

Master Customer Value Modeler (CVM®, 2013)

Prosci® Change Management Certification (2013)

ThinkBuzan® Licenced Instructor—iMindMap® (2012)

Certified Pricing Professional (CPP) (2009)

Certified Facilitator for DDI Learning Systems (2009)

Breakthrough Thinking (Gap International ECC 2007)

Six Sigma Green Belt (2007)

Over the past few years, Stephan has published academic articles in the *Journal of Revenue and Pricing Management, Business Horizons, MIT Sloan Management Review,* and *Industrial Marketing Management.* He has also written many articles on strategic pricing issues for the *Journal of Professional Pricing.* Stephan sits on the Advisory Board of Professional Pricing Society and Leverage-Point Innovation.

Over the past nine years, Stephan has edited or published nine other pricing books:

Pricing Strategy Implementation: Translating Pricing Strategy into Results (Routledge, 2019)

Monetizing Data (VIA Publishing, 2018)

Value Mindset (VIA Publishing, 2017)

Dollarizing Differentiation Value (VIA Publishing, 2016)

The Pricing Journey (Stanford University Press, 2015)

Pricing and Human Capital (Routledge, 2015)

The ROI of Pricing (Routledge, 2014)

Pricing and the Sales Force (Routledge, 2015)

Innovation in Pricing: Contemporary Theories and Best Practices (Routledge, 2012 & 2017).

All books are available on Amazon.com. Please connect on LinkedIn or contact through the website at stephanliozu.com.

www.ingramcontent.com/pod-product-compliance
Lightning Source LLC
Chambersburg PA
CBHW060749220326
41598CB00022B/2378